MIKE TYSON

The Release of Power

This book is dedicated to the memory of the Gutteridge Twins who taught Reg left from right; and to George Giller who taught Norman right from wrong.

MIKE TYSON

The Release of Power

REG GUTTERIDGE OBE
and Norman Giller

Queen Anne Press

A QUEEN ANNE PRESS BOOK

First published in 1995 by
Queen Anne Press
a division of
Lennard Associates Ltd
Mackerye End
Harpenden
Herts AL5 5DR

A catalogue entry is available from the British Library

ISBN 1 85291 567 6

Cover design: Paul Cooper
Cover photographs: (Front) Colorsport
(Back) Mike Brennan, Scope Features
Colour photographs: Mike Brennan, Scope Features
Editor: Alison Bravington
Assistant editor: Roy Mathers
Typesetting and design: Norman Giller Enterprises
Origination: Leaside Graphics

Printed and bound in Great Britain by
Butler and Tanner, Frome and London

CONTENTS

ACKNOWLEDGEMENTS

Nobody can visit the life and times of Mike Tyson without leaning heavily on the help and advice of those closest to him. Cus D'Amato and Jim Jacobs, both sadly now departed, were a constant source of information and inspiration; our thanks to Bill Cayton, Don King, Kevin Rooney, Teddy Atlas, José Torres, Bobby Stewart and a procession of good pals on the American boxing beat who passed on facts and whispers; particular thanks to the omnipotent Nigel Collins, Bristol-born Managing Editor of *The Ring,* who kindly allowed us to quote from his fascinating one-on-one prison interview with Tyson. Thanks, too, to Harry Mullan, Editor of *Boxing News*, for producing a magazine that is invaluable for anybody wanting to know the exact facts of what goes on in the fight game. Previous books on Tyson, and in particular *For Whom the Bell Tolls* and *Tyson* by Peter Heller were excellent points of reference, as was the controversial biography by José Torres. Publisher Adrian Stephenson, of Queen Anne Press, also has the gratitude of the authors. Without his support and encouragement this book would never have reached your hands. There will never be another quite like Mike Tyson. The man is unique. Read and enjoy.

Seconds Out

Reg Gutteridge OBE

MY co-author Norman Giller and I were introduced to a new sport some 15 years ago: *Tyson Watching*. Cus D'Amato, a legendary character in boxing who had guided Floyd Patterson to the world heavyweight title, told us in his Bronx drawl: "I've got a kid who's going to take over from Floyd Patterson as the youngest world heavyweight champion of all time. Note the name. It's Mike Tyson. Watch out for him." Tyson was then barely 14 years old.

So we started watching, first with casual interest and then with fascination followed by excitement as he began to develop into an extraordinary fighting machine. What we did not realise is that our Tyson Watching would turn into a frightening, stomach-churning experience. Suddenly it was like watching a runaway truck, and there was nothing we could do to stop it. Many of us in boxing wanted to reach out and help him, but he was a law to himself and always had a finger on the self-destruct button.

We – we shall use the royal 'we' throughout the book – knew that Tyson was on a crash course with disaster early on in his career. The village world of boxing was alive with gossip, rumour and innuendo about his sexual practices. He was continually getting into trouble with girls, stories that were stifled by people protecting him and the millions of dollars he promised to earn with his brutal fists.

Hush money was paid to keep girls – and at least one mother – quiet. Too much was riding on Tyson's broad shoulders to allow him literally to screw the well-laid plans for him to rule the world's heavyweights. His co-manager Jim Jacobs, sadly no longer with us, confided: "Mike is a highly-sexed guy. He does everything with high energy, and one of the reasons we like to keep him busy in the ring and the gym is that it burns off that desire to go out and get laid."

Cus D'Amato and Jim Jacobs were the men who did most to protect Tyson. When they both died he was suddenly left without cover and without control. The rape case that ended with his being sentenced to prison for six years was a disaster just waiting to happen.

Tyson has been a prisoner for years. A prisoner of his past.

As experienced Tyson Watchers, we knew that he was not going to be able to escape from his ghetto grounding. You can take the man out of the ghetto, but you cannot take the ghetto out of the man. Never has the old saying been more sadly proved than by Michael Gerard Tyson. He had been taught from an early age that this was a cruel world in which you have to snatch what you want because nobody would give you a thing. If you walk round the mean back streets of Brooklyn where he grew up, as we have, you will realise that you need an animal instinct to survive. And it was the animal in him – the one we applaud in the ring – that got him locked away for three years.

This is Tyson Revisited for Norman and me. We were his first biographers just a month or two after he became the world's youngest heavyweight champion at the age of 20 years, four months and 22 days. So much has happened to him since that it cried out for another book to record the life and times of one of the most extraordinary sportsmen of the century. We have great affection for Tyson, and consider him right up there with the immortals of the ring. That's Tyson the Fighter. Tyson the Man is such a cocktail of a character that nobody knows which of his many personalities will surface now that he been released from prison to continue his one-man war on the world's heavyweights.

In the following pages we will introduce you to Tyson the Man and Tyson the Fighter. Even if you don't like boxing, you will find this a fascinating study of what happens when a ghetto boy suddenly becomes one of the most famous and fêted people in the world.

We want him to be a kingly beast in the ring and a pussycat outside. But it doesn't work out like that. Not when you're Mike Tyson and you have been down in the gutter. Here he comes now, warts 'n' all.

Reg Gutteridge

PART ONE

Tyson the Man

1: A Walking Time-bomb

MIKE Tyson planned a $250 million smash-and-grab raid while incarcerated in prison for a rape that he still contends he did not commit. He had an ex-convict in the mountainous shape of boxing promoter Don King as his accomplice as he plotted a comeback to the ring that could, once again, make him the richest sportsman in history.

Inmate 922335, who for three years lost his identity to a prison number, was a walking time-bomb when released from jail in the early spring of 1995 after serving half the six-year sentence handed down to him in an Indianapolis court. 'Time-bomb Tyson' was ready to explode in the ring in a bid to release the pent-up anger that had built up inside him since a jury found him guilty of raping an 18-year-old black beauty contestant. His smash-and-grab raid will be on the heavyweight division that he is determined to rule once again, and the $250 million is a reasonable estimate of what he will earn if he can recapture the punching power and precision that made the rest of the world's heavyweights live in fear of him. Those of us who have been fascinated Tyson Watchers since he was just a 14-year-old schoolboy were worried as he walked out a free man that 'Time-bomb Tyson' could explode *outside* the ring.

There are many faces to the man who, at just 20, became the youngest world heavyweight champion of all time. If you asked the real Mike Tyson to stand up, there would be at least four personalities fighting to claim centre stage. You will meet all four Mike Tysons in the following pages:

The ghetto thug and controlled killer in the ring;

the wife beater and out-of-control woman molester;

the man who fancies feathered birds, loves his four-year-old daughter and looks after his 90-year-old surrogate mum, Camille Ewald,

and, our favourite, the likeable, self-educated charmer with an encyclopaedic knowledge of boxing history.

Which Tyson came out of jail in March 1995? Even Tyson could not answer that one. It could take him years to find himself. One thing for certain is that free man Tyson will be a much changed person from the one locked away in March 1992. He went in holding a Bible and came out with the Koran in his hand as a fight developed for his soul. In mileage terms, Tyson did not travel far during his three years in prison: 25 miles in fact – from the Marion County court to the high-security Indiana Youth Centre in the town of Plainfield, Indianopolis, where he served his sentence. But Tyson travelled a long, long way mentally. A major change was his consideration of a conversion from born-again Christian to the Islamic religion. At one stage during his introduction to his new faith he toyed with changing his name to Mikhail Abdul-Aziz, but no doubt Don King would have made him see that, commercially, this was not a good idea. Tyson's Baptist church associates maintained that he would remain a Christian, while Chicago-based Muslims insisted that while in prison he had taken *shahada*, the Islamic statement of faith, and that, like Muhammad Ali, he had converted to Islam. The claim and counterclaim will just add to Tyson's torment as he tries to come to terms with his new life outside the prison walls.

Uppermost in the minds of both Tyson and Don King, while the former champion was locked away, was the thought of restoring the Tyson fortunes. The $60 million he earned during his first blitz on the world heavyweight championship had been largely eaten away by legal fees, a divorce settlement, alleged mismanagement of funds and a crazy, earn-it-spend-it lifestyle. Tyson thought nothing at his out-of-control peak of buying two or three luxury motorcars at a time, spending fortunes on jewellery and house furnishings, and dazzling beautiful foxy ladies with his wealth. He admitted to being so vague about finances that he had no recollection of where the little matter of $10 million had disappeared to during a court investigation of his finances. For several months, he allowed his then wife, Robin Givens, and his mother-in-law, Ruth Roper, to take over his financial affairs. He later claimed that this had been a grievous mistake, and he has come out of prison a much wiser man. The fighter who can re-establish himself as the biggest earner in sporting history is determined not to have anybody else's hands in his pockets other than his own.

It was not only Tyson's fortune that shrank. The man who walked free from prison looked a shadow of the 17-stone colossus who was handcuffed and led away to the cells in March 1992. He had kept himself fit in the prison gymnasium with daily work-outs, but the awesome physique that used to promote fear in his opponents was much reduced. This led to the anti-Tyson brigade dragging up old allegations that he owed his enormous physical presence to steroids, and that the effect had now worn off. Their argument is that his dangerous mood swings that got him in trouble in the first place were the classic symptoms of somebody going down the steroid road. Tyson – "fit, but not yet fighting fit" – has always denied the claims and, even down to around 15 stone on his release from prison, he still looked a formidable force.

Perhaps the biggest change in Tyson from the man who ruled the world heavyweight division with frightening ferocity was that he was no longer a trusting person. "I have been screwed too many times in my life to trust anybody again," he said during one of several interviews he gave while serving his time. "Now Mike Tyson hates the world. That's a fact. I hate everybody."

Tyson's bitterness is understandable if you look at things through his eyes. He is convinced he did not get a fair trial when found guilty of raping Sunday school teacher Desiree Washington in an Indianapolis hotel in the summer of 1991. We give a full breakdown of the court proceedings in a later chapter but, several months before his release from prison, there was convincing evidence that Tyson was less than fairly treated.

Lawyer Alan Dershowitz, a high-powered attorney acting for Tyson, told an appeals court that the trial judge who sentenced the former champion, Patricia Gifford, was selected by the prosecution, giving the state a clear advantage. "If the defence had had a choice, it would have been anyone other than Judge Gifford," Dershowitz said.

He made the sensational revelation that, as the trial neared its conclusion, the defence learned of three women who said they saw Desiree Washington "engaging in foreplay with Tyson in a limousine just before they entered the Indianapolis hotel where she claimed she was raped".

Dershowitz revealed that Judge Gifford did not allow the witnesses to testify because she believed the defence delayed in notifying the prosecution of this development. "The witnesses," Dershowitz told the court, "would have corroborated Tyson's testimony that he had reason to believe that Miss Washington would be a willing sex partner once in the hotel room".

It is reasonable to assume that if these witnesses had been allowed to testify it could have swung the verdict of a jury that had to vote three times before finding Tyson guilty.

Dershowitz made further inroads on the prosecution case that had ended with Tyson found guilty and shamed in the eyes of the watching world: "Miss Washington was wearing a sequin-studded outfit, which she claims Tyson 'yanked' off her as he 'slammed her down on the bed'. If that had happened, there would have been sequins all over the hotel room. Indeed, at the trial when the dress was gingerly introduced into evidence, sequins fell off on to the courtroom floor. But only a *single* sequin was found in Tyson's hotel room after the alleged rape."

We present more of the Dershowitz counter-arguments in the rape trial chapter. Everything points to Tyson having had a raw deal, and this is why he was a walking time-bomb when he was granted his freedom.

Even in prison Tyson could not avoid assaults on his character. He had been inside only a matter of weeks when a story broke that added yet another dark shade to the portrait we shall be painting of Tyson the Woman Molester. Erinn Cosby, 25-year-old daughter of entertainer Bill Cosby, revealed on a television show that Tyson had agreed to undergo psychotherapy three years earlier. This was at the urging of Bill Cosby, after his daughter had told her parents that he had tried to sexually assault her.

She claimed that Tyson later reneged on the therapy agreement. She told interviewer Jane Whitney on *Night Talk* that she went with Tyson from a New York nightclub to his home. There, she claimed, he knocked her to the ground and began groping her, but she was able to break away. "I told my parents," she said. "They said they would handle it – and they did. I put myself through therapy. The agreement was that my parents wanted him to go to therapy for a year." She told viewers that she ran into Tyson several weeks later at a nightclub. "He came in there looking for me – deliberately looking for me – because he was so upset that he had to go to therapy for a year. Not upset over what he had done to me. He was screaming, 'How dare you do this, I am not going to go to therapy.' I couldn't believe that this man was not even concerned about anything that he had done."

We cannot claim to have been too surprised at the way Tyson's gargantuan sexual appetite continually got him into trouble. The late Jim Jacobs, his co-manager and an intoxicating influence on him both as a man and as a fighter, confided to us early on in his career: "We've got to keep him busy in the gym and in the ring to try to burn off his energy. He has a high-powered sex drive and while he's training and fighting he can't get laid."

Jacobs was talking soon after shelling out several thousand dollars to buy the silence of a mother in Catskill who had complained to him that Tyson had sexually assaulted her teenage daughter. A couple of years later, Jacobs had to pay out $105,000 to settle out of court with a car park attendant who claimed Tyson had clobbered him when he went to the aid of a girl who Tyson had lewdly propositioned.

Another little-publicised incident led to Tyson breaking with his then trainer Teddy Atlas, who had looked after him from his earliest amateur days. It was reported to Atlas that Tyson, then a 16-year-old unknown, had abused a 12-year-old girl. Atlas, like Tyson, was from the ghetto and he decided to use ghetto tactics to try to frighten him into behaving properly. Legend has it that he got hold of him in a deserted gymnasium and put a gun to his head. "You step out of line once more and I'll blow your brains out," he told a quivering Tyson. The outcome was that Atlas was sacked as trainer, and Tyson continued on down the slippery slope that finally led to prison.

Little did Tyson know just how prophetic he was being when he said in the summer of 1990 after being sensationally dethroned by Buster Douglas as ruler of the world heavyweights: "I believe a lot of people want to see me self-destruct. They want to see me one day with handcuffs and walking into the police car, going to jail. They'll say, 'Look, I told you he was headed for that.' "

It was Tyson's ex-wife, Robin Givens, who predicted that Tyson would turn out to be the "all American tragedy". Perhaps that was the path he was on from his first breath of life in the ghettos of New York.

2: Out of the Ghetto

TO know Mike Tyson, you must know the environment in which he spent his formative years. New York legend has it that, in the mid-1960s, a slab of concrete was pneumatically drilled out of a Brooklyn sidewalk, was sprayed with black paint and then left to dry . . . and it became Mike Tyson. Looking at the cliff-wall-face of a body that had been honed to awesome muscular shape long before the downhill run to prison, it would be easy to take the legend as fact. But when you get inside Tyson's 71-inch reach – as we intend to in the following pages – you discover that this is no slab of concrete. He is flesh, blood and brains; a living body with feelings and emotions that have filled out his character and personality to produce a human being far more sensitive and thoughtful than you would imagine possible when watching him brutalise opponents in the ring. But the disturbing experiences of his early life have left a deep mental scar, and even when he became, at the age of 20 years, four months and 22 days, the youngest world heavyweight champion in history, those close to him knew that he was an earthquake waiting to happen. When, as was alleged, he brutally raped a girl in an Indianapolis hotel room in the early hours of the morning in July 1991, many considered that the seeds of the deed had been sown during his days as a juvenile ghetto thug.

Academics would consider Tyson poorly educated, but he has street intelligence of Mastermind magnitude and he has developed a vocabulary that makes him sound mature beyond his years. He has added to his knowledge while in prison by reading 'heavies' like Friedrich Nietzsche, Tolstoy and Alexandre Dumas. "I must have read over a hundred books while I was inside," he told *The Ring* Managing Editor, Nigel Collins. "Some of them nearly drove me out of my mind. They made me look at things in a new perspective. Nietzsche told me there is no God, there's just superman. Man, I don't want to hear that crap. Tolstoy told me women ain't s***. Machiavelli told me don't trust nobody. That I know already!"

The way Tyson talks is an echo from beyond the grave, because he sounds and thinks exactly like the man who moulded him, the late Cus D'Amato, of whom we will have much to reveal in the following chapter. But first, let us go back to the beginning and the legend of how Mike Tyson was quarried rather than born.

In truth, Michael Gerard Tyson was born on 30 June 1966, in the tough Bedford-Stuyvesant section of Brooklyn, the youngest of three children. His father was James Kirkpatrick, a massively built construction-site labourer who walked out on his family after a heart condition stopped him working. Kirkpatrick never married Mike's mother, Lorna, and she registered his birth in her maiden name of Tyson.

One of Tyson's regrets is that he did not get to know his father better. He died of a heart attack at the age of 68 while his son was serving his prison sentence. They had a reunion in 1989, but never became close. Kirkpatrick said that he walked out on two-year-old Tyson, his mother, his brother and sister because he "wasn't the marrying kind". He explained that he and Mike's mother were not getting on after being together for seven years, and so he thought it better that he got out of her life. "I didn't just abandon them like has been made out," he said. "I used to pay them visits and give Mike's mother money when I had it."

Tyson was said by prison officials to be "distraught and upset" when told of his father's death, but he did not request time out to attend the funeral. He only got to know his father after he had become champion, and the biggest influence on him in his formative years was Lorna, who had always been totally opposed to violence. Sadly, Lorna died of cancer in 1982 without seeing her son prove that, in the ring at least, he could control violence and turn it into a legitimate and accepted way of making himself one of the richest and most famous sportsmen of the twentieth century; on the other hand, she was saved the anguish of seeing him shamed by his prison sentence and suffering the despair of his divorce to Hollywood actress Robin Givens as he rode a nonstop rollercoaster of controversies.

In his earliest years, Mike was being fed messages of pacifism and was taught right from wrong, rather than left hook from right cross. His mother preached a love-thy-neighbour code as young Mike struggled to grow up in an area where rob-thy-neighbour was too often the rule. "My mother detested violence," Mike recalled in an after-fight interview, while not a dozen yards away his battered opponent was being repaired after suffering grievous bodily harm. "She was a very timid and gentle person. I had only my sister, Denise, to play with because my brother, Rodney, was five years older. So I guess I picked up a lot of gentle, sort of effeminate habits. In fact when I was a kid they used to call me a 'little fairy boy.' " Only a volunteer candidate for the funny farm would dare call him that to his face today, despite his occasional lisp and quiet, almost apologetic tone of voice.

Tyson confessed that violence came naturally to him from as early as he could remember. "I was in a Brooklyn hospital when I was about four, and an aunt brought me a toy gun and a doll," he recalled. "I broke the gun by accident and I was so angry that I smashed the doll against the wall and ripped its head off. That gave me more pleasure than playing with the toys."

The real toughening-up process started unintentionally for Tyson when his penniless mother, scraping by on welfare, moved her family from the tenement apartment in Bedford-Stuyvesant to a rundown apartment block in another district of Brooklyn, Brownsville, where the streets are so mean that they say even the birds are armed. Mike was ten when he arrived in Brownsville and was pitched unsuspectingly into a world where the strongest survived and the weakest were walked on. "I was always getting set on," he recalled. "You'd be walking along a street when a couple of big guys would stop you and steal anything you had – your sneakers, your clothes, your money. They'd take anything and then give you a whipping just for laughs."

Mike remembers his first fight like most of us would remember our first kiss. "I was into raising pigeons," he said. "I love those birds. I'm really at peace when I'm with them. Anyways, this particular day an older boy tried to steal one of my birds. No, to tell you the truth he ripped its head off. I was 11 at the time and had never given any thought to using violence. But I just blew. I threw everything at the guy – fists, feet, head. I became an animal and beat the living crap out of him. And d'you know something? I found I loved every second of it. I had found a way of letting all my frustration out."

This first fight launched Tyson the Wild Boy and, instead of crossing the street when the muggers came his way, he joined them. He became a member of The Jolly Stompers. No, not a traditional jazz band. They were a notorious street gang committed to stomping on anybody who got in their way. Mike was the youngest in the gang, but had the respect of the older boys because of the way he could hold his own in fights. Included among his catalogue of crime was pickpocketing, house breaking, mugging and even armed robbery. "The older kids had the guns, while I was given the job of bag-man," he said. "We'd go into stores and while they did the sticking up I would fill the bags from the shelves. It was really exciting and I have to admit I got a real buzz out of it. It wasn't so much the violent stuff as outsmarting the store people. That's what I enjoyed best, showing I could beat 'em by cunning."

The police records suggest that Tyson was not that clever at outsmarting the people he was trying to rob. He was caught and questioned more than 30 times during a period when he admits that he got a liking for liquor, drinking stolen booze in a bravado act to show that he could keep pace with the older boys in the gang. By picking pockets and robbing stores, Tyson got some self respect within the laws of the concrete jungle in which he was operating. He was able to buy himself decent shoes and clothes, rather than suffer the humiliation of being given second-hand clothes by charity workers at Public School 396, where he was noted more for his long absences than any academic input.

Within a year of moving to Brownsville, Mike became completely beyond the control of his distraught mother. "I used to break my mother's heart," he admitted shortly after winning the world championship. "I was always getting into trouble, and she'd cry and say 'How can you do such things. I never stole a thing in my whole life.' She had so much pride, and I just kept hurting and embarrassing her. My mother always wanted me to turn the other cheek, but a neighbour who I called Aunt Liz used to encourage me to stand up for myself and fight back when bigger kids picked on me. She would tell me to go back outside and fight back, and when I used to hesitate she would say, 'Come on, Mike, I'll go out there with you. You've got to learn to fight back or get eaten alive in this world.' My mother, though, preferred me to forgive and forget. It really hurts me deep down that she never lived to see what I achieved. She was never able to say with real pride, 'Look, that's my little boy Michael. Look what he's done. He's champion of the whole wide world.' All she knew me as was a wild kid causing nothing but trouble."

After sentences at a succession of detention centres, and more than 30 arrests before he was 12, Tyson was finally ordered to the Tryon School, a viciously hard correction centre for juvenile delinquents in upstate Johnstown, New York. It was a prison in everything but name. Ernestine Coleman, a New York social worker, recalled: "I was appointed Mike's caseworker after he had been adjudged a juvenile delinquent. He acted up when first sent to Sopporth Juvenile Center, and it was necessary to send him to Tryon where it was hoped he would respond to the much harder discipline of that school. It was clear there was a nice person somewhere below Mike's surface, but it would need somebody to win his trust to bring the best out of him. He could be very surly and suspicious with anybody he didn't know."

Tyson was just 13 when he arrived at the Tryon School, but he was a boy in a man's body and the staff struggled to control him. He was wild and undisciplined, and wanted to fight the system that had been designed to try to put him on the right road and point him away from what looked a certain path to major crimes. Bobby Stewart, a former professional fighter and a counsellor at the School, has vivid memories of the first time he saw Tyson. "He was in handcuffs," he recalled. "Two members of the school staff were marching him across the grounds towards Elmwood Cottage, which was my base as counsellor. Elmwood was known as the 'bad' cottage because it was where the real troublemakers were sent to be ironed out. Suddenly this powerfully built youngster, with shoulders that went on for ever, was brought dragging and protesting into the cottage and he was brimming over with hatred for the world. He had beaten up another boy at the school and now we had charge of him. Everything about his aggressive manner and bad attitude suggested he was going to be a tough handful."

Little did Tyson and Stewart know it at the time, but his arrival at the cottage was to be one of the most important of all milestones in Mike's life. Social worker Stewart looked for common ground on which he could meet Tyson, who was considered by some members of the staff to be retarded because of his total lack of communication. "I had nothing to say to anyone," is how Tyson put it when looking back on his early days at Tryon. "I nearly went crazy when they first sent me there. It was in the middle of woods in upstate New York and a million miles away from the Brooklyn streets where I'd grown up. I was so frustrated that I used to start fights every day. You do that, they isolate you. So they kept locking me up, and by locking me up they just made me more angry and frustrated. I didn't want to communicate with nobody. There was nobody I trusted. In truth, I have to admit I had become obnoxious. Then I had the luck to meet Bobby Stewart. I owe Bobby so much because he was the first person to *listen* to me. He opened the door to a new life."

The patient Stewart opened up a line of communication by talking boxing to the young rebel without a pause. He had been the National Golden Gloves light-heavyweight champion in 1974 and a good-class professional. Tyson sat up and took notice from the minute Stewart started to recall his boxing career. His interest in the fight game had been briefly awakened six years earlier when he was shown a picture of then world champion Smokin' Joe Frazier in boxing pose. It had captured his imagination but, before he could find out how to turn his fascination into action, he got caught up in the street gang environment where there was no room for Marquess of Queensberry rules. Queensboro rules were more the style. A year before being sent to Tryon he had got a fleeting glimpse of Muhammad Ali, then heavyweight champion of the world, during a goodwill visit to one of the juvenile centres to which Tyson had been sentenced. He was captivated by Ali's magical presence and for the first time tried to imagine what it must be like to be the heavyweight champ. Now, in Bobby Stewart, he had found somebody who could introduce him to the world of boxing where he would be able to find an identity and a purpose.

It was Tyson who made the first move. He was in solitary after threatening a teacher, and he asked his guard if he could see Stewart. "I had been told that he was an animal and so I was really aggressive when I first went to see him," Stewart recalled. " 'What the fuck do you want?' I shouted after banging on his window to frighten him. He said he wanted to be a boxer. 'So do the rest of the assholes in here,' I told him. 'What makes you think you're any different? How do I know you're not just full of bullshit like the rest of them?' "

Tyson pleaded to be given a chance. "I want you to show me how to box, properly," he said. Stewart struck a bargain with him. "I'll give you boxing lessons in return for 100 per cent effort from you in the classroom," he said. "I don't care if you flunk every subject, just as long as you give it your best shot."

Within weeks of Stewart starting his boxing lessons there was a visible change in Tyson. He lost his sullen, 'I-hate-the-world' attitude and other teachers commented to Stewart how much better he was behaving and cooperating in class. From being close to illiterate, he suddenly started to read and write at seventh-grade level. And, from being a novice boxer, he began to develop into an accomplished ring craftsman.

"I found I was having to get myself back into shape just to stay with him in sparring sessions," said Stewart. "It was obvious within just a few days of working with him that he was a natural, and his power even at the age of 13 was phenomenal. I remember him hitting me right between the eyes with a left jab, and it was as if there was an explosion in my head. I went home with blackened eyes and a puffy nose. 'Who on earth did that to you?' my wife said, and I told her that there was a young boy called Mike Tyson who was as good a boxing prospect as I had ever seen."

Tyson looked back on his first sparring session with Stewart with a grim smile: "I was one of the school bullies and Bobby set out to humiliate me in front of the kids. He wanted to show them that I was nothing. He hit me in the body with a real pro shot and I went down. For a moment I couldn't catch my breath and I thought I was dead."

Over to Stewart: "What impressed me was that instead of throwing off the gloves and deciding he didn't want to take any more, Mike got up and asked me to show him how to throw that body punch. I knew then that here was a kid who had something special."

It was quickly plain to Stewart that he had unearthed a jewel of a prospect, and he knew just the man who could give him the polish that could turn him into a champion.

He picked up the 'phone and rang a man called D'Amato. Cus D'Amato.

3: The Court of 'King' Cus

NOBODY can begin to tell the Mike Tyson story without making a lot of room in it for Cus D'Amato. To know Tyson you have to know D'Amato. We feel qualified to write in depth about him because, over a period of more than 30 years, we got about as close to him as he allowed anybody to be. Our first meeting with Cus was back in the mid-1950s when he was parading Floyd Patterson as the then youngest world heavyweight champion in history. The parallels between Patterson and Tyson are uncanny to the point of being almost eerie. Both were raised in Brooklyn. Both grew up on the wrong side of the tracks and finished up in juvenile delinquent centres. Both used boxing as a launching pad to respectability. And both had the eccentric Cus D'Amato as their guiding light.

In those mid-50s, D'Amato – then stocky and sprightly like a pugnacious Spencer Tracy – showed the sort of courage and willpower that would have earned him a championship had he revealed it inside the ring. With the all-important world heavyweight title held by Patterson as his calling card, he stood out alone against the monopolistic International Boxing Club that was proved to be under the controlling influence of notorious gangster, Frankie Carbo. The IBC virtually ran boxing in America. But they didn't run Cus D'Amato.

It was D'Amato who bravely exposed the IBC as a corrupt organization, refusing to allow Patterson to fight for any promoter who had connections with them. He made his stubborn stand despite late-night threatening 'phone calls and menacing, side-of-the-mouth talk from men in wide-brimmed hats who were uninvited guests to his Gramercy gymnasium above what used to be a dime-a-dance ballroom at 116 East 14th Street in a rundown section of New York City. This man of deep suspicions and shifting moods took to sleeping on a single camp bed at the rear of his gymnasium with a ferocious German guard dog as his only company.

D'Amato was obsessed with the idea that gangsters were out to get him. He used always to insist on having any chair he sat in away from home facing the door so that he could see who was entering. New York fight promoter Al Braverman had known him since the late 1930s and said: "Any strange room Cus walked in he would look round it like a sniffer dog. If it was a hotel bedroom he would look under the bed and in the closet to make sure there was nobody there. He was a strange one all right. But what a manager. He could make a good fighter great and a great fighter unbeatable."

Perhaps we got to the bottom of D'Amato's phobia about gangsters. He told us of when one day two 'heavies' walked casually into his gym when he was a young manager and sat either side of him. They had been excited by the potential of one of his fighters.

"You can count us in," said one.

"In what?" asked Cus, acting dumb.

"In as partners," said the other. "We like the kid and we want part of the action."

Cus told us that he rolled up his sleeve and held out his hand. "You can start here," he told the hoodlums, miming as if hacking his fingers off. "Then you can chop my wrists off and then my arms. You can cut me up piece by piece. But you ain't having any part of the kid. Now get your asses outta here."

The two men, according to D'Amato, looked at him as if he was mad and left the gym. "All my life," said Cus, "I've stood up to the crooks, the cheats and the villains because I detested everything they represent. Maybe I shoulda been a priest, eh?"

One fighter who did get away from him was a young middleweight called Rocky Graziano, who went on to become a legendary world champion. Cus never forgave him for walking out on him, and described him to us as "gutless and a lousy fighter". This showed the sour side of D'Amato because Graziano was one of the bravest men to climb into the ring and was a formidable fighter. The odd-ball manager was also a mass of contradictions because, for all his fierce criticisms of the crooks in boxing, it was well known in the fight game that he kept the company of many shady characters, and among his closest confidants were known

Mafia bosses and underworld heavies.

D'Amato's stand against the rotten-to-the-core IBC ended in outright victory. They were declared to have an illegal monopoly on boxing and were disbanded on the orders of the United States government.

You didn't have conversations with D'Amato. You had sit-ins. He would do the talking and you the listening and occasionally, when he paused for breath, you could get in with a question. He talked like a man who had swallowed a volume of Shakespeare mixed in with a little Clarence Darrow, Mark Twain, Bertrand Russell and any number of philosophers, and every sentence was delivered in a Bronx drawl that lulled you into thinking you had walked on to the set of *On the Waterfront*. Any moment you expected Marlon ('I coulda been a contender, Charlie') Brando to walk in with Rod Steiger at his side . . .

Were you ever a fighter, Cus?

"Only all my life. Every day I'm a fighter. I fight to live. I fight to breathe. I fight for what is right. I fight for the kids out there on the street to try to give them some hope in life."

Okay, were you ever a boxer?

"I had dreams of being another Tony Canzoneri. God, could that guy fight. But my career stopped before it had started. Got in a fight in the street with this bully. Must have been ten years older than me. I was 12. He kicked me about and left me virtually blind in one eye. End of boxing career, but not the end of my dreams. Take away a man's dreams and you might as well take away his oxygen."

Where were you born?

"In the Bronx, where else? Have you heard of the Frog Hollow section of the Bronx? That's where I grew up. Me and thousands like me kicking and fighting for a way up and out. Dutch Schultz came from there. You know, the gangster. There were hundreds of others who made it to 'wanted notices' fame but I guess Dutch was the best – or worst – known. I got my education in the streets of the Bronx. School did nothing for me. I quit in my second year. Most of what I learned came from ducking and diving to scrape a living. Hunger can make you pick up knowledge damn quick. Then I discovered books and realised that the written word could transport you to new worlds and could give you a whole new outlook. I am fascinated by the stories of that English king of yours. Arthur and the Knights of the Round Table. There's a moral in the stories. The good guys can win. Camelot. That's what we're all after, ain't it. Camelot.

"Mark Twain was one of the first authors I read, and he remains one of my all-time favourites. He was full of good sense, the sort of good sense that I hope I've been able to transmit to my fighters. A couple of quotes I'd like to pass on to you: 'Keep away from people who try to belittle your ambitions. Small people always do that, but the really great make you feel that you, too, can become great.' That's Twain – and so is this: 'Work and play are words used to describe the same thing under differing conditions.' Ever since reading those wise words, I have tried to make my work seem like play, that's why I've never fallen out of love with working with boxers."

Who has been the biggest influence on you?

"My father, I guess. I was the seventh of eight sons of Italian immigrants. My father scraped a living delivering ice in a horse-drawn wagon. Even with his little business there were guys from the mob trying to cut themselves in. I recall my father telling them where to go just the way I did those two 'heavies' who came to the gym that day. My mother died when I was four so everything fell on poppa's shoulders. They were strong enough to take the heaviest load. Believe me, he was a man of granite but, underneath, very soft. Three of my brothers died when I was a kid as well as my mother, so – as you can imagine – there was a lot of sadness around when I was growing up. Worst of all, I guess, was the way my oldest brother, Jerry, died. He got in an argument with a policeman, who shot him dead. Jerry was just 17. That was just terrible. But my father got us through the bad times. He was the hardest, yet kindliest, man I ever knew. He would bullwhip me when I did wrong. It was good for me and gave me the discipline that has carried me through life."

You're a great stickler for discipline, aren't you Cus?

"You've gotta be. Show me an undisciplined man and I'll show you a bum. D'you know, when I was 16 I deliberately went four whole days without food or drink. It was a deliberate act of self-denial so that I would know how to cope if anybody tried to intimidate me with threats of starvation. And I took that discipline into the army with me when I was drafted at the start of the Second World War. I used to stand to attention for hours on end and sleep on the barracks floor rather than on the bed. I wanted to make things as tough as I could for myself so that when the bad times came I could get by. I cheated on the eye test to get myself in because I wanted to be part of America's fight for the freedom of others. I got through the war with no problems."

What brought you into boxing?

"The love of the sport – the fitness factor, the character-building it gives youngsters and, above all, the discipline. If a fighter ain't gonna be disciplined he shouldn't be in boxing. I tell all my boxers, 'Don't worry if you're feeling fear before you climb into the ring. Fear is good for you. Heroes and cowards experience fear. It's how you react to it that's important. Boxing can teach you to control your fear and to feed off it.' D'you know, I get more satisfaction seeing a six-round kid giving his all for a two-bit purse than I do outta seeing a guy winning a huge bank roll for a championship victory. I've never been in this game for money. To me, money really is the root of all evil."

D'Amato had such disregard for money that he got himself into all sorts of financial tangles after hitting the jackpot first with Floyd Patterson and then world light-heavyweight champion José Torres, who later became the New York boxing commissioner and talks of Cus with the sort of deep feeling that a son reserves for his father. "Cus didn't just prepare his fighters for the ring, he prepared them for life," José said with the sort of poetic feel for words that shone through in his riveting, under-the-skin book on Muhammad Ali, *Sting Like A Bee*. "He helped me make close to a million dollars during my career and do you know how much he took for his cut? Zero! Not a cent. He was an incredible man." José tried to write an Ali-style book on Tyson, but it boomeranged on him and cost him his close friendship with Mike. Among the shocking revelations in his book – all since denied by Mike – were that Tyson and a friend once bedded 24 prostitutes in one night, and that he liked to "really hurt women and make them bleed" when in bed with them. But back to D'Amato.

Cus (an abbreviation, by the way, of his real name, Constantine) finally gave up what he considered the distasteful pursuit of money and nose-dived into bankruptcy, owing the government more than a quarter of a million dollars in taxes. He ducked out of the mainstream of boxing and moved into a white-washed 14-room Victorian house overlooking the Hudson River in Catskill, NY. He lived with a gentle, congenial Ukrainian-born woman called Camille Ewald, whose sister had been married to one of D'Amato's brothers. She was Cus's common-law wife for more than 40 years and encouraged him to keep his boxing interest alive. He started to run a small gym in a room above the Catskill Police Station on Main Street, and he launched the Catskill Boxing Club. Out-of-pocket expenses were paid for by wealthy fight historian Jim Jacobs, a longtime admirer of D'Amato's principles and coaching techniques. He and his partner, Bill Cayton, were confident that eventually he would discover a champion.

All local youngsters were welcome to use the gym and listen to the advice and guidance of the now ageing but agile D'Amato. He liked best to help the dead-end kids, and Camille's home was always overflowing with young boxers bed and breakfasting at what was now virtually a training camp. Managers across the States were excited to hear that 70-year-old Cus was back in the business he knew better than anybody. He was flooded with requests to train their fighters. They wanted Cus's Midas touch, but he was happiest working with the boys who did not have the big-money managers behind them. He wanted to feed the hungry fighters with all the knowledge he had collected from the University of Life and from the hundreds of books he had devoured from cover to cover. "I'm not a miracle worker," he said. "Any kid comes to me for help has to have a spark before I can do anything with him. I discover and then I uncover. If I find the spark, then I get to work teaching the kid things about himself that he never knew. I can make any kid believe in himself and reach his potential, but he has to meet me halfway. He's got to bring the perspiration and I supply the inspiration. I light fires in fighters, but they've got to be able to fan the flames themselves."

Secretly, D'Amato hoped that one day he would find another Floyd Patterson or a José Torres. Somebody he could shape and sharpen and then turn over to Jim Jacobs as a gesture of thanks for his help and encouragement in the bad times. It was his dream. His oxygen. And nobody could take it away from him.

Then, one day in 1980, he got a telephone call. It was from ex-fighter Bobby Stewart.

"I've got a kid I'd like you to look at," he said. "His name is Mike Tyson."

Cus D'Amato was a harsh critic of fighters. "Too much praise makes them complacent," he said. "Complacency can get you hurt in the ring. There's no such thing as a perfect fighter. Everybody has room for improvement. You will never hear a fighter getting false praise from me. I criticise to be kind."

So it was with some trepidation that Bobby Stewart climbed into the gymnasium ring over the cop shop at Catskill for what was virtually an audition sparring session with Mike Tyson. "I had no idea how Cus would react," he recalled. "He could have a very cutting tongue and I wondered how Mike would take to a brutally honest assessment of his promising but raw ability."

It was the early summer of 1980 and a shirt-sleeved D'Amato positioned himself just below the ring apron watching Stewart and his powerfully built 13-year-old pupil sparring. He stood there like a film director studying the rehearsal of a major scene, his hawk-like eyes never leaving the swinging, perspiring Tyson as he tore two-fisted after the taller, heavier Stewart, who had told Mike to "fight for real".

"I wanted Cus to see Mike going flat out," Stewart explained. "The kid took me at my word and I had to fight my head off to stay in there with him. In the second round I caught him with a counter punch that blew his nose all over the place. Cus's trainer, Teddy Atlas, suggested that we should call it off, but Mike insisted that we go the full three rounds."

When they had finished sparring, Tyson went to the showers while Stewart waited for the old man's verdict. D'Amato had seen it all and done it all, and even in his younger days was never noted for getting excited over a fighter. It was easier to get a stone out of a horse's hoof than praise out of D'Amato. "I was hoping that Cus was going to say I could bring Mike along a few more times," Stewart recalled. "My thinking was that, after seeing him five or six times, he might take a liking to him. But he took my breath away when he said to me after the very first sparring session, 'That's the future heavyweight champion of the world. If he wants it and is prepared to listen to me, it's his.' I waited until we were alone outside the gymnasium before I told Mike the verdict. 'What d'you think Mr D'Amato said?' I asked, teasing him. Mike did not have total belief in himself then and replied, 'I guess he called me a punk.' He would not believe me when I told him exactly what Cus had said. Then when it dawned on him that I was telling the truth he hugged me like a little boy who had just got what he wanted for Christmas."

D'Amato repeated his remarkable prophecy a few days later to Jim Jacobs who, like everybody else in the fight trade, knew that Cus was miserly with his compliments. From then on Jacobs took a particularly close interest in the progress of Tyson. He sensed that he was in on the ground floor of boxing history.

Stewart got permission from the Tryon school for Tyson to spend a probationary fortnight at Cus and Camille's imposing house on the outskirts of Catskill. They needed to see if they could get on with each other before a full commitment was made by either side. "It wasn't easy at first," Camille recalled. "Mike was a very rebellious and angry young man, rude even. He was deeply suspicious and we had to win his trust."

But slowly, like a sculptor working patiently on a masterpiece, Cus chipped away at him until he had earned first of all his respect, then his loyalty and, ultimately, his love.

D'Amato was already satisfied that Tyson had the attacking artillery to become a world champion. In their early sessions together, he put the emphasis on defence. "Any guy can punch another guy," he said. "What's clever is to punch the other guy and not be there when he punches back. I teach my fighters elusiveness."

This for Tyson meant round after round of sparring with partners much smaller and faster than him. "I had to try to make them miss without hitting them back," he said. "Even little guys can hurt if they connect and so I quickly learned to be fast and smart on my feet, and how to duck and weave."

D'Amato wanted Tyson – to paraphrase Muhammad Ali – to dance like a butterfly and hurt like a bull. Included among his lessons in the gym were many on the anatomy. Cus could sound like a surgeon about to perform a cutting operation when showing how to mount a body attack. "These have got to be the main target areas," he would say, chalking on a punchbag as if giving a guided tour of a corpse. "There's the liver, the kidney region, the heart, the floating rib, the abdomen, and take special notice of the solar plexus. These are the internal organs and soft spots that you must have as a target. Sure, hunt to the head. But when you're in at close quarters – and with your short reach that means a lot of the time – go for these spots, and really dig in, with lots of follow-through." D'Amato gave each organ a number and he or trainer Teddy Atlas would call out combinations of numbers, with willing pupil Tyson responding by throwing clusters of punches in a blur of action. It was boxing by numbers, and one day they would help Tyson hit the bingo jackpot.

Patiently, D'Amato won Tyson's confidence; first as a fighter and then as a friend. He filled his head with his self-taught philosophy and encouraged him to "live life rather than battle with it". Within months of their first meeting, Tyson had allowed the wise old man into his life as the father figure he had always lacked.

Cus needed Tyson just as much as Mike needed him. "The kid has given me an extension of life," he told us. "I've got my old interest and enthusiasm back because everything I do with Mike is a step forward. We're achieving things. I was sitting around waiting for the undertaker to call. I was mentally preparing myself for death. Many of my old friends had already gone. I wasn't afraid of dying. It happens to everybody. There ain't no defence against it. You can't go into the gym and work out how to duck out of the way of it. But a lot of people in boxing thought I had already gone under. When I suddenly started to pop up at ringside with Mike, they'd say 'Jeez, we thought you were dead.' I was able to quote my writing hero Mark Twain and say, 'Reports of my death are greatly exaggerated.' It was Mike coming into my life that stopped me thinking of death, and I started to think of living again. It's all in the mind, y'know. When you're my age – past three score years and ten – and you want to lay down and die, all you have to do is find a convenient corner. But it's just as easy to live provided you've got the motivation. Mike Tyson has given me that motivation."

Cus arranged for Tyson to leave behind the suffocating strictures of the Tryon school to live with him and Camille at Catskill where he would spend hours talking to him about a whole series of subjects ranging from great old fighters to the meaning of life. He organised private tuition to help him with his reading, and then introduced him to his extensive library that covered all subjects under the sun. As quick as you could say Ray Robinson, Tyson was up to his eyeballs in boxing books featuring the lives and times of the likes of Joe Louis and Jack

Dempsey. Then Cus got him interested in great figures of history like Napoleon and Alexander the Great. He talked at length to him about King Arthur and the nobility of knighthood and the values of honour and virtue. It was like being at the Court of 'King' Cus, and Tyson was being shown the route to Camelot.

It was the boxing history lessons that Mike liked best, and Jim Jacobs was always on the scene to bring his heroes to life. Every night a projector and screen were set up in the D'Amato living room, and Tyson would watch fight films from the Jacobs library, the most extensive collection in the world. This explains how Tyson gained an encylopaedic knowledge of boxing. It was all feeding and fuelling his dreams and ambitions.

"I knew", said Cus, "that a kid who loved pigeons couldn't be all bad. You had to peel away a few layers of mistrust and prejudice left by his tough experiences in Brooklyn. But then, underneath all the anger and suspicion, you found this kid wanting and willing to learn. I've had to show him how to deal with people. Few had ever really bothered to try and converse with him and so he didn't know how to react except in a hostile way. I taught him to talk to people and to be nice to them, but warned him to be careful about who he trusted. One of his major problems had been one of communicating but, once I got him opening up, I knew that here was not only a helluva fighter but also somebody worthwhile as a human being. And d'you know something, that was just as satisfying and rewarding to me as discovering that the kid could fight."

This from-the-heart dedication to Tyson made nonsense of the cynical stories that D'Amato was interested in him only because he could fight. There was also a school of thought that he wanted to adopt Mike just to keep him out of reach of other managers who were beginning to wake up to his potential. If that is true, then Cus deserved an Oscar because he certainly convinced us that he had fatherly feelings for Tyson that went beyond the boundaries of boxing. But there was no doubt that Cus, who was half blind, turned a blind eye to the bullying side of the two-faced kid from Brooklyn.

When his mother, Lorna, died in 1982 Cus became Tyson's legal guardian. Camille recalled, "I remember Mike coming to me one day and asking if he could call me his mother. It was one of the most moving experiences of my life. He used to introduce Cus and me to people as his mum and dad, and there were a lot of raised eyebrows when they used to look at our white faces! On Mother's Day I would get a bunch of flowers from him and, on Father's Day, he would send Cus a card. That really touched Cus. He calls me Ma, and when Cus died he put a comforting arm around my shoulders and said, 'Don't worry, Ma. I'll always look after you.' That's the sort of nice, caring boy he is. That's the boy you should be telling the world about, not this monster who I don't recognise. I don't believe half the things that are said and written about him. He's a good boy, believe me."

Once he moved full-time to the D'Amato academy, the aggression that Tyson had used in street muggings and against teachers and schoolmates was channelled exclusively into boxing. D'Amato set him up with a series of learning contests on non-sanctioned, unofficial fight cards known in the States as 'smokers' and he had 35 recorded amateur contests plus at least 20 that did not find their way into the record books. Cus was looking to get him as much experience as possible against all types, sizes and styles of fighters. Jim Jacobs even paid as much as $1,000 a time for seasoned professionals to visit the Catskill gymnasium to spar with the young prospect, and he would get the better of all of them. If any overseas heavyweights were visiting the States they would get an invitation from Cus to workout with "my kid, Mike". Frank Bruno was among the fighters who accepted. They came together for a series of sparring sessions in the summer of 1983. Tyson was 16, Bruno 21. Just a handful of spectators watched them work out, and international boxing entrepreneur Mickey Duff prophesied, "One day you two could be fighting each other before a worldwide audience and with millions of dollars at stake." It would take nearly six years for that prophecy to be proved correct.

Teddy Atlas, one of the best corner motivators and trainers in the business, was assigned by D'Amato to look after Tyson in his early amateur days. It was a winning partnership broken by an incident that provided an ominous warning of things to come. 'What I saw in Mike away from the ring was an ability to manipulate people," said Atlas after a bust-up that ended with him losing his job. "Cus had always made it priority number one that his boxers should be disciplined both in and out of the ring. I know because I lived with him just like Mike did, and he helped straighten me out from when I was a wild kid. Nobody was tougher on discipline than Cus. But when Mike started to get above himself with his behaviour Cus compromised himself by refusing to hand out his usual treatment. Once, after Mike had got physical with a teacher at his school in Catskill, I decided to punish him by taking away from him the thing he loved best, access to the gymnasium and his boxing training. I suspended him from the gym, but Cus reversed the decision and that was a sign that Mike was getting too many things his own way. There was no doubting his enormous potential as a fighter. That was beyond question, even though there were times when he felt intimidated before getting into the ring. I remember clearly him once crying with a mixture of tension and apprehension before the final of the Junior Olympics in Denver in '82. He then went into the ring and won in devastating fashion."

The incident that led to Atlas parting from Tyson and D'Amato has a telling place in the inside story on Tyson. It was reported to Atlas that Tyson had made an improper suggestion to a 12-year-old local girl and had allegedly abused her. This was the breaking point for the tough but honest trainer, who has a scar running the length of his face as a permanent reminder of a knife attack in what he admits was his reckless youth. Legend has it that he put a gun to Tyson's head in the deserted gymnasium and warned him that if he did not start behaving himself he would blow his brains out.

Asked for his version, Atlas – who, like Tyson, had been as close to Cus as a son and had lived in D'Amato's Catskill home – shrugged and gave a knowing smile. "Let's just say I took what action was necessary at the time," he said. "Mike was not showing sufficient respect to people and I wanted to stop him going any further down the wrong road. I did it in the way that I knew he would understand best. You have to understand that I saw it as a duty to protect my people."

D'Amato seemed to be siding with Atlas when he sent Tyson back to the Tryon reform school. But within a matter of days he was back living and training in Catskill, and Atlas was on the sidelines.

Tyson had heard time and again the boxing legend of how Floyd Patterson had won an Olympic gold medal at the age of 17 in 1952 and then, under the guidance of D'Amato, had gone on to become the world's youngest heavyweight champion four years later. Now he had the dream of following in Floyd's footsteps. Olympic champion first, then the world heavyweight title. And quicker than Patterson.

But it was a dream that died in Las Vegas in 1984. He was matched with Henry Tillman in a final tryout for the US Olympic team for the '84 Games in Los Angeles. They met in a return showdown in Las Vegas on 6 July 1984, after Tillman had scored a narrow points victory in the Olympic trials at Fort Worth the previous month. A lot of people – including Tyson – thought he had fought his way to a revenge points win and into the Olympics. But the judges ruled that Tillman was the winner and he went on to golden glory in the Olympics. Tyson was seen later that evening smashing his bare fists against a tree in downtown Las Vegas, and screaming out with anger and frustration. The judges had robbed him of his dream, and they had made him doubly determined to become professional heavyweight champion of the world. Cus was as crushed as Tyson by the decision because he knew there was no better platform for an American fighter than winning a gold medal in an Olympics staged on home soil.

"That was when Mike really showed his strength of character," said Cus. "The Olympics would have been something really special. They only come round in your own country once in a blue moon. Believe me, Mike was the best amateur in the world at the time of the Games. But in three rounds they could run away from him and steal the points. Henry Tillman fought him as if he was trying to get into the track and field team. Mike would have been a sensation in the Los Angeles Games. That would have meant a lot to both of us. Mike knew that Floyd – followed by Ali, Frazier and Foreman – had won Olympic gold medals and had then gone on to win the world heavyweight crown. By rights, he should have been in Los Angeles to represent the United States and he would have won the gold medal in style. He was bitterly disappointed at first, but then shrugged it off and said, 'Let's go for the professionals.' "

This was the signal for Cus to summon Jim Jacobs to tell him that the time was right to launch Mike Tyson as a professional.

4: Enter the Historymakers

JIM Jacobs knew virtually everything there was to know about fast hands – and Mike Tyson had the fastest in the business. In the 1950s and 1960s, Jacobs was to handball what Babe Ruth was to baseball or Don Bradman was to cricket. He was 'The King'. Known to his army of fans as 'Fast Hands Jimmy', he won a place in the *Guinness Book of Records* by winning a record 16 American handball titles. He was the four-walls singles champion six times between 1955 and 1965 and in doubles he and his partner Marty Decatur were undefeated for an astonishing stretch of ten years.

Representing first the Hollywood YMCA and later the Los Angeles Athletic Club, Jacobs dominated the sport just as one of his heroes, Rocky Marciano, monopolized the world heavyweight championship. Like The Rock, Jacobs got out of his sport while at the top. He retired at 40 and never returned to the game he had graced with some of the most skilful play that had ever been seen in a sport that calls for quick reflexes, fast hand-and-eye coordination and rapid footwork. He retained his deep love of sport in general and boxing in particular. Along with partner Bill Cayton, he was the brains behind the brawn of Mike Tyson.

Jacobs was a mystery man when it came to the extent of his wealth. There was no doubt that he had accumulated a lot of money with shrewd business deals, but he himself spread the story that he was mega-rich from a family inheritance and there was never any real evidence of this vast wealth. He was, however, rich enough to be able to indulge what was originally just a hobby of collecting old fight films and he put together the greatest collection in the world. Shortly after Tyson had become the youngest world heavyweight champion, Jacobs showed us around his humidity-controlled vaults in New Jersey where his precious films were kept locked away under the eye of a 24-hour security guard.

He told us that his obsession with boxing films began in the 1940s when he was growing up in Los Angeles. "Joe Louis was then heavyweight champion of the world and my idol," he recalled. "I used to buy 8-millimetre films of his fights. Among my favourites were his victories over Billy Conn, Arturo Godoy, Max Baer and 'Two Ton' Tony Galento."

In 1954, Jacobs joined forces with former New York advertising executive Bill Cayton, a dapper, dignified man whose love and knowledge of boxing and fight films was equal even to that of Jacobs. He had been the man behind the *Greatest Fights of the Century* television show that ran in the United States from 1948 until 1954. Together, Jacobs and Cayton formed a company called *Big Fights Inc.* and they built up a virtual monopoly of the world's fight film business that has attracted more and more collectors now that television video recorders have made the showing and the saving of them so easy.

We have given this background to Jacobs and Cayton so that you understand into what caring hands Cus D'Amato was placing Mike Tyson. They were as much interested in history as profit (well, almost), and they saw in Tyson a fighter who they were convinced could rewrite the boxing record books. Jacobs and Cayton considered Tyson a throwback to the old-style champions, both in his style and his attitude. With a PR campaign that was quite brilliant in its concept, they deliberately resisted launching Tyson with the sort of showbiz fanfare that has become the norm with any exceptional prospect entering the professional ranks. They knew that Tyson's fists would do the talking quickly enough to get him noticed and so they kept his early fights at a low-key pitch. While most of the fighters were climbing into the ring preening like peacocks in multicoloured robes and with knee-length socks and tasselled boots, Tyson deliberately made his entrance looking more like 'golden oldie' Sam Langford – the Boston Tar Baby — used to look back in the first quarter of the century.

He had black trunks, no socks, old-style ankle-high boots and just a white towel thrown around his shoulders. He looked just as if he had stepped out of one of those old, flickering black and white Jim Jacobs films. Even his hair was cut 'pudding-basin' style as with the fighters of the 1920s. The effect was quite startling. He had an intimidating warrior look about him and oozed power and menace before throwing a single punch. The only people not exactly ecstatic about his appearance were sportswear manufacturers. If every boxer started to drop to the stark and simple basics like Tyson they would have an output crisis on their hands! Mike said of his all-black attire: "In the old cowboy movies the good guys always wore white and the outlaws black. I'm not a bad guy but that's the impression I like to give." His opponents were not slow to get the message. To them, he was all bad. Jacobs and Cayton let Tyson move quietly and quickly through his first five fights – won in a total of nine rounds – and then opened the publicity floodgates. They had exclusive films made of each contest and then skilfully edited them into an introductory video. Five hundred tapes were sent with a covering biographical sketch to every major television company, sports agency and newspaper in the United States. We were included in the mail-shot as European boxing writers, and international commentators and columnists were sucked into the 'Watch out for Mike Tyson' promotional campaign. Suddenly the boy from the Brooklyn ghetto was as well known as any of the major heavyweights.

Inevitably, there were some critics soon out sniping at Jacobs and Cayton for allegedly pushing Tyson too hard. It was a widely held view that their fight-a-fortnight plan was asking too much of the teenaged Tyson. "It was Cus D'Amato who chose the game plan and nobody knows boxing and boxers better than he," Jacobs told us in response to the criticism. "He felt that because Mike was so young he needed to know what it was like to get your hands taped before a fight, to get used to the tension of that drive to the arena, to listen to last-minute instructions and to experience that special gut-churning atmosphere that can make or break a fighter. It can destroy your nerves if you are not accustomed to it. You can't keep a kid like Tyson buried in the gymnasium. You'll take all his emotional drive away from him. We preferred him doing his fighting in the ring than in the gym. It's in the gym where fighters become stale. There's an old saying that fighters leave their fight behind them in the training camp. We were not going to let that happen to Mike. We wanted him to fight often, just like the great champions used to in the old days. There was no danger that we were going to burn him out. Mike thrived on the action, just as the greats of the ring like Gavilan, LaMotta, Louis, Robinson and Basilio had before him. We had to weather some vitriolic press, but we knew exactly what we were doing. Mike enjoyed every minute of it and was coming along nicely like a true thoroughbred. The kid was a natural."

Jacobs had a powerful supporter for his 'fighting fit' theory in José Torres, then the New York boxing commissioner who had once been guided to the world light-heavyweight championship by D'Amato. "I think this constant fight action is the best thing in the world for Tyson," José said after his tenth rapid victory in just seven months. "It's not as if he is having tough fights. He is winning all the time in one or two rounds. He's one of those types who needs to fight as much as possible. The more you win, the more you tend to win. It is going to take somebody very special to stop his winning streak. He is as exciting a prospect as I've ever seen. He's got the punching power of George Foreman but is much faster with his fists. His style reminds me of Marciano but he is much bigger and more powerfully built. And he's got a left hook like Frazier, but it's even more potent. Getting together with Cus was just about the best possible thing that could happen for him. Nobody could have matched Cus for bringing out all Tyson's potential. I see the D'Amato touch in everything that Mike does. He could be the best thing that's happened to boxing for years, since the young Ali first came on the scene."

While we're quoting Torres, we cannot resist passing on the story he tells about his early days under the D'Amato banner. Normally a model citizen, José stepped out of line once when he got involved in a street brawl with somebody who had insulted him. It led to him being arrested and taken down to the local police precinct. He was allowed the customary 'phone call and, of course, 'phoned Cus at the Gramercy gymnasium. You didn't need a lawyer when you had a street-wise man like D'Amato to consult. Nervously, he dialled Cus's number.

"Cus," said Torres, embarrassed and apologetic, "I'm in the police precinct. I got into a street fight."

"José," said D'Amato, with deep concern coming down the line into the ear of Torres, "did you keep your chin down?"

Torres became closer to Tyson than almost anybody, and it was he who first rang public alarm bells about his wild behaviour outside the ring. In a book while he was still world champion, he made startling allegations about Tyson's sexual appetite and his rough treatment of women that would weigh heavily against Tyson at a future date. Not surprisingly, Tyson felt he had been betrayed by a man he had counted as a close friend. He said on American television show *A Current Affair*: "In my view, Torres is a traitor who is worse than a murderer."

But back to the early Mike Tyson story. With D'Amato becoming frail in his mid-70s, Tyson's everyday training preparation was put into the capable hands of Kevin Rooney, another D'Amato-tutored fighter just coming to the end of a professional career in which he had risen to a world junior welterweight title contender. Like his former friend Atlas, Rooney had lived with and worshipped D'Amato. He and Tyson became as close as brothers. "I know Mike as well as anybody can know him," Rooney said during the lightning journey towards the world championship. "He's capable of winning the title because he's learned so much from Cus including that vital inner confidence, like a Zen thing. He has got tremendous will and heart. You've gotta have that if you're going anywhere in this business. Also, he secretly likes the attention. He enjoys climbing into the ring. That's his stage and, while he never shows off normally, he can be extrovert out there under the ring lights. And he loves every second of it."

A few years later Rooney would not have a kind word to say for Tyson after he had been sacked during a perplexing period when the then world champion seemed intent on purging his past.

Floyd Patterson, the fighter Tyson knocked out of the record books as the youngest heavyweight champion of all time, was not allowed to be part of Tyson's past. He was never invited to get close to the young man who had followed in his fighting footsteps. The feeling in the totally professional Tyson camp was that they did not want to risk any of the self doubts that used to assail Patterson creeping through the Tyson armour.

Patterson admitted quite freely that he failed to come to terms with his success. "I didn't know how to handle it," he said. "I was full of complexes and suspicions." He had so many hang-ups that he became known in the fight game as 'Freudian Floyd'. After his first-round knockout defeat by Sonny Liston in their first world title fight in 1962, he felt so ashamed of himself that he crept out of the stadium through a back exit, wearing a false beard and glasses as a disguise. Yet we can say without fear of contradiction that Patterson is the last man on earth who ever had reason to feel shame. He was always a credit to boxing with his dignity and behaviour, in and out of the ring, and his record as a fighter stands comparison with all but a handful of Hall of Fame greats. He might have matched any of them if he'd had more body weight and if his chin had been as strong as his heart.

One thing is for certain, and that is that Patterson was too much of a sportsman and a gentleman to be caught saying the sort of thing that brought Tyson a torrent of criticism after his eighteenth straight victory over Jesse Ferguson. He knocked Ferguson down with a sweeping right uppercut, and said in the dressing-room later: "I wanted to have one more shot at him so that I could punch his nose up into his brain." Ernestine Coleman, his former social worker, captured the mood of many people when she sat down and wrote a letter to Tyson telling him how upset she was by this sort of talk. "I told him that he should try to behave like a man, not an animal," she said.

Jim Jacobs, Bill Cayton and Kevin Rooney attempted to build a protective wall around Tyson to try to block at least some of the pressure that had torpedoed Patterson during his days as a D'Amato fighter. It was the sort of protection Patterson could have done with when he won the world heavyweight title vacated by Rocky Marciano. He knocked out 'Ageless' Archie Moore in five rounds at the age of 21 in 1956. "Like it or not, Mike Tyson and I are bound together by our pasts," said Patterson after Tyson had replaced him as the youngest ever heavyweight title holder. "We both know what it's like down there at the bottom of the heap. I admire him enormously as a fighter. If you put him in the ring with a gorilla I wouldn't bet a cent on the gorilla. But how will he react to all the attention he is going to get? If anything, it's even tougher today than when I was the youngest champion because everywhere you turn there is a television cameraman, a press photographer and a reporter analysing you from every angle. He has come so far so quickly that he has got to be a very special person to be able to handle it all."

Patterson knew exactly what he was talking about because he and Tyson followed the same route to the top. Born in Waco, North Carolina, on 4 January 1935, Floyd was the third of 11 children whose parents never knew where the next penny was coming from. The family moved to the same Brooklyn district where Tyson was born and Floyd got into the wrong company and was sent to a rehabilitation school for juvenile delinquents. As for so many kids who have wandered on to the wrong side of the tracks, boxing proved the salvation for Patterson. When he was 14 he followed two elder brothers to the New York gymnasium run by our old friend Cus D'Amato, and that was where his career and new way of life started. Thirty years later, the same script was being written for Mike Tyson,

But Tyson's handlers were determined that the similarities between Tyson and Patterson went no further. They fed Tyson's ego and his confidence to help him avoid the complexes that were Patterson's biggest enemies. Every time he climbed into the ring for a major fight Floyd had himself to beat as well as his opponent. But Tyson had total confidence in himself and his ability. This is best illustrated by his quote to Jim Jacobs a couple of hours before his 1986 world championship challenge against Trevor Berbick, which was the most important fight of his life and in which he was bidding to take over from Patterson as the youngest ever champion.

"How are you feeling?" he asked Jacobs.

"My hands are a little sweaty and I'm beginning to feel a bit nervous," admitted his co-manager, who was used to the pressure of big sporting occasions.

"Don't worry about it," said Tyson, as calm as can be. "It's quite normal to feel that way before a world title fight."

Jacobs laughed as he told us the story. "It's the sort of thing I should have been saying to him," he said. "But there was this young kid trying to build up my confidence. I have so much faith in him when he climbs into the ring that I have zero trepidation."

Did Tyson worry about the sort of pressures that were such a burden to Patterson? "The world championship seemed to be a weight on Patterson's shoulders but I'm enjoying every second of being the champ," he said after a year as the title holder. "I don't think Floyd really knew in which direction he was headed, but I know exactly what I want to do and how I want to do it."

He was helped in handling the pressures in and out of the ring by sessions of hypnosis treatment. "He has been getting mental as well as physical training," explained Kevin Rooney. "It's just a question of tapping into the subconscious mind to help him think positively. It is, of course, a Cus D'Amato idea. I had the treatment myself when I was fighting and it helped me enormously."

The man who could boast that he managed to send Tyson to sleep was 71-year-old New York City hypnotherapist John Halpin. "It was Cus who first brought Tyson to me," he recalled. "I had worked with several of his fighters including José Torres. Mike was a good hypnotic subject straight from the start. Cus had told him to give me his complete trust and confidence and so he was quickly relaxed. The subconscious mind is exceptionally powerful and can dominate your thinking. It is down there that fears and inhibitions lurk and my objective is to help my subjects bypass their doubts and fears. When you hear any boxers, or anybody for that matter, say they have no fears you can bet they are lying. We all have hidden fear but you can come to terms with it with the right approach and attitude. Mike has learned to overcome his apprehensions and knows how to handle his fear."

As well as introducing him to hypnotherapy, D'Amato taught Tyson never to waste time worrying about past mistakes. "Don't think about the past except to apply its lessons to the present," he used to say. "I want to teach you that fighting is much more than hitting a bag and then getting into the ring and hitting an opponent. It is as much about psychology as physical effort. Always think positively and never, never waste time on negative thoughts about what might have been. Today and tomorrow matter. Yesterday is history."

Jacobs, Cayton and Rooney continued where D'Amato left off. "When Cus died," said Jacobs, "we wanted to continue everything that has contributed to Mike's success. This included the hypnotherapy sessions. If Cus said it was the right way to prepare for boxing then who am I to argue? Nobody, but nobody, knew better than Cus about anything to do with a boxer's preparation."

What Jacobs and Cayton knew – possibly even better than D'Amato knew – is how to get the best possible packaging and presentation for their fighter. They were carefully selective with the marketing of Tyson and deliberately projected him as a man of dignity and sensitivity, a world away from his bullying ring image.

A secret that Jacobs kept from Tyson, and from everybody else following the death of Cus D'Amato, was that he himself was a dying man living on borrowed time.

Everywhere he went in his early days as the champion Tyson had at least one minder with him, and often he was accompanied by Steve Lott, a world-wise man from Manhattan who knew how to diplomatically steer Mike through avenues of demanding fans without causing any hassle and aggravation. "I'm proud to have all these people interested in me," said Tyson. "When they shout 'Hi Champ!' it gives me a terrific feeling. I want to give them all hope because hope is what can lead you out of the sort of depression that hits you in the kind of place that I've come from. Take it from me, because I know it's a fact. Give somebody hope and they've got something to cling to."

"This guy is so popular that you have to see it to believe it," said Lott, who carried the title of assistant manager. "He is mobbed wherever he goes in New York. He likes to go back to his old neighbourhood after fights. It gives him a buzz, and he encourages all the kids with words of wisdom. He is really sincere in wanting to help them escape the poverty trap just like he has. I get worried for him when he's walking those mean streets of his childhood, but he knows how to handle any situation. He's been there and has done it all."

But it was not long before Tyson was in bigger trouble than he had ever experienced during his days as a ghetto thug. And Cus D'Amato was not around to show him how to wriggle out of it. He had missed the signpost to Camelot. The champion was headed for Doomsville.

On the sad day in November 1985 when Cus died of pneumonia at the age of 77, all eyes were on Tyson to see how he would react. A lot of people – those who did not really know him – thought he had quickly come to terms with it when he insisted on going ahead with his twelfth fight just nine days later, but Tyson hid his feelings. "He was grievously hurt, and deep down he still suffers greatly," Jacobs told us after Tyson had dedicated his world title victory over Trevor Berbick a year later to the memory of D'Amato. "Mike had grown to love Cus but he didn't realise just how much. Suddenly it was as if his head was cut off."

Camille Ewald added to the evidence of how Tyson had been devastated by D'Amato's death. "Coming back from Cus's funeral," she recalled, "Mike broke down and cried. He said, 'I never knew what love was until now. He taught me so much.' It was the first time I ever saw him cry."

Tyson and Jacobs, along with Floyd Patterson and José Torres, were among D'Amato's pall bearers. On his gravestone was carved the quote:

The boy comes to me with a spark of interest.
I feed the spark and it becomes a flame.
I feed the flame and it becomes a fire.
I feed the fire and it becomes a roaring blaze.

Just two years and three months later, Jim Jacobs died of leukaemia, the illness that he had been secretly fighting for nine years. "He battled the illness with great courage and dignity," said his widow, Loraine. "He was convinced a cure was around the corner, but it was not to be. Jim believed in fighting adversity from within himself, and his attitude was a lesson to us all." A Jim Jacobs Leukaemia Research Fund was set up as a memorial.

Mike Tyson had lost the two people who had done most to give shape and meaning to his life.

They were the two men who had put him on the right path. He had nowhere near the same rapport and understanding with Bill Cayton. Suddenly he was like a runaway car, and a crash seemed inevitable. It was two women who finally sent him spinning out of control.

5: Beauty and the Beast

IT was a beautiful, fragile-looking actress who helped bring Mike Tyson to his knees, something all but one of his opponents failed to do. He was put through an emotional wringer by Robin Givens, his wife for 12 turbulent months until a divorce finalized down in the Dominican Republic just 11 days before his 1989 title defence against Britain's Frank Bruno in Las Vegas.

Robin, and her formidable mother Ruth Roper, had to live with continual accusations that they were gold diggers following a secret wedding ceremony in Chicago after Tyson had become infatuated when seeing her starring in the television sitcom *Head of the Class.* It was like window shopping on a grand scale. He saw her on his television screen, rang up for a date and they were married after a passionate romance. There was time enough, it appeared, for Miss Givens to become pregnant. Tyson was devastated when four months into the marriage she informed him that she had miscarried.

The wedding ceremony may have been secret, but the marriage was conducted in the full glare of publicity. Robin always refuted the 'gold digger' charge, claiming that what had been true love was poisoned by Tyson's violent and unreasonable behaviour and, ultimately, her failure to steer him away from his deeply embedded ghetto influences.

It was quickly clear that Robin and her mother were trying to build a wall between the champion and his oldest friends, who they saw as a bad influence on Tyson. They persuaded him to set up home in a luxurious $5 million mansion out in Bernardsville, New Jersey, which became no-go territory for anybody that they considered as 'unsuitable'.

The events over the 12 months following their marriage could not have been conjured up by an over-imaginative Hollywood writer preparing a script for Robin. This is a catalogue of just some of the extraordinary episodes that kept the headline-hungry media fully fed as they focused on what, predictably, became tagged the 'Beauty and the Beast' affair:

6 February 1988: Tyson and Robin Givens are married in a top-secret ceremony in Chicago. The bride is 22, the groom 21. He had gone to Chicago on the pretext that he wanted to watch a basketball match. Even his closest friends are not told of the wedding plans. Just two weeks earlier Tyson had pulverised Larry Holmes in four rounds in Atlantic City to record his thirty-third consecutive victory and his sixth world championship triumph. Bill Cayton says: "Mike seemed pretty serious about three women in his life, and he invited all three to see him fight Holmes. That took some juggling on our part, I can tell you. We sat Miss America, Suzette Charles, in one section, Robin Givens in a second section and a beautiful British model called Naomi Campbell in a third section. Mike and I had a laugh about it after the fight, and he said he was going off to the coast for a few days. The next thing I heard he was married to Robin Givens." Paid $500 for his first professional fight in 1985, Tyson could now command more than $10 million a contest. He had a seven-fight, $26 million exclusive TV contract with Home Box Office, and it was conservatively estimated that he would, over the next five years, earn an extra $50 million from commercial activities. The ink is hardly dry on the marriage certificate before those who claimed to have Tyson's best interests at heart are questioning whether Robin's motives for marriage are love or money. We Tyson Watchers, who had seen plenty of boxers knocked over by women, wondered whether the champ would have misgivings about marrying Miss Givens.

21 March 1988: Watched from the ringside by his wife, Tyson knocks out Tony Tubbs in two rounds in a world title defence in Tokyo. He says that he now wants to spend more time with his bride before his June title date with number one challenger Michael Spinks. Tyson confides to close friends that Robin is expecting his child. Missing from the ringside for the first time since he launched his professional career is co-manager Jim Jacobs, who lies seriously ill in a New York hospital. The champion is unaware that it is a fatal illness. Jacobs told him that he would not be at the fight because he had a pressing business engagement in Texas.

23 March 1988: Jim Jacobs dies in New York from lymphocytic leukaemia, a condition from which he had secretly suffered for nine years. Tyson is devastated but also bewildered by the news of his co-manager's death at the age of 58. "I had no idea he was a sick man," he says. "I just cannot believe this has happened. First Cus. Now Jim. I find it hard to take." He had been forced to break training for the fight against Tubbs when summoned to an urgent meeting in Albany with Jacobs and his partner Bill Cayton. With José Torres as the witness, Tyson signed contracts that – in the event of the demise of Jacobs – would make Cayton his sole manager, with a third of his ring earnings going to Cayton and Loraine Jacobs, Jim's wife. This would soon become a matter for bitter legal fisticuffs.

26 April 1988: The village world of boxing is alive with talk that Don King, the shock-haired, larger-than-life promoter, is about to muscle in on the Mike Tyson empire following the death of Jim Jacobs. Bill Cayton issues a 'hands off' warning. He says that he has a watertight contract with the champion that runs until 1992, and he confirms that it entitles both himself and Loraine Jacobs, the widow of Jim Jacobs, to a third of Tyson's ring earnings. The furnace of media attention is now turned up and focused on the part that Robin's mother, Ruth Roper, is playing in the Beauty and the Beast affair. A high-powered businesswoman and president of a New York computer company, she is reported to be taking more than a passing interest in Tyson's finances. She encourages Robin to get right of attorney over Tyson's business affairs, and they openly challenge Bill Cayton's right to take a third of his ring earnings. Cayton said: "I got a telephone call and the voice on the other end of the line said, 'This is Mrs Mike Tyson. From now on I'm handling his business affairs.' " Robin says in angry response to the 'gold digger' claims: "When his management met me they thought I would make a good Mrs Tyson, I was pretty enough and well-spoken enough. They never realised that I wasn't just interested in shopping but that I happen to love Michael and I care about what happens to him. They didn't think I was a hustler until I started asking how much money Michael had in the bank and why he was giving them 33 per cent of it. We had noticed a discrepancy, and decided that on Mike's behalf we should take a closer look. Our view was that if Mike had, for instance, been entitled to $70 million and he had received only $50 million then something was seriously wrong. They don't seem to understand that we're not interfering outsiders. We're family, with only Mike's interests at heart. I'm his wife. He is my husband, and my mom has become his mother."

19 June 1988: Rumours that all is not well in the Tyson marriage are given weight when Stephanie, Robin's tennis-playing sister, makes startling revelations in an interview during a tournament in Madeira. She claims that Tyson has "emotionally and physically" abused her sister, and that the stress of the relationship has caused Robin to have a miscarriage. "The marriage was a mistake from the beginning," she says. Robin refuses to comment on the allegations but admits, "It has been very hard, but I love Mike and I hope we can have a life together." Tyson shrugs his huge shoulders when told about Stephanie's comments. "I can't understand it," he says. "Maybe I'm not man enough for them. But I'll get by somehow. I always find a way to get by." The evidence is piling up against Tyson and his state of mind. Police had earlier reported that he crashed his $100,000 silver Bentley into two parked cars, and that when they questioned him he said, "Take the damn car. You can have it. I don't want it." It was alleged that Robin Givens had been in the car with him and that they were having an argument when he ran off the road and crashed. The champion was also having to face claims from a parking lot attendant that he had hit him when he tried to stop Tyson making advances to a terrified girl. It had been settled out of court with a $105,000 payment. Bill Cayton was one who could not believe that Tyson was a wife beater. "He is totally obsessed by Robin Givens," he says. "I have never seen anything like it. He worships her. It is ridiculous to suggest that he's been using violence against her."

27 June 1988: Tyson makes nonsense of the theory that his domestic troubles will affect his boxing when he knocks Michael Spinks cold in just 91 seconds of unbridled fury in Atlantic City's Convention Centre. Butch Lewis, bubbly, extrovert manager of Spinks, who wears a bowtie but no shirt, says: "I like to try to put a little pressure on the opponents immediately before a fight, and so I called into Tyson's dressing-room to see if I could rattle him a little. I made a fuss about a bump in his bandages and tried to get him riled up. But I wish I'd never gone in that dressing-room. I could not believe my eyes. He was so motivated that he was punching holes in the wall. I couldn't get out of there quick enough. I knew my man was in trouble, and sure enough Tyson gave one of the most potent performances ever seen in a heavyweight championship fight. The critics crucified my man, but nobody would have lived with Tyson that night. Nobody." There is more action outside than inside the ring. Bill Cayton is served with legal papers in which Tyson contends he was duped into signing a new four-year contract with Cayton and Jacobs a month before the death of Jacobs. Tyson claims it was the duty of both men to have disclosed to him that Jacobs was already a dying man when he signed. Mike is unable to take on board the possibility that Jacobs kept the seriousness of his condition from him because he did not want to cause him any distress during his build-up to a title fight. The lawsuit charged that Tyson's signature on the contract was 'induced by fraud, material misrepresentations and material omissions'. Tyson insists: "I would never have signed that contract had I known Jim Jacobs was dying." At the after-fight press conference, Tyson erupts over what he sees as media invasion of his private life following increasing scrutiny of his marriage and his alleged wife-beating and drinking binges. "You're assholes," he says. "You are trying to disgrace my family."

29 June 1988: Just 48 hours after his stunning victory over Spinks, Tyson makes an astonishing announcement that he is retiring from the ring because he is feeling burned out. "I'm willing to sacrifice, to give up boxing to save my family," he tells an incredulous media audience. "I just feel it is the best thing to do. My personal and professional lives are so vastly different that I can't manage both of them. So I'm giving up boxing. I'm depressed, unhappy and I've put my wife through a lot of stress. I've had fun. I live to fight when I'm in that ring, but I'm not a happy guy. I know people will think I'll come back. They think I can't stay away from boxing. But I can do it if I want to do it." The feeling in boxing is that the retirement announcement is a tactic aimed at putting pressure on Bill Cayton in their contract dispute. "If I have a flaw," says Tyson, "it's that I am too trusting. But in future I won't be a sucker for anybody. I'm through trusting people. What I've discovered is that people basically suck. They are always trying to screw you. I am now suspicious of everybody who comes to me with any sort of a suggestion. 'What are they after?' I have to ask myself."

7 July 1988: Property tycoon Donald Trump announces that he has agreed to act as adviser to Mike Tyson. He reveals that he has had meetings with Tyson's lawyer, Michael Winston, and with his mother-in-law, Ruth Roper, and he has now agreed to work with the champion. Trump has been involved with Don King as co-promoter of three of Tyson's title fights. The champion is contracted to fight Britain's Frank Bruno in an open-air show at Wembley Stadium on 3 September, but this fight is in doubt.

18 July 1988: Tyson reverses his retirement decision and says that he will fight on. In future, he reveals, he will manage himself. "I shall call the shots," he said. "Mr Trump is kindly acting as my adviser and he will be putting together a consortium of businessmen to help me with all aspect of things outside the ring, but I'll be the man in charge." It is clear that Tyson will need all the advice he can get. An unsubstantiated story has broken that, during a holiday in the Caribbean, he beat up his wife in their hotel room, making such a racket that the guests next door summoned the security guard.

25 July 1988: The Wembley fight with Frank Bruno is put on hold as Tyson reaches a compromise agreement with Bill Cayton, who will, in future, take 20 per cent of Tyson's ring earnings instead of the previously agreed 33 per cent. "I intend to fight only when I want to fight," says Tyson. "In the past I fought Tony Tucker and Larry Holmes when I didn't really feel like fighting. I don't feel like fighting at the moment so Frank Bruno will have to wait for his chance. I'm glad the legal business is out of the way. Now I can give all my attention to running the show."

23 August 1988: It seems that Tyson is determined to push the self-destruct button as he makes worldwide headlines again, this time with a bizarre, unscheduled fight that leaves him with a fractured right hand.

He receives the injury in a brief street brawl with a former opponent, Mitch 'Blood' Green (there's a report of their official 1986 fight in Part Two). Amazingly, the clash takes place at around 4.30 in the morning outside Dapper Dan's, a men's fashion boutique in New York's Harlem district. According to Tyson, he was visiting the store to collect an $800 made-to-measure white leather jacket emblazoned with the words: 'Don't believe the hype.' He claims he just happened to run into his old rival Green, who had once been a gangleader in the ghettos where Tyson used to run wild. "Green started ranting and raving when he saw me," Tyson told a hastily called press conference. "He kept shouting that Don King and I owed him money. Green came at me and I pushed him off. I've not had a street fight in seven years and I was nervous. He ripped my shirt and started throwing punches. I had to defend myself, and hit him just once." Green suffered a five-stitch gash on the bridge of his nose and a swollen left eye. Tyson had to go to hospital to have his fractured hand put in plaster. According to Green's version of the 'fight' – made to the police – the altercation took place outside a nightclub next door to the fashion boutique. "I told Tyson that Don King done took my money," said Green. "Tyson said, 'You saying I didn't beat you? Then let's get it on again.' Then he suckerpunched me, and ran off like a big sissy." Green dropped assault charges on the understanding that he would get an official return with Tyson, who agreed provided he managed to beat a rated contender. "I can beat that punk anytime anywhere," said Tyson. "He hit me first and then I hit him back. It was quicker than Spinks." The biggest loser on the night was Frank Bruno. His rescheduled October date at Wembley with Tyson was again postponed. The question many people were asking is, "If Tyson has such a strong marriage, what is he doing on the streets of Harlem at 4.30 in the morning?"

4 September 1988: Exactly what happened on this Sunday morning in the tiny town of Catskill in upstate New York is shrouded in a mist of rumour, half-truths and gossip. The certain fact is that Mike Tyson was knocked unconscious when he drove his wife's BMW at full speed into a tree outside the home of his surrogate mother Camille Ewald. He had been staying with Camille and feeding his beloved pigeons while Mrs Tyson was in New York with her mother watching the US Open tennis championships. He had regained consciousness by the time he was taken on a stretcher by ambulance to the local Catskill hospital before being transferred to a Manhattan medical centre for neurological tests. It was reported as a driving accident in wet, skiddy conditions until a sensational story surfaced in the *New York Daily News* that Tyson had told his wife on the telephone before getting behind the wheel that he was going to kill himself by crashing the car. When Robin visited him in hospital, he is alleged to have said: "I told you I'd do it. And when I get out of here I'll do it again." The suicide-bid story might have died with the strong denials that came from the Tyson camp, but it was given new impetus when it was revealed that Robin's mother, Ruth Roper, had requested that he should get urgent psychiatric treatment. Then it emerged that, as a youth, Tyson had been on medication to correct a chemical imbalance. It was later learned that blood tests had shown he was clear of this problem, but he could not shake off the belief of spectators watching his amazing adventures that here was a young man bent on self destruction. A lawyer for the Tysons issued a statement saying they would not comment on the suicide rumours, although privately Tyson was dismissing the story as "total crap". The lawyer was not quite so to the point. His statement read: "The champion and his family love each other very much. They are very supportive of each other and they would like the privacy that is the entitlement of any other citizens in America."

8 September 1988: A New York TV station gets an exclusive telephone interview with Tyson. He tells them: "I've got too much still to accomplish in the ring and in my private life to even think about killing myself. No one loves living more than I do. It's funny, but why can't I be successful, have money and have a wife and be happy? It's very difficult. Me and my wife just love each other and are just trying to live a basic life. I'm never going to leave my wife. My wife is never going to leave me. So whatever somebody's trying to do by spreading all these stories, it's never going to work out." Once again, the Frank Bruno fight was postponed.

17 September 1988: A fit-again Tyson turns up in Moscow of all places, visiting his wife while she is on location making an episode of *Head of* *the Class*. It is reported that he has several losses of temper while in Moscow, and is alleged to have chased his wife, mother-in-law and a secretary through the hotel in blind rage. Another report suggests that he threatened to kill himself by hanging from a hotel balcony. On his return to the United States he gets involved in a bust-up with a television news crew filming his early-morning run. He smashes their camera to the ground, and the TV station threaten to file charges with the police. Tyson is undergoing counselling with psychiatrist Dr. Henry L. McCurtis, who is reported to be of the opinion that the world heavyweight boxing champion is a manic depressive. "I guess I was born with this disease," says Tyson. "I am out of control at times. I can't help it. This is the way it's been all my life. Maybe that's why I'm successful at what I do. It's like going through a metamorphosis – changing from very, very depressed to very, very highly strung. You're just paranoid. It's abnormal." Later, another medical specialist dismisses the manic depressive theory as incorrect. "I would agree that he suffers from a mood regulatory disturbance," said New York psychiatrist Dr. Abraham Halpern after a clinical examination of Tyson. "But his condition is a far cry from a major mental disorder." This is a relief to Tyson because it means he does not have to take the calming drug, Lithium, which could have had an effect on his boxing plans.

30 September 1988: Millions of American television viewers see Mike Tyson publicly humiliated by his wife on the coast-to-coast show *20-20* when she gives a no-holds-barred interview to Barbara Walters. With her husband sitting impassively alongside her on the sofa at their sumptuous New Jersey home, Mrs Tyson indicates that perhaps all the rumours of wife-beating and the suicide attempt are true when she says: "It's been torture. It's been pure hell. It's been worse than anything I could possibly imagine. I'm not talking about once a week. Every day there has been some kind of fight. Michael is intimidating to say the least. I think there's a time when he just cannot control his temper, and that's frightening . . . frightening for me and for my mother. I don't know where Mike Tyson would be if it were not for my mother. I don't know where I'd be. It is my mother who has been the glue that has held this marriage together. For the first time, I can understand about abused women. Recently I've become afraid. I mean very, very much afraid.

Michael is a manic depressive." She expresses concern that, if she left him, Michael would be "more deliberate and kill himself or hurt somebody else". Tyson, wearing a brightly coloured open-necked shirt, has a sheepish smile on his face like a little boy caught misbehaving in class. It does not seem to sink in with him that his wife is publicly destroying his carefully cultivated image as world heavyweight champion; that he is being emasculated in front of the nation. He gently strokes his wife's neck and tells America: "I love my wife, but I wouldn't stand in her way if she wanted to leave. She can leave right now . . . take everything I have and just leave. She has the right to do that. She has the power to do that." The sudden wind whistling through America was the sound of the intake of breath of hundreds of divorce lawyers with dollar signs sweeping before their eyes.

2 October 1988: The final, inevitable breaking point in the doomed Beauty and the Beast marriage comes with Tyson raging through his New Jersey mansion hurling furniture through the windows and terrorising his wife and mother-in-law. He chases them out of the house, allegedly striking the actress with his open hand and then a closed fist. The police are called, and they report it as "a domestic dispute". This terrifying Sunday morning eruption follows his slow reaction to the humiliation he had suffered on the *20-20* show. His 83-year-old surrogate mother, Camille Ewald, told him from her Catskill home: "If I'd been sitting there on the sofa alongside that woman I'd have put my hand over her mouth." Camille later confided to friends: "Mike is very unhappy with his marriage. That wife of his and her mother have made him an emotional captive."

7 October 1988: Robin Givens files for divorce in Los Angeles, citing irreconcilable differences. Acting for Mrs Tyson initially is the flamboyant celebrity divorce lawyer Marvin Mitchelson, who describes the actress as "a devoted wife who has done as much as anybody could possibly do to help her emotionally disturbed husband. This is a very, very sad day for her, but she has taken as much as a wife can take." The divorce papers carry the statement: "My husband has been violent and physically abusive and prone to unprovoked rages of violence and destruction." It was stated that he had "lost control of his emotions while visiting me in Moscow . . . [and] started throwing champagne bottles around our room. At the peak of his manic state, Michael went down to the bar and started drinking vodka glass after glass, like it was water. He then returned to our room, grabbed a handful of Lithium and locked himself in the bathroom, saying he was going to kill himself." Mrs Tyson also stated in the divorce papers that Tyson had hung from a hotel balcony in Moscow for ten minutes, threatening to kill himself. She further alleged that during the flight home he called her a "whore" and a "slut", and said that "he was going to kill me, that he had got guns at home." She added: "He told me that the world would forgive him because he had succeeded in making everyone think that I was the bad one." She also alleged that during the outburst in their New Jersey home on the previous Sunday, Tyson had jumped on her in bed while drunk and punched her in the head and body. Mrs Tyson later switches to New York lawyer Raoul Felder after a disagreement with Mr Mitchelson.

11 October 1988: Tyson counters his wife's divorce demands by moving to have the marriage annulled. He files papers in New Jersey State Superior Court alleging that Givens entered the marriage "motivated solely by personal aggrandizement and a need to enhance her level of public recognition". Tyson also alleges that his wife sought to humiliate him publicly and that she had tricked him into marriage. The papers claim that Givens has caused Tyson severe emotional distress and prevented him from attending to his boxing career. A doctor acting for Mrs Tyson releases a document stating that the actress suffered a miscarriage in June when in the second month of her pregnancy. Yet Tyson had told close friends in March that she was pregnant. Lori McNeil, American tennis star and Mrs Tyson's close friend, reveals that rumours that Tyson had beaten up his wife during a holiday in the Bahamas in July were true. She had originally denied the story when ace reporter Mike McAlary had published it in the *New York Daily News*. Miss McNeil, who was in the Bahamas with the Tysons, says: "I lied because I was afraid of the whole situation. I'm still afraid, but I think it is something that should be told. People need to know the other side of Mike Tyson." She claims that Tyson had been drinking heavily – "he always does" – and Robin, she says, claimed he had been flirting with another woman in the bar. "He kicked in the door to my room and dragged Robin out and back to his room," she tells McAlary. "I went in there and he was hitting Robin and dragging her and saying he was going to kill her. He was choking her and she was screaming, so I called security. They chased him out into the hall and he made a big scene. He was totally out of control and hit me in the mouth and busted my lip. I was trying to stop him from hitting Robin."

20 October 1988: To rebut her husband's claim that she married him for his money, Robin Givens announces that she will not accept any money in a divorce. Her New York lawyer says that his client had given up a property claim that could have been worth up to $10 million.

21 October 1988: Tyson signs an exclusive promotional contract with Don King and also grants him limited power of attorney. Bill Cayton, the champion's manager, claims that the four-year contract is illegal because Tyson teamed up with King without first consulting with or informing him, as is required under New York State boxing regulations. According to Cayton, Tyson and King telephoned him from a Chicago lawyer's office to tell him about the contentious contract. Cayton says Tyson told him: " 'You're my manager and Don King is my promoter.' Mike sounded defiant and disrespectful. I had never heard him like that before, but I realised he had been brainwashed by that man Don King." Tyson has been staying with King at the promoter's farm in Ohio since his wife sued for divorce. King, who once served a prison sentence for manslaughter, has told Tyson that they are "brothers" who have a "background, a history and the colour of their skins" in common. It has time and again been whispered to Tyson that he has been living in a white man's world since the age of 13, always with white people in charge of his destiny. Once again, it is Frank Bruno who loses out. Tyson decides that he does not want to fight abroad while his divorce is pending. His championship defence against Bruno is rescheduled for the United States in the New Year, with the British challenger receiving extra money as compensation for losing home advantage. King announces that Tyson will become his promotional partner. "Mike is going to work with me, not for me," he says. "He will get a share of everything."

7 November 1988: Tyson accuses Robin Givens of trying to "steal" his money. He states: "It turns out she was lying when she said she didn't want anything from me." He claims that she wants to keep the New Jersey mansion, now reckoned to be worth close to $8 million following all the improvements and refurbishments made since they moved in. Tyson also claims in an interview with the *New York Post* that his wife wants to keep more than $1 million-worth of jewellery, and that: "She wants me to forget about the $5 million that went missing during the shifting of one bank account to another." Mrs Tyson responded by hitting her husband with a libel suit for $125 million. Her lawyer was demanding $25 million for damages and injury to Robins "good name, professional reputation and social standing", plus $100 million in punitive and compensatory damages.

28 November 1988: Watched by a congregation of 700 including the Reverend Jesse Jackson and Don King, white-robed Mike Tyson is immersed in water and baptised at a Baptist church in Cleveland. Pastor Henry Payden tells him after the ceremony: "Mike, now your job is to take the message of Christ to the people. You have a way of knocking men down, but Jesus has a way of picking people up."

9 December 1988: Kevin Rooney, Mike Tyson's trainer since his first professional fight, is sacked by the champion just two months before his defence against Frank Bruno at the Las Vegas Hilton on 25 February. Tyson decides to part company with the man many had considered as close to him as a brother after Rooney remarks to reporters that it would be "a good idea" if Tyson began dating his estranged wife. The champion is also irate that Rooney mentions his wife's mother, Ruth Roper. "Doesn't Kevin know what I went through with those women?" Tyson says, when announcing his decision to look for a new trainer. "How many times did I talk to Kevin? How many times did I tell him only to worry about me and him?" Rooney has also been outspoken about Tyson's involvement with Don King. "We knocked off all his fighters on the way to the championship and then in the defences of the title," he says, "so now he has decided to steal Mike. Surely Mike knows that this is a man who bleeds fighters dry." Rooney reacts to his sacking by issuing a $10 million writ.

31 December 1988: Tyson's year ends with the sort of confusion and controversy that has marked it from day one. Not one but two women have come forward to accuse him of sexual harassment on the same night at a night club in Manhattan. He will have to go to court to answer charges from at least one of the women.

11 January 1988: Under oath, Tyson gives a deposition at a court hearing in Las Vegas as he continues his bid to break from Bill Cayton. He paints a picture of himself as being vague about his fight finances. When presented with documents showing that he had received a total of $11,578,000 for his title defence against Michael Spinks, he claimed that he did not know whether he had received all the money. Tyson accused 70-year-old Cayton of "having a slavemaster mentality . . . he would not let me do anything, basically, that I wanted to do". He revealed that Cayton had objected to him buying the New Jersey mansion in which he set up home with his bride because he considered it overpriced. "If the house is worth one million dollars and I want to pay ten million, that's my prerogative," said Tyson. Cayton's case is that he has always acted in Tyson's best interests, and that he was refusing to sanction the deal making King the champion's exclusive promoter because he suspected that it would be loaded too much in the promoter's favour. The extrovert King made his deposition in New York, launching a tirade against Cayton. "I called him Satan in disguise," he shouted in typically theatrical style. "The disguise has now gone. He's just Satan." King, showing what an acrobatic man he could be, added that he would not rule out working with Cayton in the future. "Boxing breeds strange bedfellows," he boomed.

13 January 1989: Less than six weeks before his title defence against Bruno, Tyson takes time off from training to make a secret trip to Vancouver to see his estranged wife during a break in shooting a made-for-TV movie. Tyson is followed to a local hotel and reacts in familiar fashion when a photographer from the *Vancouver Sun* tries to snap him, snatching his camera from his hands and hurling it to the floor. Then he turns on a TV cameraman. He tears the viewfinder off his hand-held video camera. With an enraged Tyson in full pursuit, the cameraman runs off and escapes through the revolving door while a hotel security guard attempts to restrain the champion. Charges are filed by the police. The film being made by Mrs Tyson is called *Penthouse*, about a young woman terrified by a man who has a history of throwing women off balconies. Nobody dared whisper any jokes about typecasting.

14 February 1989: Valentine's Day, and Tyson performs the less than romantic act of flying down to the Dominican Republic aboard Don King's private jet to finalise his divorce from Robin Givens. The papers are signed in Santo Domingo and Tyson flies back to the United States a single man. The divorce was said to be "by mutual agreement" and no terms of settlement were disclosed. It was rumoured that Robin Givens had received $20 million, but neither party would comment on what was pure conjecture. They married in secret, and one year and eight days later kept secret the conditions of their divorce.

So there was no fairytale happy ending to this Beauty and the Beast story . . . and there was an even more horrendous experience waiting to engulf Tyson on the female front. For those of us watching from the ringside, we were saddened by the disintegration of the marriage made in hell but even more concerned by the champion's acrimonious divorce from Kevin Rooney.

In boxing circles the advice to Tyson would have been: "By all means get rid of the wife but for luck's sake hang on to your trainer!" Or words to that effect. Rooney, a Runyonesque character who could have stepped off a Bowery Boys film set, knew the champion better than anybody; his strengths and, more important, his weaknesses. He talked the same street language and had been to the same Cus D'Amato school of boxing. Tyson would miss not having him in his corner.

Despite all the self-inflicted wounds and the crushing pressures, Tyson overcame the brave challenge of Frank Bruno in five rounds. But there were warning signals that he had lost the dynamic edge to his punching speed and accuracy. A disaster was waiting for him in the bulky shape of James 'Buster' Douglas.

6: Busted in Tokyo

JAMES 'Buster' Douglas was carefully selected as a pushover opponent for Mike Tyson's tenth world title defence because a $30 million showdown had been arranged against number-one challenger Evander Holyfield. Nobody believed that Douglas could throw a spanner – or rather, a sledgehammer – into the works. His tenth round knockout victory in Tokyo in 1990 could not have caused a greater sensation had he mugged the President.

Since turning professional in 1981, Douglas had won 29 of his 35 fights, and defeats by David Bey, Mike White, Jesse Ferguson and Tony Tucker lured the Tyson camp into thinking that here was an easy defence. They made the elementary mistake of completely underestimating the challenger at the Tokyo Dome in the early hours of Sunday, 11 February 1990. Douglas, a 6 foot 4 inch tall former basketball player who often had a problem with wildly fluctuating weight, came in at a trim, for him, 16 stone 7 pounds (231 pounds) and had obviously got himself in good shape. There were understandable doubts about whether he was mentally right for the contest. His mother had died suddenly during his early training preparation, and the mother of his 11-year-old son Lamar, who was at the ringside, was seriously ill at home in Ohio.

But, from the first moments of the fight, it was clear that Douglas was in the mood to go all out for an earthquaking victory, while Tyson was struggling to get into anything like his usual rhythm. The champion's head was continually rocked back on his 20-inch neck by jolting left jabs, and the following rights kept sitting him back on his heels. Tyson was not throwing his usual explosive combinations with 'bad intentions', and was thrashing away with single punches that lacked their customary timing and deadly accuracy. He fought as if his mind was elsewhere.

Douglas had one moment of real crisis, and through no fault of his own it caused a controversy that threw a shadow over his victory. Tyson was under heavy attack in the eighth round when he produced just one lightning flash from his old artillery – a crushing right uppercut that screwed Douglas's head around on his shoulders and dropped him like a sack of potatoes. The roar of the crowd was so loud that the referee struggled to pick up the timekeeper's count and he was trailing three seconds behind as the challenger pulled himself up on to one knee and listened to the referee tolling the seconds. When he heard "nine" he rose and braced himself to meet the following attack from Tyson. Just then the bell rang . . . and it was Tyson for whom the bell tolled.

It was a desperate final fling by the champion. He took a terrible tanking in the ninth round, and in the tenth was forced to retreat under assault from a procession of left jabs before a furious flurry of lefts and rights sent him crashing backwards. His mind clearly in a mist, he was scrabbling around on the canvas for his gumshield as the referee counted him out for the one and only time in his career. He had been well and truly busted. Douglas, at 29, six years older than Tyson, wept as he was named as the new heavyweight champion of the world.

The boxing authorities, under pressure from the many-tentacled Don King , tried, shamefully, to take the title away from Douglas because of the long count, which could not be blamed on him. All he could do was listen to the seconds being called out by the referee and, when he shouted "nine", Douglas was not to know that it was in fact 12 seconds since he had been knocked down. King and his associates quickly climbed down when they saw the outraged public reaction to their 'strip the champion' suggestion.

There had been a hint that all was not right with Tyson when he was knocked down while sparring with Greg Page during a training session in Japan. It was dismissed as a publicity stunt, but those in the know said that it was a genuine punch that had dropped the 'Iron Man' of the ring. Tyson, who had always thrived on action, had boxed only one round since his victory over Frank Bruno, a first round stoppage of Carl 'The Truth' Williams in July 1989. So he was ring rusty when he climbed into the ring, but even then nobody gave Douglas a chance of beating a fighter who was considered invincible.

In defeat, Tyson must have silently cursed himself for sacking his trainer Kevin Rooney. His new cornermen, Aaron Snowell and Jay

Bright, were unable to motivate him when the going got tough. They seemed overawed by him, and kept making sycophantic noises in the corner when what Tyson needed was somebody to bully him into producing some high explosives. Rooney, with his intimate knowledge of what makes Tyson tick, could have made all the difference. He was a sad shadow of the fighter who had frightened the life out of the world's heavyweights for the previous four years. "I just didn't recognise him as Mike Tyson," said Rooney. "He got into the ring like he didn't want to be there. I'd heard he had virtually been training himself and it looked like it. He just wasn't in the right shape, mentally or physically. They were giving him all the wrong instructions in the corner. After the first round they told Mike: 'You're doing good.' You never tell a fighter a lie like that if you want to get the best out of him. I would have said, 'Okay, Mike, if that's the way you want to fight I'm gonna throw in the towel before somebody gets hurt in there. And that somebody is you.' "

Rooney was of the view that Tyson was a beaten man before he got into the ring. "Deep down, psychologically, I think he didn't want to win," he said. "All the things we'd worked on for years, he didn't do. Hit-and-slip is how I've always taught him. Punch, and then you're gone. Your opponent will always hit where he last saw you, so you mustn't be there for him. Throw your shot and then move your head. That's the way Mike had been taught to fight. Both Cus and I had hammered it into him night and day. 'Hit but don't get hit. Hurt but don't get hurt.' But against Douglas all the basic things we'd taught him were forgotten and he was just standing there to be hit. No bend in the legs, no side to side movement – nothing."

Tyson took his defeat badly, and bleated about the long count. He had clearly been stirred up by Don King, who was yelling "We wuz robbed" long into the night and the following days and weeks. "I am still the legitimate champion," Tyson said at the after-fight press conference. "I knocked the guy down, went to a neutral corner and saw he was down for more than ten seconds. According to the rules I'm still the champion. You guys know me. You know I walk like I talk. I've never cried or bitched about anything. I knocked Buster Douglas out fair and square. All I know is that I still think of myself as the champion of the world. This isn't going to change. I ain't making excuses. I'm just giving it to you straight. You saw what happened. The guy did not beat the count, and that's the truth. Just look at the video of the fight and count from the moment Douglas hit the floor. It should have been 'nine, ten . . . out!' I can handle a loss. I just want to lose fairly. The record books should show that I won by knockout."

Most people would have liked Tyson to have accepted defeat more gracefully.

The reaction to Tyson's defeat in the American media could not have been greater had he landed on the moon. It was not exactly a quiet news time. Nelson Mandela's release from prison, the reunification of Germany and even Donald Trump's trumpeted divorce all took a back seat to the news of Tyson's sensational defeat. It got more space in newspapers and on television screens than any of his victories, and it must have hurt the fallen champion to see that almost unanimously his defeat was greeted with a mixture of relief and joy. His year of collecting all the wrong headlines while married to Robin Givens had turned the public against him, and there was a general feeling of satisfaction that a man who had, by all accounts, bullied and beaten his wife had himself been on the wrong end of a good hiding.

Tyson had lost the world title. That was bad enough, but even worse, he had lost the affection and the respect of the public.

Bill Cayton, the man who had been in at the ground floor of Tyson's career, watched sadly from the sidelines as he came crashing down. Two months after the humiliation by Douglas, he wrote an open letter to Tyson pleading with him to come back under his wing. "Don King," he wrote, "has cost you your title. He's costing you your career. He has cost you getting endorsements and TV commercials. He has already cost you more than $50 million."

Cayton's letter warned against the fight programme mapped out for him by King, which included a rearranged contest against Razor Ruddock. The letter went on: "As far as you and I are concerned, I want you to remember through all your comments about me, I have never said one bad word about you. I am your manager. I will continue to protect you. Not just for you, Mike, but for my own integrity and self-respect. It's up to you, Mike."

Cayton concluded by saying that his old team of trainer Kevin Rooney and assistant manager Steve Lott were waiting to welcome him back with open arms. He wrote: "The team that brought you from your amateur days, from your first professional fight to recognition as the greatest fighter in the world, are ready to prepare you for your comeback. You can do it again and go on to be fully recognized as not only the greatest fighter in the world but the greatest of all time."

Cayton's plea fell on deaf ears, and Don King continued to be the man who pulled the Tyson strings. The hold of King on Tyson needs to be explained. For a start, King is one of the most persuasive people you could ever meet. He and his ego can fill a room, and he mixes a cocktail of charm, sinister menace and street-wise intelligence into a personality that is loud, brash and, if he wants something from you, quite intoxicating. King speaks like a man who has swallowed half a dictionary. His malapropisms have made him a legend on the American fight circuit, and he is continually misquoting the likes of Shakespeare and Twain. He has a catchphrase, "Only in America", and it's only in America that you could expect to meet such an engaging, infuriating and over-the-top character.

King has been a leading player on the world boxing stage since helping to bring Muhammad Ali and George Foreman together for their legendary 'Rumble in the Jungle' in 1974. Just three years earlier he had been released from prison after serving nearly four years of a ten-year sentence for manslaughter. He used to run an illegal numbers racket in Cleveland, and in 1954 shot dead a man who was trying to rob his numbers house. The killing was ruled a justifiable homicide. In 1967, he got involved in a street brawl with a numbers runner who he claimed was ripping him off. The man died from brain injuries sustained when his head hit the ground. King was charged with second-degree murder which was later reduced to manslaughter. While in prison he read everything he could lay his hands on, and came out in 1971 with a vastly increased vocabulary and a burning ambition to get on the Muhammad Ali bandwagon. He saw boxing as the gravy train that would take him to a more acceptable lifestyle than the numbers game.

King, with his giant frame crowned by an electric shock of greying hair, has a powerful physical presence and, for neutral onlookers, can be wildly entertaining and mind-blowingly arrogant. We like the man, but we have never had to do business with him. It was Mike Tyson who once said, "When you shake hands with Don King count your fingers afterwards to make sure they're still all there." That was in the days when he was protected from any King influence by Jim Jacobs. There are some champions and contenders who swear that King has swindled them out of money. One the other hand, there are many others who swear by him, and insist that no promoter has given them a better deal. It was Kevin Rooney who best summed up Tyson's attraction to King, the man Bill Cayton continually warned against as if he was a boxing bogey man. "It's because of King's black ghetto background," Rooney said. "He talks jive talk, and will have convinced Mike that he is one of his own. Mike is out of reform school. He looks up to King because he's done the ultimate . . . he's been to the big house for murder [later reduced to manslaughter]. Mike can't see that all King wants him for is the money and the power he will bring him. He has made him cut all his ties with what I call the Cus D'Amato line. That was the line that made Mike Tyson."

King spends thousands of dollars in legal fees fighting a string of battles with fighters and managers alleging financial chicanery, and he has also had to sweat through Grand Jury investigations of his affairs. But, as we write, the King is still on his throne and he has the ear and the affection of the man they all want to control, Mike Tyson.

Asked in prison why he remained loyal to King despite a chorus of voices warning him to make the break, Tyson said: "Don King is a good man, and a damn good businessman. Like everybody else in big business he's competitive. He has broken all the records, all the P.T. Barnum and the Ziegfeld records. He can be ornery and arrogant, and he's not under any sort of control. He gets caught up in being suspicious of everybody. I think sometimes he even distrusts his friends. But he's the best at what he does."

An unpublicized story that we can pass on shows a little-known side of Don King. After Oliver McCall had shocked Lennox Lewis by taking the WBC world heavyweight title from him at Wembley in September 1994, King (McCall's promoter) picked up a bundle of money in a side-bet on the fight. The day after the contest he quietly sent a huge cheque – and we do mean huge – to Great Ormond Street children's hospital. King will not thank us for publishing this, but he often gets mauled by the media. This puts a balance on the criticism, and reveals the caring side of King.

Following his divorce from Robin Givens, Tyson relaxed in the company of 24-year-old Los Angeles divorcee Natalie Fears and, in May 1990, he became a father for the first officially recorded time when she gave birth to a baby girl in a Catskill hospital. Tyson said he had no plans to marry, but that he was "very happy" to be having a family. He was unable to see his daughter straight away because he was in strict training for his comeback fight against old amateur rival Henry Tillman under the experienced eye of his latest trainer, Richie Giachetti. The appointment of Giachetti caused raised eyebrows in the world of boxing. Giachetti and Cus D'Amato had been sworn enemies and used to criticise viciously each other's training methods. "This is an insult to the memory of the man who did most to make Tyson the fighter he is," said Bill Cayton. "It is a disgraceful and stupid appointment by Don King. Cus D'Amato, the greatest trainer who ever lived, ridiculed Giachetti's way of training fighters. I am appalled, and I have to say that I am surprised that Mike has gone along with it. Kevin Rooney is the man who should be training him."

Beaten twice by Tillman in his amateur days, Tyson got sweet and savage revenge with a first round demolition job in which he looked like the terminator of old. Uncharacteristically, Tyson showed concern for Tillman after the ten second count had been completed and helped him to his feet. Was this a new, caring Tyson trying to win back the affection of the fans? "Henry and I are old friends," he explained. "We just happen to be in the same business. I'm glad he's okay. I have a home in Los Angeles now, and we see each other there all the time. He is still a good fighter, but by rights he should be in the cruiserweight division. Anyway, I'm just glad to be back with a win. I was ready to go all night if necessary. I want my title back and I'll be happy to fight Buster Douglas again just as soon as it can be arranged. He did well to beat me, and I can't take that away from him. But let's see if he can beat me twice. The test of who's the better fighter is who wins most out of three or four fights, not one. I've paid my dues, and I'll never lose again."

Tyson's plans to fight on his old regular pattern were hit by a training injury while sparring with Greg Page, the former WBA world champion who had floored him in Tokyo. Tyson received a facial injury that required 48 micro stitches, and his scheduled fight against London-born Alex Stewart was put back three months to December.

His dreams of regaining his world title from Buster Douglas died on 25 October when the man who had been a lion in Tokyo folded like a lamb against Evander Holyfield in Las Vegas. Holyfield knocked out a fat and less-than-enthusiastic Douglas in the third round. "That wasn't the same guy that beat me," said Tyson. "He looked as fat as a pig."

Meantime, Tyson's concentration on boxing was interrupted by another court case that revealed that he seemed to be heading for a financial crisis. His finances were made public in a New York courtroom during his trial for allegedly fondling Sandra Miller at a Manhattan disco. It was pointed out that the former champion's $100 million fortune had dwindled to only $15 million. Tyson looked confused and uncomfortable as the mind-boggling figures were read out, and when questioned he was unable to explain the whereabouts of his enormous career earnings.

It was nothing new for him to be vague about money. The previous April, for example, he was questioned about the multimillion-dollar worldwide TV rights fees he had received. "I never understand anything as far as the closed-circuit rights," he said. "I don't understand anything about the foreign affairs and those sort of things. I just go in and fight and hopefully get the fee." Interrogated in 1989 about his earnings for the title defence against Michael Spinks, Tyson said he did not know where a $10 million cheque had been deposited. "I don't understand the money game," he said. "The money's coming in millions. I can't count that high."

The financial statement read out in the New York courtroom, detailed up to February 1990, was both fascinating and somewhat frightening for we experienced Tyson Watchers. It showed that most of his wealth was tied up in his sprawling New Jersey mansion (valued at $6.2 million) and a second 60-acre home in Ohio (worth $831,612). He had life insurance policies valued at $2,244,376 and his stocks and shares totalled $2,016,958. His cash bank account stood at a recorded $2,322,138. His luxury lifestyle was spotlighted in the valuation of his eighteen cars ($843,668), furniture ($988,159) and jewellery and furs ($645,054).

The jury found Tyson guilty of fondling Sandra Miller, but she was awarded just $100 in damages because the jury decided that Tyson's behaviour was "not outrageous". It was a victory of a kind for the fallen champion, but did nothing to lessen his reputation as a "serial buttocks fondler", a tag hung on him by the media after a procession of women had made allegations about his wandering hands.

A power-propelled Tyson blasted Alex Stewart to defeat in just two minutes 27 seconds of the first round at the Convention Centre in Atlantic City on 8 December 1990. "I never lost my confidence in myself like the majority of people expected," said a triumphant Tyson. "I've shown beyond argument that I'm still the best. I was ready to explode tonight because I was so anxious to impress. I've lost none of my power. When I connect they have to go."

But when Tyson connected against Canadian-based, Jamaican-born Donovan 'Razor' Ruddock in his next fight in Las Vegas on 18 March 1991, he refused to go. In fact for seven rounds he gave Tyson all the trouble he could handle, before a controversial decision was made by referee Richard Steele to stop the contest after Donovan had been sent reeling back into the ropes under a two-fisted attack. Most observers thought the referee had been premature in calling it all over, and a free-for-all fight broke out in the ring between associates of the two boxers as Donovan's followers disputed the decision.

Asked in the televised after-fight interview whether Ruddock could punch, Tyson astonished viewers with the blunt comment: "Yeah, like a fucking mule. Pardon my French." Donovan stressed that he was in a position to defend himself when the referee stopped the fight. "He hit me with his best shots that you media guys said would kill me," he said. "But look, I've got no bumps or bruises and I felt no pain. I swear to God that I can beat Tyson. He's gotta give me a rematch and I'll show that he can be beaten."

Three months later, Tyson cleared the way for a mega-bucks world championship showdown with Evander Holyfield when he outpointed Ruddock over 12 gruelling, uninspired rounds in a return fight in Las Vegas. He was a clear-cut winner on the scorecard of each of the three judges, but it was the tamest performance of Tyson's ring career. The explosive power was missing, and he was laboured and predictable with combination punches that used to zip to their target in a blur of atomic action. What was even more worrying for Tyson was that Ruddock found him an easy target, and he took a lot of unnecessary blows that, in his peak years, he would have comfortably avoided.

"I was not happy with my performance," admitted Tyson. "But it will be different against Holyfield. That fight will really motivate me. This is the one I've been waiting for. He stands between me and the championship that I believe by rights belongs to me. I have set my sights on regaining the title ever since that terrible night in Tokyo against Douglas."

He was all set to pick up a $15 million purse for his title fight with Holyfield, a dream duel that had been torpedoed in Tokyo when Buster Douglas so rudely interrupted.

Then, on a fatal day in July 1991, Tyson was the celebrity guest at the annual Miss Black America Pageant in Indianapolis. It was the beginning of a nightmare that would end with the former world heavyweight champion behind prison bars.

7: The Rape Trial

THE courtroom knockout of Mike Tyson was watched world-wide as if there had been a nuclear explosion, and the fallout scorched the already heavily scarred sport of boxing. His trial for alleged rape was given greater media exposure than any other sports-linked court case in history . . . until O.J. Simpson came along. Like Simpson, Tyson was a colossus of sport. Unlike Simpson, he did not have a groundswell of public sympathy to cushion him as he faced up to charges that he had raped a beautiful black American beauty queen contestant. He had been a walking time-bomb since the break up of his marriage to Robin Givens, and experienced Tyson Watchers were able to say "I told you so" when 18-year-old Sunday school teacher Desiree Washington screamed that most terrifying of all four-letter words: "RAPE!" Tyson had often called himself "the baddest man on the planet". Now he seemed to be trying to prove it.

This time, there was no Jim Jacobs or Cus D'Amato to get him off the hook, as had been the case with previous sex-driven incidents. Jim Jacobs had confided to us that he had once paid the mother of a girl alleging uninvited sex with Tyson several thousand dollars to hush everything up. This was while Tyson was still a young amateur. Six or so years later Jacobs coughed up $105,000 to settle a case out of court after Tyson had been accused of thumping a car park attendant following a lewd approach to a girl. "Mike is a highly-sexed guy," Jacobs told us. "He does everything with high energy, and one of the reasons we like to keep him busy in the ring and the gym is that it burns off that desire to go out and get laid!"

We were completely spellbound by the court case because of our inside knowledge of Tyson and his lifestyle. We give this full account of what happened because much of what was uncovered in the courtroom is so relevant to the life and times of Michael Gerard Tyson. It does not make pretty reading.

The girl making the accusation of rape against Tyson was an eight-stone beauty queen called Desiree Washington, from the small town of Coventry, Rhode Island. The picture painted of her was that of a daughter of middle-class America, the sort of girl all parents long to produce. Beautiful, bright, popular, the classic storybook teenager from an idyllic background. Butter would not melt in her mouth. But then on the eve of the trial in an Indiana courtroom the portrait suddenly became blurred when it was sensationally revealed that the so-called model student had suffered years of watching her mother being brutally beaten by her father. It promised to be the first round of revelations in a bout of legal fisticuffs that, instead of having a referee and three ringside judges, would have a judge and 12 ordinary men and women scoring the most important fight of Tyson's life. The judge was a formidable lady called Patricia Gifford, whose previous courtroom role was prosecuting sex crimes.

In the accuser's corner stood Miss Washington, who had seemed to be living the dream teenage life in smalltown America. She had been voted most popular girl in her graduating class and had just won a scholarship to university. Desiree – whose pert, good looks and toothy grin made her look considerably younger than her 18 years – was the youngest contender for the Miss Black America title. Tyson, in the defendant's corner, was guest celebrity at the beauty pageant in Indianapolis in July 1991. When Miss Washington first met him, he was wearing a *Together with Christ* badge and was praying with the Reverend Jesse Jackson. But, if her story was to be believed, the Christian was about to turn into a lustful lion. The accusation was that, at 2 a.m. on 19 July in room 606 at the Canterbury Hotel, Tyson raped Desiree Washington. If found guilty, he could face a jail sentence of up to 60 years.

On day one of the trial, in a tense, crowded Marion Superior Court, Miss Washington called on all the skill she had learned as the star of her school's debating society as she confronted Vince Fuller, one of America's toughest lawyers. The jury noted that she gave as good as she got under cross-examination.

Desiree described how she and her roommates at the Miss Black America Pageant had been star-struck by Tyson. It was, she said, this enthusiasm that persuaded her to leave her own room to join the former world champion in his hired limousine at about 1.20 a.m.

At first, she claimed, she had been reluctant when he summoned her with a call from the hotel lobby. But he had "begged" her with the repeated assurance that he "just wanted to talk", saying he was leaving town early in the morning. Her roommates persuaded her there were still parties to go to and she agreed to get dressed and meet the boxer. She agreed that he had embraced her when she stepped into the car, and tried to kiss her on the mouth. She said she had "jumped back". "But," asked Fuller, "was that not a clear signal of the nature of the date?" "No, he wasn't like dirty on me or anything like that," she replied.

In his opening argument, Fuller said, in a booming bass voice for which he is renowned in courtrooms across the country, that he would show that the young woman schemed to start a relationship with Tyson so she could take money from him. She denied telling roommates that Tyson was "dumb, but good for $20 million".

There was rapt attention in the courtroom when Fuller asked her the question most of us had on the tip of our tongue: "Don't you consider a man's invitation to join him in the bedroom an invitation to sex?"

"No, I was fooled," she replied quickly, as if well prepared for the question. "It was the way he said it. He said: 'Come in and let's watch TV and talk.' He said it really nicely." At that point, Desiree glared from the witness seat across the courtroom at Tyson, who was absent-mindedly gnawing on a pencil.

She then switched her gaze directly on to the jury. "Anyone can be fooled," she said. "I look back now and say 'Yes, it was stupid.' "

Miss Washington told how Tyson had turned on the television and lay down to watch a Western film. She had sat at the bottom of the bed because she would not have been able to see the screen from the chairs at the other end of the room.

Fuller again questioned her intentions when she went back to the Canterbury Hotel with the former heavyweight world champion in the early hours of the morning. Desiree's eyes blazed and, for a moment, she lost the little innocent girl look. "That was no reason to do what he did to me," she said.

The famous Washington defence lawyer, with a string of victories behind him as impressive as Tyson's ring record, could not shake Desiree. She kept calm under his expert attack, refusing to be drawn away from her story – that Tyson attacked her at lightning speed and pinning her down on the bed like a rag doll as he raped her.

Fuller wanted to know why, when Tyson told her "You're turning me on" as they both sat on the bed, she didn't just get up and walk out? Why had she decided that was the time to go to the bathroom, when only 20 minutes earlier she'd been to the bathroom at her own hotel?

Asked if Tyson's comment to her on the bed was an explicit sexual statement, Desiree replied "Yes". She pointed out that she went to the bathroom because: "I was upset. I couldn't believe he'd said it." She said that she believed as soon as she came out of the bathroom they would leave immediately for a promised sightseeing trip round Indianapolis.

Fuller's only reference to the alleged attack was when he asked her if Tyson had held her legs "pretty tight" while they were on the bed. She agreed. He nibbled away at her story by asking her if it was true she had wanted Tyson to walk her out of the hotel after the alleged rape. She denied it, adding, in an icy tone of voice: "I didn't want him to. I didn't want him near me."

Desiree remained calm and assured under a bombardment of questions from Fuller, occasionally smiling at the jury like a schoolgirl currying favour with her teacher. "Do you recall Tyson saying: 'I'm willing if you're willing'?" "No."

"Did Tyson say to you, 'I can't see your figure with your clothes on'?" "No."

"Did Tyson ask: 'What do you hide under those clothes?'?" "No."

"Do you recall Tyson saying to a fellow Miss Black America contestant: 'I'd like to get into a sexual act'?" "No."

Fuller sustained his attack, firing questions with the speed that Tyson throws combinations. But they were having no effect on the opponent.

"Did Tyson urge you: 'Bring your roommates too'?" "Did Tyson ask for sex?" "Do you remember Tyson saying: 'You've got to give it, you've got to give it up'?" The demure Miss Black America contestant answered each potentially damaging question with a soft but assured "No."

Now Fuller moved on to some of the things the defence claims she

said prior to her meeting with Tyson. "Do you recall describing Tyson to one of the girls as, 'I like the money, the build and the weight'?"
"No."

"Did you observe, during pageant rehearsals, at the sight of Tyson that 'He's good for 20 million dollars'? 'Did you make a comment about Tyson's ex-wife Robin Givens saying, 'She got plenty of money and besides he's dumb'?" "Did one of the girls tease you by saying, 'Here comes your husband, pity he can't talk'?" "Did you respond by saying, 'I'll do the talking, as long as he makes the money'?"

Miss Washington maintained her dignified but firm "No" replies throughout the quick-fire exchange, but then felt an explanation was needed when asked: "Didn't you, during the opening ceremony of the pageant, say as Tyson appeared, 'Money, money, money'?" "All the contestants," she said, had "sung this as a jingle to greet Tyson".

She then returned to the "No" responses as Fuller tried to break her account of what happened with more claims of things she'd said, this time after the alleged attack. "Did you tell one of the girls that Tyson's bodyguard had left the suite as you arrived?" "Did you tell another that Tyson took advantage of you as soon as you got in the room?" "Did you tell yet another contestant that Tyson held your wrists over your head?" "Did you tell four separate people that you screamed?" "Did you tell someone else that you couldn't scream because he put his elbow in your mouth?" "Was yet somebody else told that he put his hand over your mouth?" Her reply was always the same. "No."

But Miss Washington answered "Yes" when Fuller asked: "Do you recall Mr Tyson saying to you, 'Is it still on tonight?' "

There were also "Yes" responses when he asked: "Isn't it true that within minutes of meeting Tyson he was hugging you and asking for a date?" "Isn't it true you went to meet him at 1.30 a.m., and as you jumped in his limo he hugged and kissed you?" "Isn't it true you willingly went to the hotel, willingly went to his suite, willingly went into the bedroom?"

There were the first signs of Desiree losing her cool as Fuller brought up the subject of physical contact. She insisted that there was no physical contact in the bedroom . . . "until he raped me".

For his last shot of this opening round Fuller asked: "Isn't it true you chose to go to the bathroom rather than leave?" Desiree seemed to think about this one before answering: "Yeah".

Fuller then retired to his corner, and most observers considered that Miss Washington had scored a clear points victory. She had given her evidence in a clear, confident but almost little-girl voice. Desiree lived up to her image as the teenager whose dream date with a hero had turned into a nightmare.

The Tyson fight back after the shaky first day started when the defence produced a witness who claimed that Miss Washington was excited about going out with him because he was "rich and dumb". Madelyn Whittington, a fellow contestant in the Miss Black America contest, told the court she talked to her in the bathroom shortly after Tyson invited her out. She said that Desiree had been "primping" and putting on lipstick, clearly thrilled to be going out with the former heavyweight champion. Miss Whittington said: "I asked if she was really going out with him, and she replied, 'Yes, of course I'm going. This is Mike Tyson. He has a lot of money and he's dumb. You saw what Robin Givens got.' She seemed very determined to go out with him, but I didn't think it was any of my business."

She said she had avoided Tyson at the pageant because she was appalled at his behaviour among the women, which was described as "serial buttock fondling". Miss Whittington claimed that at one point Tyson approached her with the words: "I know I'm not going to get nothing from you, but I'm going to ask you anyway." She had turned her back, keen to hear a speech by the Reverend Jesse Jackson, the civil rights campaigner and former presidential candidate. Then, she said she heard Tyson say about her: "Who does she think she is, that little Catholic *******.'

The defence called a senior gynaecologist who said the abrasions found on the alleged victim could not be considered proof of rape. Dr Margaret Watambe doubted that the young woman's injuries would cause significant pain or bleeding. She said that she frequently found similar minor injuries on women who had engaged in normal, consensual intercourse. She told the court: "It is much more common to see scratch marks on the back and face in a rape case, more than genital injuries alone."

The trial had resumed after a day's delay following a fire at the hotel where the jury were staying. Three people were killed in a blaze that started in mysterious circumstances.

Tyson's limousine driver, Virginia Foster, a key witness for the prosecution who was also a trained counsellor, testified that the boxer had seemed to her to show the symptoms of a "manic depressive", and that she had informed Desiree Washington of that impression as she drove the distraught accuser back from the Canterbury Hotel in the early hours after the alleged rape. She described in detail how Miss Washington had rushed in agitation and disarray from the hotel and sat in the limousine in a clear state of distress.

At least two of the jurors were seen to wipe tears from their eyes as Miss Washington's mother told the court how the alleged rape had become her daughter's recurring nightmare. Gregory Garrison, a smart lawyer with a homespun air whom the local District Attorney had hired as special prosecutor, played a tape recording of the accuser's call to the police emergency number 911, in which she reported the assault approximately 24 hours after she had left Tyson's room. All the jurors listened intently as they heard the emotional voice of Miss Washington describing how Tyson had raped her.

It was considered that one of the weakest parts of Tyson's testimony when he took the stand was his assertion that he had "definitely" told Washington, "I want to fuck you," at a dance rehearsal earlier on the day of their date – an approach which, if believed by the jury, would have been sufficient to acquit him on its own. But what weighed against Tyson was that he had omitted to make this vital point at his Grand Jury arraignment 11 months earlier. He recalled that, on the night before his 'date' with Washington, he had had sex with the rhythm and blues singer B Angie B in his hotel room.

Tyson testified that he and Miss Washington made love in his hotel room, insisting that he didn't force her and that she never protested. "I didn't violate her in any way," Tyson told the court. "She never told me to stop, or I was hurting her, nothing." He said that he and his accuser kissed and touched each other in his limousine on the way to his hotel and continued kissing and touching in his suite. "As I'm kissing her, she's taking off her jacket, fast," he said. "I performed oral sex and we had intercourse. Afterward, I invited her to stay. I said, 'I would really love for you to spend the night,' she said she didn't want to, and I said

I didn't want to walk her downstairs, that I was too tired. 'She said, 'You're not going to walk me downstairs? I don't believe you!' She was irritated."

Under earlier questioning by defence attorney Fuller, Tyson said he made his intentions clear when he first met Miss Washington at a rehearsal for the Miss Black America Pageant. He said they agreed to go out, and when she suggested a movie or dinner, he said he replied, "I don't want to do that. I just want to be with you. I want you."

"Did you say anything else?" Fuller asked. Tyson replied that he told the woman directly that he wanted to have sex with her. "I want to fuck you," he told a hushed and shocked courtroom. He added: "She said, 'That's kind of bold,' and then she said: 'Sure, give me a call.' "

Earlier, a parade of pageant contestants testified that Tyson could be a foul-mouthed lout one moment and a congenial gentleman the next. Tonya Traylor said the former world heavyweight champion went from one Miss Black America contestant to the next, asking all of them for dates. She told the jury: "He said, 'Do you want to go out and go back to my room for sex or a kiss? A kiss will do, but sex is better.' "

Defence witness Traylor said she refused a photo session with Tyson after he made lewd remarks to them and insisted the contestants sit on his lap. "I didn't want a picture of him that bad," she said. Later, at a concert, she revealed that Tyson had behaved like a gentleman and gave her a friendly hug, which she returned. "At that time, I did think he was a nicer person. He was congenial to me," she said. "He was very down-to-earth."

Prosecutor Garrison asked Miss Traylor: "His behaviour could be very bad at one time and very acceptable at another?"

"Yes," she replied. "He was very respectful. He does use four-letter words when he talks, but it's just part of his normal vocabulary."

The defence maintained throughout the trial that his accuser should have known by his crude behaviour at the rehearsal that he wanted to have sex. Singer Johnny Gill, who accompanied Tyson to the pageant rehearsal where he met the accuser, said the boxer was grabbing the women's buttocks while he signed autographs. "Mike was basically being Mike," Gill said. "He was putting the moves on some of the contestants."

Contestant Jacqueline Boatwright said Tyson called her pretty and gave her a kiss on the cheek when they first met. She said when she saw him later: "He patted me on the rear, and I gave him one of those looks that could kill, and he stopped."

Under cross-examination, she admitted that she was afraid to rebuff Tyson further. "You were afraid because he was big and powerful and a boxer?" Garrison asked. "Yes," she said.

Tyson later testified that he wanted to have sex in his limousine with Miss Washington and urged her to wear something loose. Under cross-examination by Garrison, he said he telephoned her in her hotel room to invite her to the limo and discouraged her from wearing tightfitting clothing. Garrison asked him why, and Tyson replied, "Because I had intentions of doing it in the limo."

"You figured she was coming down to have sex with you?" Garrison asked.

"Yeah," said Tyson, who said he presumed she was willing from an earlier conversation where he bluntly asked for sex. "If she was wearing something like tight jeans, it'd be difficult to take off," Tyson said. "Gets complicated."

Tyson was cross-examined for about an hour and did not give an impressive performance under interrogation by the skilled prosecutor who had been brought in like a hired gun to shoot down 'the baddest man on the planet'. Watched by his 86-year-old surrogate mother Camille Ewald, Tyson was a halting, hesitant witness and twice had to be told to keep his voice up. Garrison hammered away at Tyson's assertion that Miss Washington, an honour student and Sunday school teacher, had chirpily agreed to have sex with him just 20 minutes after they met. Garrison then had Tyson stumbling and stammering when he asked about his sexual encounter with rock singer B Angie B on the night before the hotel incident. The singer had recalled it vividly in her deposition, yet Tyson said he couldn't recall the details. "Yet," said Garrison, "you purport to remember the smallest details of a brief meeting with Miss Washington."

The jury chose not to believe Tyson's story. They believed instead the case of the State of Indiana, which, unusually, had been prepared with the help of seven FBI field officers and three out-of-state senior investigators.

Miss Washington was in court to hear Garrison's closing argument, her first appearance since she had given evidence. The prosecutor made a point of walking across the courtroom to her, taking hold of her hand and saying: "The fight's over for you, so just loosen up. We've kicked his ass."

The jury were swayed by a highly emotional closing statement by Garrison. He claimed it was "virtually impossible" that vaginal abrasions suffered by the accuser had been caused by consensual sex; that it was "telling" that Dale Edwards, the Tyson bodyguard who might have been able to corroborate the boxer's version of events, had not turned up to testify; and that the "fatal flaw" in the defence argument was that, if Desiree Washington had been so covetous of a long-term relationship with Tyson, as Fuller claimed, then why, when Tyson had asked her to stay the night, had she instead fled the room in terror?

Garrison convinced the jury that they should not believe the woman doctor who said that it was impossible to be certain whether or not the abrasions were caused by forced entry; nor that Dale Edwards had not been called because he had already impeached himself in earlier written testimony, and would therefore have been a sitting duck for the prosecution; nor that Desiree Washington might have had to turn down Tyson's offer of staying the night because she feared her absence would be noted at a wake-up call for pageant contestants which, she had herself testified, took place between 4 a.m. and 5 a.m.

Earlier, Garrison had persuaded Miss Washington to give a graphic account of the alleged rape. In a voice often shaking with emotion and even more childlike than Tyson's, she described the "excruciating pain as he jammed his fingers into me". You could have heard a feather drop in the court as she said: "He was laughing, like it was a game. He performed oral sex on me. I was trying to get him to move so that I could get away. He just said, 'So we'll have a baby,' and he jammed himself in." Later, she testified that he withdrew and ejaculated. "I told you I wouldn't come inside you," she quoted Tyson as saying: "Don't you love me now?"

Garrison, seeming to have the jury in a hypnotic trance with his spellbinding delivery, saved his most telling point until last in true Perry Mason fashion. He pointed a quivering, indignant finger in the direction of defence counsel Fuller, who he claimed had just made perhaps his biggest mistake of the whole trial by daring to suggest that when Desiree Washington said she just wanted to go sightseeing, she could hardly be believed because "after all, what sights are there to see in Indianapolis at two o'clock in the morning?" That carried enormous weight with the jury from Indianapolis.

Fuller argued in his summation that Tyson's accuser was a gold digger. He contended that Tyson was telling the truth when he testified that, after the woman had consensual sex with him in his hotel room, she spurned his invitation to spend the rest of the night with him.

Tyson faced the jurors on the final day of the trial knowing a quick verdict could mean a conviction. He sat slumped in his chair, struggling to control his fears. If it had been a fight and this was his appearance on the stool, the referee would have stopped the contest. It was the most tense and nervous any Tyson Watchers had ever seen him, including during the last moments before his most important fights when he used to come alive and alert. Here, in court, he was lifeless and wore the look of defeat. He wrung his huge fists, staring fixedly at the table, and his chest heaved as he struggled to control his breathing. The jury were out for around nine hours and had three votes before reaching a unanimous verdict.

He rose unsteadily as the judge called the jury. Don King sat close by with a Bible in his hands. Tyson's $5,000-a-day lawyer, Vince Fuller, who had conducted the defence without emotion, moved into the chair next to the boxer and put a comforting arm around his giant shoulders. At one point he massaged that enormous neck. The jury avoided Tyson's eyes, the old signal of a conviction due. The foreman, looking like a funeral director in collar and tie and gold-rimmed glasses, handed a slip of paper to the judge. She pursed her thin lips, and read out three guilty verdicts. Tyson slumped as if he had just taken a right to the solar plexus. His head moved from side to side, as it used to do before fights. Miss Kathleen Begg, assistant defence lawyer, wept at the verdict.

Greg Garrison, the prosecutor brought in especially for the celebrity trial, cited the severity of the hearing and demanded the withdrawal of Tyson's $30,000 bail bond. The sheriff's deputies, handcuffs and pistols on their belts, stood by the rear door of the court. But Fuller said flatly that Tyson could not abscond, even if he wanted to. "My client is an international celebrity; he has nowhere to hide," he said. Judge Gifford took one hard look at Tyson and called for his passport, and it was hurried to her hand from Don King as if any delay might prompt her to change her mind. King knew better than most how Tyson was feeling. He was once sent down for manslaughter.

A few minutes later, Fuller helped Tyson to rise and, with his arm around his waist, led him stumbling from the court. Garrison, a colourful character whose folksy style did much to persuade the jury in a case where hard evidence was thin, stood on the court steps to hail the case "A victory for women". He said: "It was a moral triumph. The accusing witness was truthful, and she has been believed. But, in victory, I have a sense of compassion for Tyson. That is what separates us from the jungle. I feel sorry for Tyson the Man, but not for Tyson the Celebrity."

At an impromptu press conference the jury foreman, flanked by fellow members of the jury, described how the verdict had been reached. "We felt that the girl had made a stronger case," he said with an openness peculiar to the United States legal system that allows jurors to discuss cases after they are over. "There were questions about both the defendant and the complainant. But when it was all weighed up, we felt the plaintiff was more believable."

For one juror it came down to a straightforward detail, almost a throwaway line during the evidence given by Miss Washington: "She testified that when she rushed from her room to join Tyson in his limo, she had taken her camera. She really did think that Tyson was going to show her the town and escort her to some of the celebrity-packed parties being held on the eve of the pageant. We asked ourselves, 'Why did she take the camera?' It was clear that she thought she was going to go out and see the sights, as Tyson had promised."

The jury had taken three votes to reach a unanimous verdict. Race, they said, had played no part, with the two blacks on the jury voting either way before agreeing at the third vote. One man on the jury backed the appeal for women to report date rape cases that had begun to look uncertain after the acquittal of William Kennedy Smith at Palm Beach. "We all agreed that we would like to see more people come forward with date rape," he said. "But we took this as a case on its own, and did not worry about the ramifications."

Miss Washington sat with her mother in court during the closing arguments, but stayed away for the verdict. There were reports that she planned to sue Tyson for damages in a civil court. Two lawyers acting on her behalf were in court for parts of the trial.

The verdict had been a crushing defeat for Vince Fuller. He took two extraordinary gambles, and both failed. First of all he made the mistake of putting Tyson on the stand, and then he depicted him as a notorious sexual predator in an attempt to persuade the jury that any women who went with him should surely have known that he was so ravenous that he would expect to have sex with them. Any strangers in the court would have thought they were listening to the case for the prosecution rather than for the defence.

Mike Tyson's life as a free man ended on 27 March 1992 as Indiana Judge Patricia Gifford rejected pleas for leniency and sent the former heavyweight boxing champion to prison for six years for the rape of Desiree Washington. Judge Gifford, saying Tyson was capable of raping again and had not expressed sufficient remorse for the crime, sentenced him to ten years on each of three felony convictions, then suspended four years for 'mitigating' circumstances. Gifford refused to free Tyson on bond pending appeal.

A disconsolate Tyson gave a rambling 11-minute statement midway through the two-hour hearing, insisting he had not raped Miss Washington. "I have not raped anyone. I did not rape anyone by any means," Tyson said in a soft, timorous voice. "I'm sorry to Miss Washington. I by no means meant to hurt her or do anything to her. I'm sorry Miss Washington took it personally. I'm sorry Miss Washington isn't here so I could apologize to her."

The fallen champion conceded that his behaviour towards the contestants during the pageant had been "kind of crass" and he accepted blame for "saying some things that were horrible". He told the hearing: "I got carried away and I got into a situation that got way out of hand. We made an arrangement and the situation happened. Miss Washington is very sophisticated, and it is incredible to believe that I could take her upstairs and do horrific things to her."

Tyson said prosecutors, and some witnesses, portrayed him unfairly. "I was devastated listening to people say how stupid I was," he said. "I kept reading things that weren't true, that were vindictive and ferocious, that weren't fair. Things that were said by the prosecutors were distasteful and disdainful. I thought a lot about the case and was nervous and slightly afraid to be in court because I was not guilty of committing a crime."

He looked up at Judge Gifford and said with as much sincerity as he could muster: "I don't come here begging for mercy, ma'am. I expect the worst. I can't see anything good coming out of this. I've been crucified and humiliated worldwide. And socially with women. Rape is a bad thing, an extremely bad thing. The situation that occurred was not meant harmfully at all. There were no black eyes, no bruises, no scars."

He wound up the most important speech of his life by saying: "Ma'am, I will accept whatever you offer me."

Judge Gifford was unmoved. "From everything I've read and heard so far, we're looking at two different Mike Tysons," said the 53-year-old judge, who had specialized in rape cases as a prosecutor. She seemed to be swayed by the seriousness of the crime and Tyson's apparent failure to understand the magnitude of what he had done.

She told him: "You have been given many gifts. Your background and what you have done with yourself is a mitigant. You are to be commended. You have done a lot."

But as to whether Tyson was capable of raping again, Gifford said: "Quite honestly I'm of the opinion that you are. Something needs to be done with that attitude that I hear from you, saying that somehow she [Miss Washington] misunderstood."

Desiree Washington was not in the courtroom. But she wrote a letter to Gifford and county prosecutor Jeffrey Modisett read portions of it in court. "In the place of what has been inside me for 18 years is now a cold and empty feeling," the letter said. " . . . Although some days I cry when I see the pain in my own eyes, I am also able to pity my attacker. It has been and still is my wish that he be rehabilitated." Defence attorney Fuller asked the judge to suspend all of Tyson's sentence or place him in an alternative residential program where he could undergo counselling. He said that, despite Tyson's impoverished background and lack of education, he had shown determination by becoming a boxing success. Fuller said the boxer's life was filled with people interested only in his career. He singled out the late Cus D'Amato –

whose companion, Camille Ewald, was in the courtroom.

Prosecutor Gregory Garrison said Tyson should be imprisoned immediately because he had shown "an ongoing, practiced pattern of aggressive behaviour toward women. He is guilty, he has been convicted, he is to be remanded."

Defence attorneys argued passionately that Tyson would profit more from counselling in an alternative setting from prison. Additionally, Fuller said that, because of who he was and what he was, Tyson would be "a marked man" in the penitentiary.

Tyson, wearing a light grey suit and black and red tie, solemnly answered "Yes" when Judge Gifford asked if he understood the terms of his sentence. Then, flanked by a brood of attorneys and boxing promoter Don King, Tyson was led from the hushed courtroom with a new identity: Indiana Department of Corrections inmate 922335.

"The guys in the ghetto still love you, Mike," a man yelled as Tyson left through a rear exit. "We love you, Mike," a woman screamed as she burst out sobbing. Handcuffed and taken into custody by the Marion County Sheriff's Department, Tyson was later transferred to the Department of Corrections, where he was processed like any other felon. He exchanged his suit and tie for the standard prison attire of white T-shirt and blue jeans and had to undergo a strip search, delousing and a shower before being assigned to a two-man cell.

Prisoner 922335 had hardly had time to settle into his cell before he was back in the headlines. The FBI announced that they were investigating allegations from Desiree Washington that she was offered $1 million four months before the trial to drop the charges. Thomas F. Jones, the FBI's chief spokesman, said: "We have an investigation pending. It involves a couple of offices. We are attempting to ascertain if in fact there are any violations of federal law."

In her first interview since Tyson's conviction, Miss Washington told ABC-TV's Barbara Walters that she was offered money to withdraw the charges after the former heavyweight champion was indicted. Washington said she was "not at liberty" to disclose who made the offer.

She told viewers: "They told me to say that I was afraid because of what happened to Patricia Bowman [the unsuccessful accuser in the

William Kennedy Smith rape trial of 1991], and that I was afraid because of how Anita Hill was exploited [in the Clarence Thomas sexual harassment hearings in the Senate]." Miss Washington added on the same *20-20* news programme that triggered the Tyson-Givens divorce: "They gave me a million excuses as to how and why I could drop the charges." She stressed that she never considered accepting the offer. "I said, 'No way.' " She told Barbara Walters: "I reported it to my lawyer, who took it to a higher authority." New York *Newsday*, citing a source close to the FBI investigation, reported that the Reverend Virgil Wood, a minister in Providence, made the offer to Miss Washington. The newspaper quoted Wood as saying he had contacted her in only "a pastoral role". Wood later commented: "I categorically deny the report."

Another minister, the Reverend T.J. Jemison, revealed that he had contacted Miss Washington to ask why she was going through with the charges, and that her father, Donald, made a comment about financial assistance. Jemison said he never offered Washington money or pressured her to withdraw the charges. Jemison is head of the Nashville-based National Baptist Convention USA and led a prayer vigil on Tyson's behalf during the 13-day trial.

Miss Washington, who testified for six hours during the trial, told Walters that she decided to grant the television interview "because there were so many unanswered questions that people have judged me on without knowing all the facts and without knowing me as a person. If they still feel negatively towards me after this interview, then there's nothing that I can do."

She said it bothers her when people suggest that Tyson was a victim of a racist trial. "Our people fought for years to get in the civil rights movement for equal rights, equal treatment," she said. "And to take the side of a black man over a black woman is not equal. That's not what I believe we fought for for years."

In the interview, Miss Washington explained that she naively accompanied Tyson to his hotel room when he told her he needed to pick up something there. "Even the most street-smart person wouldn't have thought anything of it," she said. "Without thinking, I just went in there." Miss Washington described how she became distrustful and antisocial after the incident and how she prayed not to be bitter or hateful toward Tyson. "I can only pity this man, because he's sick," she said. "I feel really bad for him."

She added that she would have dropped the charges if Tyson had apologized and agreed to seek counselling. But there was no sign of contrition from Tyson. In the summer of 1994, he wrote to Judge Gifford stating that his conduct leading up to the alleged rape was "inexcusable". He said he had apologized to Miss Washington, but still denied committing any crime even though an admission of guilt would have almost certainly won him an early release from jail.

As we explained in Chapter One, lawyer Alan Dershowitz told an appeals court that the trial judge, Patricia Gifford, was selected for the Tyson trial by the prosecution, giving the state a clear advantage. "If the defence had had a choice, it would have been anyone other than Judge Gifford," Dershowitz said.

There was a shift of public opinion in favour of Tyson when Harvard law professor Dershowitz made the revelation that, as the trial neared its conclusion, the defence learned of three women who said they saw Desiree Washington "engaging in foreplay with Tyson in a limousine just before they entered the Indianapolis hotel where she claimed she was raped".

It was pointed out that Gifford did not allow the witnesses to testify because she believed the defence delayed in notifying the prosecution of this development. "The witnesses," Dershowitz told the court, "would have corroborated Tyson's testimony that he had reason to believe that Miss Washington would be a willing sex partner once in the hotel room." He said the defence first learned of the possible witnesses on a Thursday afternoon. It was Friday before the witnesses were interviewed and Saturday before lawyers received a court order allowing them to inspect the limousine to make sure someone could see into it from the outside through tinted windows. The prosecution was notified before the end of the weekend of the new witnesses, but the judge ruled that surprise witnesses that late in the trial would have been too disruptive.

Dershowitz made another powerful point. "There were no bruises, external or internal, found on Miss Washington," he said. "This was inconsistent with her account of how Tyson had forced her to have sex. She testified that Tyson 'slammed' her down on the bed, got on top of her, held her down with his forearm across her chest, and forced himself inside of her. Had the 230-pound, muscular Tyson done that to the 105-pound, slight Miss Washington there would have been bruises, contusions, welts and perhaps even broken ribs. Yet there was not even the slightest bruise or welt on her body when she went to the hospital just hours after the sexual encounter. All the doctors found were two tiny microscopic abrasions, which, according to leading experts, are perfectly consistent with consensual sex: "These tiny abrasions are quite likely to occur when two people have consensual sex with each other for the first time and are not used to one another's sexual movements and desires."

He also made the observation that, if Miss Washington was so concerned about Tyson's behaviour when she went to the bathroom, she could have locked the door and called for help from the bathroom telephone.

Dershowitz, who said he is totally committed to proving Tyson's innocence, could fill a book with the evidence he has collected. He is convinced that the jury would have returned a 'not guilty' verdict had they had heard the full story. It is tough for Tyson that Dershowitz was not representing him in place of Vince Fuller, who was heavily criticised for the way he conducted the defence.

Taking on board all that Dershowitz has to say, it is easy to understand why inmate 922335 was an angry man when he came out of prison to continue his boxing career after three lost years. The purpose of this book is not to reach judgement on Mike Tyson. If he did what Miss Washington claims, he deserved every second of his prison sentence. But the foundation of a fair legal system is that phrase 'beyond reasonable doubt'.

We wonder what reasonable people think now that they are in possession of all the facts?

8: Prisoner 922335

MIKE Tyson made a disturbing start to his six-year sentence and, within a matter of weeks, had lost his first major fight with the Indiana prison system. He was placed in solitary confinement in the disciplinary unit at the Indiana Youth Centre after getting himself involved in a bust-up with a guard.

It was leaked to the press by another inmate that Tyson had threatened to "whup" a guard, who had shouted at him to keep moving when he stopped to shake hands with a fellow prisoner. Eight other guards closed in on Tyson and he was taken to the disciplinary unit, segregated from all the other prisoners. When taken to the supervisor's office, Tyson lost his temper again and became belligerent after disputing the guard's version of the incident.

Tyson's attorney, Harvard law professor Alan Dershowitz, said that his client feared he might be provoked into a confrontation. "I saw Mike three days before the incident and he was very worried something like this could happen," Dershowitz said. "He was worried about being set up. He said that there were all kinds of rumours that people would try to provoke him into something, that people might try to plant drugs in his cell, or something of that kind."

Promoter Don King said that he was concerned about Tyson's safety while in jail. "I'm very fearful something will happen to Mike that will hold him in jail or that they're going to kill him," King told a press conference. "They're trying to destroy this man and I want the world to know it. You may wake up one day and Mike Tyson is coming out of there on a slab."

King said he would appeal to President Bush and black leaders about his fears for Tyson's safety. "It's bad enough that he is in prison for something that he did not do, without all this hassle," said King.

Prisoner 922335 was charged with disorderly conduct at a disciplinary hearing, and pleaded guilty to threatening a guard with bodily harm. He was sentenced to 30 days' loss of commission and also 30 days' loss of special privileges. The prison superintendent stressed to Tyson that it didn't matter who he was or how much he was worth, the system could put him in a solitary cell and forget him for the next six years, and if he still caused trouble, it could accommodate him with some extra time. One former prisoner said: "Tyson came back down from that hearing a sadder and wiser man. Nobody had ever talked like that to him in his life. I think that, for the first time, he realised the writing was on the wall. He had to either go with the flow or get his ass kicked in the disciplinary unit."

It was feared that Tyson was going to become a troublemaking prisoner, but proof that he settled down came shortly before his release in March 1995. Prison commissioner Christian DeBruyn lifted the penalty period added for threatening the guard after getting behaviour reports from prison staff. "I have decided, after considering all reports, that the misconduct resulted from Tyson's difficulty in adjusting to prison life in the first few weeks of his sentence," he said. " Since then, he has been a well-behaved prisoner."

Tyson came to terms with prison life by exercising his mind as well as his body. At 8 a.m. every morning, he worked out in the prison gymnasium as if preparing for a fight. The former world champion was keeping physically rather than fighting fit because no sparring was allowed. He would set himself a target of completing more than five hundred press-ups before breakfast. He was given the privileged job of handing out exercise equipment to his fellow prisoners. After each work out, he would go for an eight-mile run round the prison grounds, then he would shower and visit the prison library where the collection of books were opening a whole new world to him. Each night, Tyson did two hours homework for proposed exams, and then read until 'lights out'.

Phil Slavens, assistant superintendent at the prison, commented: "For the first time Mike Tyson is learning a discipline outside the regimen of boxing. Nobody is suggesting he likes prison, but in some ways the incarceration has lifted a tremendous weight from his shoulders. There had been a lot of pressure on him in the outside world. Now he's got the chance to find himself. He took time to adjust to the rigours of prison life, but has settled down into a routine."

It was nearly as difficult for the prison staff as for Tyson to adjust to his imprisonment. His very presence threatened to disrupt the everyday running of the prison. He was receiving hundreds of letters from all around the world every day, including marriage proposals, but mostly good luck wishes from fight fans. Both the prisoners and the warders were bugging him almost daily for autographs. Tyson was such a celebrity that the system was changed to cope with him. A prison spokesman said: "We had to do something. It wasn't fair to Tyson. He wasn't getting a chance to settle down and do his time." It led to a complaint from an inmate that Tyson was receiving privileged treatment, but this was dismissed by the authorities, who had never had a celebrity quite like Tyson under their roof before.

One of Tyson's first tasks when he arrived at the prison was to undergo educational assessment examinations for a week. The embarrassing results showed that he had the reading level of an 11-year-old. By the time he was released, Tyson could read and understand like an adult, and was able to quote from Tolstoy's *War and Peace* and works by Nietzsche, Dumas, Voltaire and Hemingway. "I particularly enjoyed *The Count of Monte Cristo*," he said. "I can really identify with that Edmund Dantes. He was unjustly imprisoned, too. And he got an education while he was locked away."

Tyson had long talks with Don King, who spent three years, 11 months in jail for manslaughter. When he was released, he had a degree in business administration. King continually stressed to Tyson: "I didn't serve time. I made time serve me." Mike dropped out of the prison education system because he was kept too busy giving interviews and seeing visitors, but when he returned to his studies it was noticed by prison supervisors that his work showed a marked improvement.

Muhammad Siddeeq, a high school biology teacher who also acts as a Moslem minister in the Indiana prison system, first met Tyson on a routine visit and discussed religion with him. He said: "I discovered that Tyson had an overwhelming desire to educate himself. His interest is really phenomenal. He has an incredibly quick, retentive mind. He absorbs everything I give him."

There were conflicting stories as to whether Tyson had converted to

Islam. The certain fact is that he made a deep study of the Muslim religion while in prison. According to Kamran Memon, spokesman for the Islamic Centre of Plainfield, Indiana, close to the prison, Tyson was a regular at the Friday afternoon Islamic prayer meetings.

We Tyson Watchers in the outside world got a good insight into how he was coping with prison life when he gave a live television interview to Ed Bradley on the CBS programme *Street Stories*. He had been locked away for just three months when he talked from inside the Indiana Youth Centre, a medium-to-high-security prison. Bradley asked him what thoughts he had when the cell door was closed and the lights went out on his first night in prison. "It wasn't realistic at that point," said Tyson. "But after a couple of days I'd just say, 'These cells are horrible.' You'll never forget them, know what I mean? Not as long as you live. Prison will have an everlasting effect on me. Especially a prison like this. I'll never forget it."

John Solberg, who worked closely with Don King, reported at the end of Tyson's first year inside: "When Mike visited schools, he always told kids that doing well at school was the most important thing in their lives. He made no secret of the fact that he had little education and secretly he deeply regretted it. When I last visited him, he was in fantastic physical shape and reading extensively. He wants to improve himself and he is using the prison time to do it."

Tyson stoked up an old romance while in prison, encouraging regular visits by Geraldine Ecclestone, a childhood sweetheart from the Brownsville back streets where he grew up. Geraldine moved into his home in Southville, Ohio, and was looking after it until his release.

When he came out of prison, Tyson had two new tattoos to show off on his muscular arms. On his right bicep he had the head of Chairman Mao. ["I read about the way he led the Long March, and admired his determination."] Tyson's other bicep, the left, is tattooed with a picture of the late tennis master Arthur Ashe. "I never knew the man and thought I never liked him" said Tyson. "But then Spike Lee sent me Ashe's book (*Days of Grace*) and I read this: 'Aids isn't the heaviest burden I've had to bear . . . it's being black . . . race has always been my biggest burden . . . it feels like an extra weight tied around me.' An extra weight tied around me. That's telling it as it is."

Our good friend Nigel Collins, Bristol-born Managing Editor of the American boxing bible, *The Ring*, acted as our eyes and ears while Tyson was locked away, and continually provided inside information in his excellent magazine. He managed to get into the prison for a fascinating one-on-one interview with Tyson when his release was just about due. These were some of the answers he got to his searching questions:

> **Q:** *Like Muhammad Ali, your boxing career has been suspended for approximately three years during your prime. Do you see any parallels between Ali and yourself?*

Mike Tyson: There was only one Ali. There is no parallel. Ali committed himself to something for a reason *[he was stripped of the title and banned from boxing for his refusal to join the US Army during the Vietnam war]*, and I did mine by making bad choices, not being careful enough protecting myself.

> **Q:** *Ali fought a different style after he returned from his exile. Will the time you spent away from boxing change your style or affect the way you fight in any way?*

Mike Tyson: No. I train every day. I feel better now than I did at any time during my career. I'm not saying that's gonna make me fight better, but I believe it should. I run around eight miles a day. I do my exercises, my shadow-boxing, all that I can do.

> **Q:** *You unified the heavyweight title at a time when boxing desperately needed an undisputed champion. How much damage do you feel splintered titles and the proliferation of divisions has done to the sport?*

Mike Tyson: I believe we have too many weight divisions now, too many titles. That's because boxing has become big business, and that doesn't allow people to become the best possible fighters they can. You no longer have to work as hard as you used to become champion. I don't like all the weight divisions. You don't even know who the champion is. At one particular time, you didn't even have to be a fight fan to know who the champions were because there were only seven of them. Now, you've got 16, 20 of 'em. It's incredible.

Q: *If I could wave a magic wand and make you czar of boxing, what would be the one change you would make to improve the sport?*

Mike Tyson: Boxers would have pensions – a percentage of their money would go for pensions. Boxing is the only sport where anybody can get involved and make money. A fighter, in general, has no other method of making money except fighting. It can take a guy of low circumstances and put him in the high ranks. But on the other hand, if a guy abuses his skills and neglects them, he can lose his title.

Q: *There have been certain people who have played an important part in both your life and your career. Let's play a variation on the word-association game: I'll give you a name and you respond with the first thing that pops into your head. Here goes. Cus D'Amato.*

Mike Tyson: An incredible teacher, an incredible man. I believe Mike Tyson and Cus D'Amato had great chemistry. That's the reason Mike Tyson was the fighter he was. He had great chemistry with his trainer, more so than Cus's other fighters that became successful, like Floyd Patterson and José Torres. I had more malice in my temperament, and I took orders well. When Cus told me what to do, I had confidence in him and executed what he told me to do.

Camille Ewald [Tyson's surrogate mother].

Mike Tyson: A loving lady. A lot brighter than people give her credit for. Everybody was always trying to manipulate her, especially the press. She just has a good heart, and when somebody comes to the door and wants to do a story, she's not rude, she doesn't fight back. That's because she's used to having Cus there to fight for her. She's very kind, and people try to take advantage of her because she's a very old lady.

Jim Jacobs.

Mike Tyson: A very different individual, very mysterious. You never knew anything about him. He lived his whole life a secret. No one knew his situation. He always played the role and never got caught up in scandal, because if there's a scandal, you have to be investigated. He never allowed himself to be in that position. No one ever knew him.

Bill Cayton.

Mike Tyson: Bill Cayton is crude and sophisticated at the same time. His main objective is Bill Cayton. I don't take it personally, like I once did when my feelings were hurt. But I put myself in that position by trusting him.

Kevin Rooney.

Mike Tyson: This is a difficult one. We used to have a lot of good times. It's sad it had to end the way it did. I was doing my thing. He was doing his thing. He got caught between something he shouldn't have been caught in between. He believed he had more power than he actually did. He believed he was in the situation to stay forever. But that wasn't necessarily true. I was only with him because of Cus. He doesn't understand that Bill Cayton and Jim Jacobs didn't want him to be my trainer. They wanted to get Eddie Futch to train me. But I was loyal to him because I knew that if Kevin didn't train me, what else was he gonna do? He wasn't that successful as a fighter.

José Torres.

Mike Tyson: An opportunist. For some reason he never liked me, though he pretended to be my friend for many years. I had a great deal of respect for him, and I couldn't believe he did the things he did. Then again, I always felt he envied me. It still hurts today that he wrote a book about me that was nothing but lies. I still haven't said anything disrespectful about him because I believe I'm better than that. But he hurt my feelings.

Q: *HBO is making a movie about you based on Torres' book. Do you have any thoughts about that?*

Mike Tyson: Well, the movie is a bunch of lies, and what José wrote is bunch of lies. He asked me one time, and I said "Yes, you can write a book about me." I was a young kid, 20, 21 years old. He discussed something about pain, and how I like to hurt women, which wasn't necessarily true. I said that when I was younger, I loved to inflict pain. He walked around with a tape recorder trying to discuss these things that were damaging. But I wasn't talking about women. When I was fighting, I wanted to hurt the guy, I wanted to break him up. And I got that from the old fighters because they used to say what they were gonna do to guys. And I'm living back in their time, and I'm not thinking about having some kind of fear for the media. I'm not thinking about becoming a corporation and making commercials. I think about Joe Gans and Battling Nelson. Those were the guys I really admired. I wasn't thinking about how my life depends on some corporation sponsoring me. That's not where I'm at.

Robin Givens.

Mike Tyson: We were two young people who weren't supposed to be married in the first place. We weren't ready for marriage, and we got caught up in the whole situation of being who we were. She got caught up in being who she was because she was with me. I don't have any hard feelings for Robin. We were two kids. Things happen. She did things I truly didn't like and don't agree with, but what can you say? When all is said and done, we're all dead anyway. I don't want to be her friend. I don't want to hug and kiss and be cordial with her, but I have nothing bad or good to say about her.

Don King.

Mike Tyson: Don King is a good man. Don King is a businessman. Don King sometimes gets caught up in being so suspicious of everybody. I think that sometimes he even distrusts his friends. I think that that's just the life he leads. I don't think he trusts me totally.

Q: *Besides the obvious, what has been the hardest part of being incarcerated?*

Mike Tyson: I don't know. It's so crazy, but I think I could do 100 years without flinching. I used to think the boredom would get to me. When I first came, I used to say, "It's killing me. It's killing me. I want to see my family." But when it really comes down to it, I really don't have anybody I want to go to. I've been alone all my life, and every time I did accept someone in my life, they've f****d me. *[Laughs.]* Who do I really want to go to? I'll always take care of Camille. Now, she's 90 years old. Come on, odds are not on her side. As long as she's all right and my little daughter is all right, I don't give a damn about anything. Me? My life is useless. I don't care a damn about my life. That's why I'm so successful and everything, because I don't care.

Q: *Despite your tough-guy image, you're still a human being, experiencing the same emotions as the rest of us. Has there ever been a time since you've been in prison when you've broke down and cried?*

Mike Tyson: I'd never do that. I can't do that. I just feel that everyone is against me. I try not to let myself get angry, and if I cried, I'd get angry at myself.

Q: *You've been studying the Islamic religion. Has that been a comfort to you?*

Mike Tyson: It's helped me a great deal. You know, if it wasn't for Islam, I don't know what I'd be into. I would become part of society in this place. I'd probably be in here with these damned faggots, getting high. Man, I'm telling you, it's a helluva world in here. It's a world within a world. Islam has given me a great outlook on life. I have to appreciate where I've been, where I haven't been. I could have been somewhere else worse. I just praise the Lord that I'm not dead.

Q: *A lot of people think you're broke. Is that true?*

Mike Tyson: I'm not broke. I'm not Mike Tyson rich, but I can do what I want. I can still buy things I want in prison. I can still send money to someone in another country if I want them to come see me.

Q: *Is it important to you how the general public feels about you?*

Mike Tyson: I don't want anyone to love me. I just want them to respect me. Nobody comes into my face and calls me an asshole or a jerk and violates me without being violated back in return.

Q: *What, besides the passing of time, is the biggest difference between the Mike Tyson who was imprisoned almost three years ago and Mike Tyson today?*

Mike Tyson: The Mike Tyson who was not in prison and was out on the street being champion loved everybody, thought everybody was nice. Now, Mike Tyson hates the world. That's just a fact. I hate everybody. I know they say, "No, you can't hate the world, don't be bitter." But I just hate everybody. Well, the majority, maybe 99 per cent.

Previous page: Mike Tyson, portrait of a fighter.
Left: Tyson with Camille Ewald, his 'surrogate' mother and Cus D'Amato's long-time companion.
Right: Young man in a hurry. Tyson has a love of fast cars.

Below: Cus D'Amato, the man who moulded Tyson and Floyd Patterson, is pictured here (left) with Patterson before a trip to London for an exhibition bout in 1958.

Tyson, as free as a bird, is happiest when he is with his pigeons in Catskill, in upstate New York.

The Tyson team (left to right): John Horne (personal assistant); Anthony (bodyguard); Mike Tyson; Don King; Tyson's personal chef; and in front, Rory Holloway (Tyson's close friend).

On the right side of the law – posing with the Atlanta Police.

Tyson the Champ . . . and he's in the money after winning the WBC belt to become the youngest-ever heavyweight champion.
Following page: Happy days for Tyson and Robin Givens, whom he married in 1988. But Mike soon had misgivings about marrying Miss Givens and their divorce was finalized on Valentine's Day, 1989.

When he was 10 years old, Tyson moved with his mother to Brownsville, Brooklyn, where only the strongest survived. He began raising pigeons. "I love those birds. I'm really at peace when I'm with them."

Above: The caring side of Tyson. Mike hands out T-shirts and Christmas turkeys at the Martin Luther King Center, Atlanta, in 1991.

Right: Tyson the Businessman, on the road and in conversation with Don King.

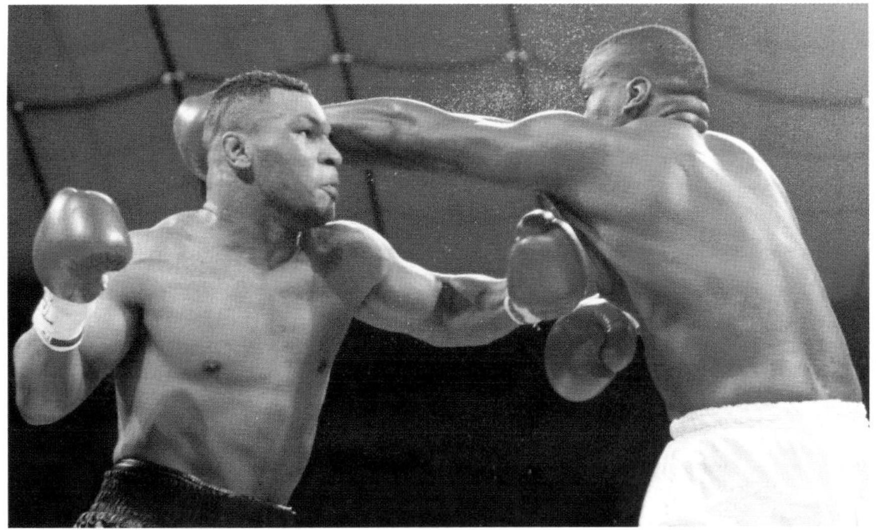

Above: Tyson prepares a big right hand as Buster Douglas misses during their world title fight in Tokyo, February 1990.
Opposite: Bruised, battered and beaten – Tyson on his stool seemed to share the amazement of the rest of the boxing world when Douglas knocked him out in the tenth round.
Below: By June, he was back in winning form against old amateur rival Henry Tillman in Las Vegas.

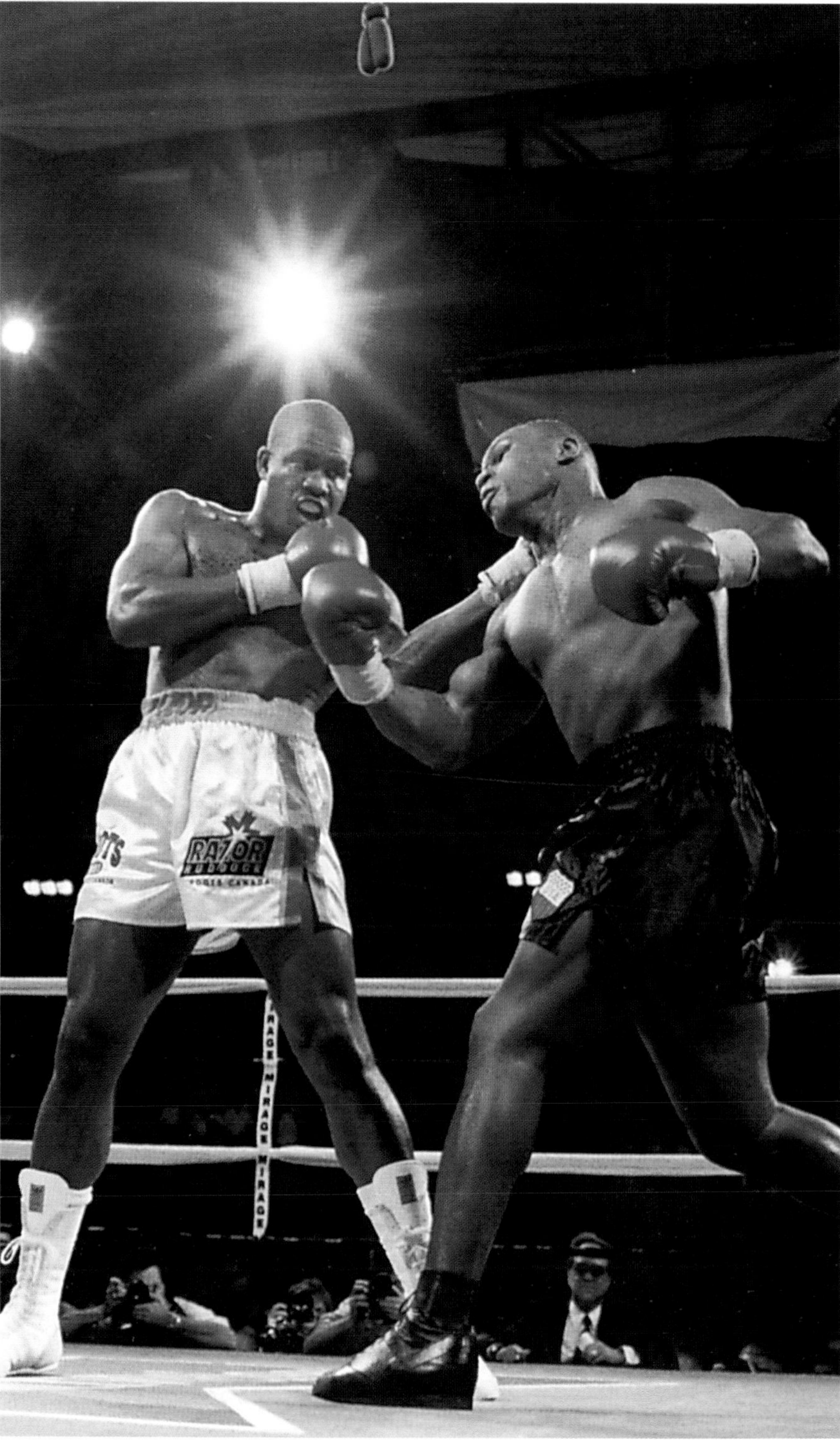
RAZOR
MIRAGE

Above: Tyson on the attack . . . with a verbal volley at the media for what he claimed were insults against his family.

Opposite: Tyson beat Ruddock on a controversial seventh-round stoppage in their first meeting in June 1991.

Overleaf: Tyson had even bigger battles to fight outside the ring. In 1992, he was sentenced to six years in prison for rape. In 1994, he went to the Appeal Court in Indiana in an unsuccessful attempt to get his release. Nevertheless he would soon be ready to swap handcuffs for boxing gloves.

ONE
WAY

Tyson came out of jail in one piece, despite Don King's fears that he would get cut up by organized gangs. But it was touch and go. He managed to stay out of serious trouble until the Christmas before his release when he got drawn into an incident that could have blown his chances of an early parole. Through no fault of his own, he got involved with a notorious gangleader who objected to him giving away presents of food and cigarettes to inmates because it cut across his contraband business. We would have loved to have been flies on the wall as spectators of what happened next. It would have been worth top ringside seat money.

The gang boss, a mountain of a man, confronted Tyson, who knocked him flat with one punch. It sparked a brawl between supporters of Tyson and the gangleader. Guards broke it up, and Tyson was cleared of any blame for the incident. It was a winning fight that will not find its way on to his ring record.

Tyson said of his three years inside: "Prison will have an everlasting effect on me. Especially a prison like this. I'll never forget it. You don't forget seeing men raping men. But I've learnt to do my time."

While in prison, Tyson officially named John Horne and Rory Holloway as his co-managers for boxing business. Both are close associates of Don King, who expects to be pulling the Mike Tyson promotional strings. There are millions of dollars to be earned from his return to the ring, but it would be foolish to push him too hard or too fast.

Tyson coped in prison by always expecting the worst. Assistant superintendent Phil Slavens revealed: "He never allowed himself to get carried away with notions of an early release. He kept setting himself up to expect the worst and was pretty surprised when something other than that happened. He got his attitude right after some early teething problems. Settling to prison life is always the hardest thing."

The Reverend Charles Williams, a friend of Tyson's and president of the Indiana Black Expo, kept in close contact with him and expects him to be a better person for his experience of prison. "Michael has matured during his sentence," he said. "He has done a lot of studying and has had plenty of time to think about what he wants from life."

Tyson agrees. "I have discovered humility," he said. "I'm at peace with myself, and it's a better person coming out than who came in here three years ago."

He sincerely wants to put something back into society. "I want to travel and talk to as many young people as I can," he said. "I don't want them to make the mistakes that I have. I shall return to boxing but not to the life I had before."

The man who used to slip diamonds under the pillow of Robin Givens and bought her a Porsche as a surprise gift had, by all accounts, learned humility and true values in prison. His lessons in being made to feel humble continued after his release. Judge Gifford ordered him to do 400 hours community service during a four year probationary period. This programme would have included sweeping local roads, helping pensioners with their shopping or digging ditches for the public works department. Whether he should wear an electronic device so that the prison authorities knew of his whereabouts was also considered. This was all part of The Taming of Tyson. But the shackles would be off when the bell rang to signal his return to the ring.

As Tyson Watchers, we hope that he can cope with the pressures that are sure to pile on him.

He has done his time. Now we want to see him allowed to adjust to his new life. When the Tyson Time-bomb explodes, let us hope it is *inside* the ring. For Mike's sake.

PART TWO

Tyson the Fighter

9: The Fight File

WE have analysed Mike Tyson the Man . . . the man who nobody, even Tyson himself, really knows. Now we come to Mike Tyson the Fighter. Here, we are on much more comfortable ground because we feel that – as dedicated Tyson Watchers – we know Tyson the Fighter as well as anybody. Our objective is to give as thorough a breakdown as possible of his fights on his way to becoming the youngest heavyweight champion of all time, and then to follow him on his rise as one of the all-time greats to his fall in Tokyo against Buster Douglas.

Tyson turned professional in 1985 after an amateur career that embraced 35 recorded contests of which he won all but five. He had at least another 19 bouts on unofficial 'smoker' shows, where Cus D'Amato pushed him through the learning process.

Two of Tyson's losses were disputed points defeats by eventual Los Angeles gold medallist Henry Tillman in the Olympic trials. Tyson also dropped a points decision to Craig Payne in the 1983 National Golden Gloves final, a coveted title that he won the following year by stopping John Littles in the first round. His one stoppage was by 26-year-old Al Evans, of Chicago, in the 1982 US/ABF tournament when, at 16, he was stopped in the third round of what was his tenth contest. The other blot on Tyson's amateur record came in the same competition a year later, when he was disqualified against Kimmuel Odom for turning away in disgust from an opponent he claimed was refusing to fight. In his last amateur contest in September 1984, Tyson had his first experience of overseas boxing. He won the Tampere International in Finland by beating Sweden's Hakan Brock. It was time for the challenge of the professional ring, and the first seven contests were little more than limbering-up tests against carefully selected opposition . . .

FIGHT No 1. Opponent: **Hector Mercedes**. Venue: Albany. Date: 6 March 1985. Tyson walked through Mercedes as if he wasn't there and was hammering him unmercifully with both fists when the referee called a halt. It was all over in one minute 47 seconds. Cus D'Amato reacted as quickly as a skilled counter puncher when a reporter commented that it was an easy win. "The term is quick, not easy," said wise old Cus. "This guy Mercedes came to fight. Mike did his job. Quickly."

FIGHT No 2. Opponent: **Trent Singleton**. Venue: Albany. Date: 10 April 1985. Singleton was overwhelmed by Tyson and the referee intervened midway through round one. Mike then cheered his trainer Kevin Rooney to an eight rounds points win over Jamie Medina.

FIGHT No 3. Opponent: **Don Halpin**. Venue: Albany. Date: 23 May 1985. Tyson's inexperience was exposed as he strove too hard to nail the strong and stubborn Halpin. He finally caught up with him in the fourth round and knocked him down and out with a vicious left hook.

FIGHT No 4. Opponent: **Ricardo Spain**. Venue: Atlantic City. Date: 20 June 1985. Spain was flattened by a volley of punches in the first round and the referee stopped the one-sided action with Tyson totally in command. "Everything at this stage is part of the learning process," said D'Amato. "Mike is wiser for every experience and having wisdom is as good as money in the bank."

FIGHT No 5. Opponent: **John Alderson**. Venue: Atlantic City. Date: 11 July 1985. Alderson took heavy punishment throughout two one-sided rounds and quit at the end of the second after having taken a count just before the bell. They were calling Mike 'Catskill Thunder'.

FIGHT No 6. Opponent: **Larry Sims**. Venue: Ploughkeepsie. Date: 19 July 1985. In the fight programme for Tyson's world championship challenge against Trevor Berbick, he is credited with a first round knockout victory over Sims. In actual fact, he was taken three rounds before the referee saved Sims from further punishment.

FIGHT No 7. Opponent: **Lorenzo Canady**. Venue: Atlantic City. Date: 15 August 1985. Tyson dropped the towering Canady with the first serious punch of the fight, a whiplash left hook and the referee stepped in after just 65 seconds. Tyson was now attracting world attention and every fight was coming under the media microscope. He could no longer be hidden out of sight.

Fight No 8
v
Michael Johnson
Atlantic City
5. 9. 85
Won RSF 1

THE table-players at the Atlantis Casino Hotel took time off from their fortune hunting to watch Tyson prove that he doesn't need to gamble to hit the jackpot. He did not keep them away from the tables for long. It took him just 39 seconds to dispose of Michael 'Jack' Johnson in what was scheduled as a six rounds contest. Tyson weighed in at his heaviest weight to date, seven ounces over 15 stone 9 pounds (219 pounds), and he was a stone and a half heavier than his outgunned opponent. The contest was screened on cable television and Johnson talked with confidence about how he felt sure he could give Tyson his first real test. "I'm not going to let him bully me," he said. "Everybody's on about his punching power. But how will he react when I land my best punches? That's the 64 thousand dollar question." It was a question that went unanswered. Tyson took Johnson's breath away with his first big punch of the fight – a scything left hook to the body that bent his opponent double. He sank to the canvas for a compulsory eight count. As Tyson was waved forward he feinted to throw a left but then crossed with a crushing right to the chin. Johnson went down like a man who had been shot and the referee instantly signalled that the brief encounter was all over without taking up the count. A doctor was summoned into the ring to treat Johnson, who was sent to hospital for an x-ray on a suspected broken jaw.

"We're going to move Mike up to eight rounds," said co-manager Jim Jacobs. "But I'm not sure it's going to make any difference. When he hits 'em they stay hit! We want to bring him along slowly, but the word is out on him now and it will make it that much harder to find opponents who can give him the experience he needs."

Yes, the word was out – and the word on the lips of most people who had seen Tyson in action was "awesome!"

Fight No 9
v
Donnie Long
Atlantic City
9. 10. 85
Won RSF 1

TYSON'S handlers thought they had found just the man to give him some stamina experience in Donnie Long, who had won 15 of 18 contests including ten-round distance defeats by high rankers John Tate and James Broad. But Tyson swept him aside with contemptuous ease in a one-sided brawl that lasted just 88 seconds. Long talked a much better fight than he fought. "I hit as hard as Tyson and I'm the superior boxer," said the 27-year-old stylist from Youngstown, Ohio. "I'm going to give him all the trouble he can handle."

Tyson didn't give him a chance to provide action to go with his brave words. A left hook in the opening seconds turned Long's legs to rubber and it was obvious from then on that the 'Typhoon' was in for another quick blow-through. Long was pounded around the ring under a non-stop barrage and took three counts before referee Frank Cappuccino rescued him as a classic combination – a left hook to the body and left hook to the chin – sent him sinking slowly back to the canvas like a drowning man at sea.

Marvis Frazier and James Broad were among the spectators at the Trump Casino Hotel. "The kid's got a lot going for him," said Broad. "He has been sparring with me and has the right attitude to make it to the top. He's got power on his side, that's for sure." Frazier was less impressed. "He is knocking over nobodies," said the son of former world heavyweight champion Smokin' Joe. "You can't judge him yet. Let's wait until he meets somebody good enough to hit him back."

The contest was screened by ESPN-TV, and the triumphant Tyson told viewers after the quick destruction job: "All you heavyweights out there watching, come on and get some. Mike Tyson's right here and he's waiting for you."

There was not a stampede to take up his challenge.

Fight No 10
v
Robert Colay
Atlantic City
25. 10. 85
Won RSF 1

THE Typhoon struck inside the first round again and, after the referee had come to the rescue of outgunned Robert Colay, fight statisticians started reaching for the record books. Had there ever been a heavyweight in history to match this explosive start to a career? Up came the answer: "Yes, Rocky Marciano." The Brockton Blockbuster had blasted out his first ten opponents in a total of 15 rounds – a record of destruction that was one round ahead of Tyson's.

Rocky's ten fight winning sequence had gone 3-1-1-3-1-1-1-1-1-2. Tyson's tally of terror read 1-1-4-1-2-3-1-1-1-1. His average time spent in the ring at this point of his career was just three minutes 16 seconds. Thanks to being exposed at a young age to the unbeatable film collection owned by Jim Jacobs, Tyson had a keen sense of fight history. He knew that comparisons with Rocky Marciano were inevitable and was aware that The Rock had won his first 16 fights inside the distance. Tyson's trainer, Kevin Rooney, had mixed feelings about his lightning strikes. "It does Mike's confidence no harm whatsoever," he said. "But from the point of view of ring experience, it would do him good to have somebody take him a few rounds just so he can find out how to pace himself. That's easier said than done because, when Mike lands his best shots, there's nobody in the wide world who can stand up to them." Tyson's get-it-over-with-quick approach to his fighting meant fans were getting short value for their money, but his rapid demolition work was making him a big box office attraction.

"The fans who come to see Mike Tyson know what to expect," he said, with that disconcerting habit of his of referring to himself in the third person. "They know what they're doing when they risk their money."

So far, nobody had been to him to ask for their money back!

Fight No 11
v
Sterling Benjamin
Latham, NY
1. 11. 85
Won KO 1

THE mighty left hook that is the Exocet missile in Tyson's wide-ranging weaponry devastated the luckless Sterling Benjamin after just 54 seconds of the first round. Now some critics were putting their heads above the waters like Jaws, snapping and biting at Tyson and saying that he was being fed on a diet of pushovers. This seemed premature knocking of a fighter whose entire professional ring experience stretched to just 11 fights and only 16 rounds.

Meantime, a rising British hope called Frank Bruno was getting similar slap-down treatment from some critics because of the calibre of his opponents. Has there ever been a world heavyweight prospect who has not met a procession of 'unknowns' on his way up the ladder? Do these names mean anything to you: Bob Jefferson, Patrick Connolly, Gilley Ferron, Johnny Pretzie, Artie Donator? They just happen to be opponents 10-11-12-13-14 on the Rocky Marciano ring record. And how about Stan Poreda, Charley Massera, Lee Ramage, Donald Barry and Natie Brown? They were little-known opponents 10-11-12-13-14 on the Joe Louis ring record. And here's another name for you: Don Mogard, who was Rocky's seventeenth opponent and the first to take him to a ten rounds points decision. Hardly household names, but The Rock and Brown Bomber Louis – like Typhoon Tyson and Frank Bruno – had to learn their trade, and it would have been madness to pitch them in over their heads against far more experienced opponents who just might have had the ring craft to destroy their confidence before they'd had the opportunity to get vital ring knowledge themselves.

When Sterling Benjamin had recovered from his assault and battery, he conceded that he had now joined the growing army of Tyson admirers. "I thought he was just being hyped," he said. "Now I know different. That left of his is pure dynamite."

Fight No 12
v
Eddie Richardson
Houston, Texas
13. 11. 85
Won KO 1

THE death nine days earlier of Tyson's mentor Cus D'Amato threw a shadow over this fight, but Tyson declared that he would go ahead with it "because that's what Cus would have wanted. I shall dedicate each of my victories to the man who meant more to me than anybody."

Lined up as his twelfth opponent was Eddie Richardson, a fighter who, on paper, looked as if he could give Tyson a tough test, but it was a different story on canvas. Richardson was a 'Towering Inferno' from Tyler in Texas. He stood 6 foot 6 inches and weighed in at 15 stone 2 pounds (219 pounds). The winner of all but two of his 14 previous professional fights, he had a seven-inch height advantage but was outweighed by seven pounds. Tyson was dwarfed by Richardson, but after just seven seconds the old saying of 'the bigger they are the harder they fall' really struck home. Richardson was chopped to the canvas with the first really solid punch of the fight. As the tottering Texan struggled up at eight, Tyson dropped into the menacing crouch position from which he likes best of all to deliver his favourite left hook. He was spot-on with the punch and he followed through in coaching-manual fashion, with his shoulder turning like a long-hitting golf professional on the tee. As the punch thundered home Richardson staggered backwards across the ring before going down and out. It was over in just 77 seconds.

"When Tyson hits it's like getting in the way of a runaway truck," said Richardson. Tyson's 12 fights had lasted a total of 18 rounds and they had been squeezed into just eight months of atomic action. Rocky Marciano's first 12 fights had also taken up 18 rounds, 11 of the contests coming in just seven months. Thanks to the boxing history lessons he had been receiving from Cus D'Amato and fight historian Jim Jacobs, Tyson was aware of his neck-and-neck running with Marciano. Now he was poised to beat his wrecking record.

Fight No 13
v
Conroy Nelson
Latham, NY
22. 11. 85
Won KO 2

THEY found another giant for Tyson's unlucky-for-some thirteenth fight: Conroy Nelson, the No 2 ranked Canadian heavyweight who at 6 foot 5 inches towered over the New Yorker. It was Nelson who was the unlucky one. The giant from Ottawa was a 27-year-old hardened professional who had won 19 fights against five defeats and two draws. He said before the fight that he respected Tyson but that he felt he knew too much for him. He knew enough to survive the first of the scheduled eight rounds, which at least meant he had done better than nine of Tyson's previous opponents.

The Brownsville assassin failed to get his timing right in the first round, but came out for the second clearly intent on getting the fight finished as quickly as possible. Nelson sensed his bobbing and weaving opponent was going for the kill and tried to smother his savage attack by getting to close quarters. Tyson then proved he could work inside by beating a two-fisted tattoo to his ribs and then whipped over that devastating left hook that was proving the most potent weapon in his armoury. Nelson took the punch flush on the jaw and toppled to the canvas like a giant Canadian timber felled by a skilled lumberjack. Tyson had won after just half a minute of the second round.

Nelson, a winner on a disqualification against Britain's Noel Quarless in London in 1984, joined the anthem of acclaim for Tyson. "When there's somebody around who can hit as hard as Tyson, not a heavyweight in the world can feel safe," he said. There were still a lot of cynics around who considered that Tyson's reputation was being fattened on easy pickings, but equally there were many fight-wise boxing experts who were beginning to think that here was a 22-carat prospect – the next jewel in the heavyweight crown. And, as they say in New York, "You'd better believe it."

Fight No 14
v
Sammy Scaff
Felt Forum, NY
6. 12. 85
Won KO 1

BRITISH fight fans had taken a panoramic view of gigantic Sammy Scaff when he tangled with 'Terrible' Tim Witherspoon on the Azumah Nelson-Pat Cowdell undercard in Birmingham on 12 October 1985. Witherspoon had pounded his way to a fourth round victory against an opponent who weighed in at a colossal 18 stone 5 pounds (257 pounds). Scaff went into the ring against Tyson claiming 13 victories in 19 contests. The fact that he had won six fights inside the first round proved that he often punched his weight, and he promised before the fight: "I'll give Tyson all the trouble he can handle. I was doing real well against Witherspoon until I got careless and took a good shot from Timmy. I like fighting in the top company, and I know that a victory over Tyson would mean a big step-up for me."

But 'Iron Mike' – Tyson's new ring nickname – didn't give Scaff a chance to show that he belonged in top company. He came roaring out of his corner like an express train and put the Kentucky Colossus under enormous pressure from the first bell. Scaff tried to jab him off, but Tyson just walked through his punches. He had rarely had such a huge target to aim at and he unloaded a two-fisted barrage of hooks, uppercuts and crosses. He ended Scaff's interest in the scheduled ten-round fight after just 79 seconds.

Scaff, whose nose was still bleeding half an hour after the fight, gave a resigned shrug of his huge shoulders as he admitted: "I just couldn't keep him off. That guy's real hungry. I've never been hit so hard in my life, and that includes by Tim Witherspoon. The amazing thing about him is his hand speed. He's got the fastest hands in the business, and they're packed with dynamite." Tyson had now attracted worldwide interest, and ABC-TV tabled a contract worth $850,000 for four fights. The hungry fighter was already guaranteed rich pickings.

Fight No 15
v
Mark Young
Latham, NY
27. 12. 85
Won RSF 1

MARK Young made no secret of the fact that he felt he was the man who could end Tyson's unbeaten run. He arrived at the Coliseum in Latham making loud noises about his gladiatorial powers. The winner of 12 of 18 professional fights, Young said: "If I didn't think I could win I wouldn't be getting in the ring. Tyson's not met anybody of any class. He'll find that I'm no pushover. I ain't in the mood to show any seasonal goodwill." Brave words, and, for just a few moments, it looked as if the big man from Charlotte, North Carolina, was going to provide the action to go with them. He came out swinging wildly and Tyson had to slip, duck and weave to avoid getting on the wrong end of a punch that could easily have wrecked his unbeaten record. Young was allowed about 30 seconds of glory and then Tyson took over. He pulled Young up in his tracks with a volley of punches to the head and a left-right combination sent him sinking to the canvas like a boat that had been suddenly torpedoed. The referee didn't bother to count but just lifted Tyson's arm to signify his fifteenth straight victory. It had lasted just 70 seconds.

Tyson said: "It went exactly the way I thought it would. I knew from the way he was talking that he'd come out fighting. I was good and ready for him, and I was in complete control of myself when I was ducking his bombs. That was the elusiveness that Cus taught me." Young didn't argue. "I went out with the intention of testing his chin and got in a couple of good shots," he said. "Then he hit me . . ."

Tyson's 15 fights to date had lasted a total of 40 minutes and 25 seconds, an average of two minutes 42 seconds per fight. Rocky Marciano had started his career with a record 16 successive inside-the-distance victories. Now all eyes were on Tyson to see if he could equal Rocky's rocketing start.

Fight No 16
v
Dave Jaco
Albany, NY
11. 1. 85
Won RSF 1

TYSON came into the New Year as the most feared heavyweight outside the top ten ratings. The hardest job was finding anybody willing to trade punches with him. Albany matchmaker and promoter Lorraine Miller, a lady who really knew her boxing, commented: "Tyson is scaring opponents away. I thought I'd found him somebody from Texas, a fighter called O.T. Davis. But when he realised who it was I wanted him to fight he said, 'I'd rather live on a street corner in Texas than climb into the ring with that man Tyson.' " Mrs Miller finally persuaded Dave Jaco to take on the job of tackling Tyson on her promotion at the Empire Plaza Convention Center. The fight was scheduled for ten rounds. It lasted two minutes 16 seconds.

A man mountain from Michigan, Jaco stood 6 foot 6 inches and weighed 15 stone (210 pounds). He was seven pounds lighter than the bull-necked Tyson but had a seven-inch height advantage. Jaco attempted to make full use of his long reach by trying to keep Tyson at a distance and spearing out his solid jab, tactics that had taken him to 19 victories in 24 fights. But it was like trying to stop a bull with a peashooter. Tyson ducked inside the jab and flattened Jaco with a left hook. Another left hook quickly had Jaco back on the canvas after an eight count, and his third trip to the canvas – this time from a clubbing right to the side of the head – brought an automatic stoppage because of the three knockdown rule.

Tyson had matched Rocky Marciano's start, but his 16 victories had come in just 23 rounds compared to the 30 rounds occupied by Rocky. In his seventeenth fight, Marciano had been taken the distance for the first time in his career before scoring a ten rounds points victory over Don Mogard on 23 May 1949. Tyson's next target was to try to beat Rocky's record.

Fight No 17
v
Mike Jameson
Atlantic City
24. 1. 86
Won RSF 5

PHIL Brown, the first boxer to go the distance with Frank Bruno, was lined up as Tyson's seventeenth opponent but pulled out with an injury. The replacement was 'Irish' Mike Jameson, a bearded giant from California, who had been a good-class American footballer before switching to boxing. To look at Jameson in the ring, you would think he had forgotten to take off his gridiron shoulder pads. He stood 6 foot 4 inches and weighed in at two pounds under 17 stone (238 pounds). The winner of 17 of his 26 contests, Jameson had been knocked out in two rounds by Bruno two years earlier. He had since proved he had staying power by going the distance with top contenders Tex Cobb and Mike Dokes.

Jameson decided that the best way to survive against Tyson was not to let him throw any punches. For four rounds he gave a good impression of a wrestler as he held and smothered, grabbed and grappled. He was deducted a point for holding in the fourth round after being bowled over for an eight count. Coming into the fifth round for the first time in his career, Tyson knocked Jameson back into the ropes with a crushing left hook and then brought him to his knees with a cluster of lefts and rights. The referee waved it all over after just 46 seconds of the round.

Tyson had beaten Rocky Marciano's start with 17 successive inside the distance victories, and it was wrongly reported that this was a new record for the heavyweight division. The main reason Tyson's peformances were being continually compared to Marciano's was that The Rock had gone on to become heavyweight champion of the world. The start Rocky made to his career was a record for a fighter who ultimately became world champion. Lamar Clark, an American who had been carefully matched, set the world record of consecutive inside-the-distance victories with 44 in the 1950s. He came apart when put into the ring against world-class opposition. Tyson still had that test to come.

Fight No 18
v
Jesse Ferguson
Troy, NY
21. 2. 85
Won RSF 6

THE entire American nation was now tuned into the progress of Tyson, and he made his coast-to-coast TV debut against Jesse Ferguson on the ABC network. Ferguson, a 28-year-old seasoned professional from the tough Philadelphian school of fighting, had been beaten only once in fifteen bouts. His one defeat had been by world-ranked Carl 'The Truth' Williams, who stopped him in the tenth and last round after twice being dropped by Ferguson's potent left hook.

"Everybody talks about Tyson's left hook as if it's something special," said Ferguson during the build up to the fight. "Well, I can hit every bit as hard with my left and I promise Tyson that he has got a real fight on his hands."

There was a near 8,000 crowd in the Troy arena and the rousing reception they gave Tyson as he came into the ring provided noisy confirmation that he was already the king of New York boxing. Ferguson's entry bordered on the farcical. He lost his footing and tripped on the way into the ring and for a brief moment it looked as if he might knock himself out. Tyson's supporters considered that this was a task that Tyson could carry out quite comfortably himself without the unintended assistance of Ferguson.

After all his positive talk before the fight, Ferguson disappointed by producing a negative performance. He appeared interested only in survival (who could blame him?), and he rarely made a decisive move. The moment there was any danger of Tyson launching a sustained attack, Ferguson would grab him and hold on as tightly as a long-lost brother. Philadelphia is the City of Brotherly Love but this was ridiculous. The pro-Tyson crowd mocked Ferguson's unashamed attempts at self-preservation and referee Luis Rivera issued four warnings for holding. Tyson tore forward relentlessly and forced his two-inch taller opponent back towards the ropes but, every time he set himself for his heaviest punches, Ferguson would cover up and then seek the sanctuary of a clinch. A couple of times in the third round, Ferguson adventured out of his shell, and landed with a right uppercut and the left hook that had caused Cart Williams so much trouble. Tyson walked through the punches as if they were little more hurtful than flea bites.

This did little to help Ferguson's morale and he was clearly suffering a crisis of confidence as he came out for the fifth round. The New Yorker showed why his fans were calling him 'Kid Dynamite' late in the round when he brought a right uppercut thundering up through Ferguson's defence to land with a jarring impact that broke his nose. Ferguson went down and showed commendable courage in climbing back up at eight. Blood was seeping from his damaged nose and he covered up on the ropes as Tyson threw punches from all angles in a bid to finish the fight, but the bell came to Ferguson's rescue.

A left hook early in the sixth unhinged Ferguson and he grabbed hold of Tyson with both arms. Referee Rivera called out to Ferguson to stop holding but was ignored. The crowd were yelling insults, but Ferguson, no doubt wisely, kept his hold on Tyson as if he knew that to let go would be suicide. The referee finally ran out of patience, pulled the two fighters apart and held up Tyson's arm after one minute 19 seconds of the sixth round. It was thought at first that Rivera had disqualified Ferguson, but he explained: "I stopped the fight. Ferguson's eyes were glassy and he just didn't have any fight left in him."

Tyson was understandably frustrated by his night's hard work. "Fighters think the way to beat me is to jab, pot-shot and grab me," he said at the after-fight interview. "But I've got all the necessary patience. I know that I'll eventually catch up with them. Ferguson gave Carl Williams all sorts of trouble with his left hook. He caught me with it and it achieved nothing."

Asked about the uppercut that broke Ferguson's nose in the fifth round, he replied with his infamous comment about wanting to try to punch the nose up through the brain. It brought a lot of protests, particularly from the anti-boxing brigade. Jim Jacobs had a quiet word with Tyson, and advised him to pick his words more carefully in future. "Everything you say now, Mike, is going to be analysed," he warned him. "You've got to think before you speak."

Fight No 19
v
Steve Zouski
Uniondale, NY
10. 3. 86
Won RSF 3

TYSON had been scheduled to fight William Hosea two weeks earlier, but he had to pull out after a fall from his 12-foot-high pigeon coop. He banged his ear and it became infected. This interrupted his training and accounted for what was, by his skyscraping standards, a sluggish display against Steve Zouski in a ten-rounds contest that was screened live as the curtain raiser to the Marvin Hagler-John Mugabi world middleweight title fight.

Zouski was from Brockton, Massachusetts – hometown of the Brockton Blockbuster Rocky Marciano. There the similarity with The Rock ended. He had started boxing professionally in 1978 when Tyson was an 11-year-old schoolboy. His peak years were undoubtedly behind him, and there was nothing on his record to suggest he had the ammunition needed to end Tyson's unbeaten run. But, for two rounds, Typhoon Tyson looked little more than a breeze. His timing was right off and he missed with more punches than he landed against his 31-year-old opponent who was an inch taller but ten pounds lighter at 15 stone exactly (210 pounds).

Early in the third round, Tyson's trainer Kevin Rooney shouted from the corner: "This guy's going to take you the ten rounds unless you start throwing some punches." The message got through to Tyson and, with his first sustained attack of the fight, he was right on target with a barrage of punches to the body followed by his favourite left hook. Zouski collapsed face down to the canvas and was bravely in the process of pulling himself to his feet as referee Arthur Mercante's count reached ten. Tyson shaped to follow up, but the referee waved that it was all over with 11 seconds of the third round remaining. "This was the worst performance of my career," the truthful Tyson said later. "I just wasn't mentally prepared for it."

Fight No 20
v
James Tillis
Glens Falls, NY
3. 5. 86
Won Pts 10

THE ear infection that had caused problems before the Zouski fight returned, and Tyson's toughest test to date – against recently world-rated veteran James 'Quick' Tillis – was put back six weeks while he went into hospital for treatment. His right ear ballooned up to twice its normal size because of a damaged cartilage and Tyson had to sit through the longest period of inactivity in his career while doctors at Mount Sinai Hospital in New York City cured the infection. When he was at last allowed back into the gymnasium, Tyson took his frustration out on sparring partners. A right uppercut during a work-out with Charlie Smith loosened four of Smith's teeth. "It was a perfect punch," said trainer Kevin Rooney. "It's just tailor-made for Tillis."

Born in Chicago in 1957 and based in Tulsa, Oklahoma, Tillis had been rated the brightest heavyweight prospect for years but was found wanting in the top company. He was outpointed by Mike Weaver in a 1981 WBA world heavyweight championship contest after winning his first 20 fights. Tillis was a smart boxer with fast feet and fast fists, hence the nickname 'Quick' – but defeats by Pinklon Thomas, Greg Page, Tim Witherspoon, Carl Williams and, most recently, Tyrell Biggs had cost him his place in the world ratings. Tillis was unimpressed by Tyson's winning record. "His opponents have all been hand-picked," he said. "I've heard of baby-sitting, but this is ridiculous!" His manager, Beau Williford, joined in the war of words on Tyson. "So far he's met fighters who are sitting targets," he said. "How's he going to cope with a boxer who has the ability to use the ring? He's going to find it tough just hitting shadows."

When the talking stopped and the fighting began, Tillis provided action to go with his brave words. Tyson was made to prove that he had stamina to go with his strength as Tillis took him the distance for the first time in his career. There was never any danger of Tyson losing the fight, but for the first time since turning professional he found out how fickle the fans could be. There were jeers punctuating the cheers as he coasted through the last four rounds after building up an unassailable lead in the first half of the contest.

Tillis boxed mainly on the defensive, concentrating on making full use of the ring by circling backwards and occasionally snapping Tyson's head back with fast counter punches. Tyson, who had a seven pounds weight advantage at 15 stone 5 pounds (215 pounds), was always forcing the pace but without ever looking as if he might overwhelm Tillis. There was just one knockdown, moments before the bell in the fourth round. A left hook to the side of the jaw dropped Tillis, but he was up quickly to take a mandatory count of eight on his feet. He grinned in Tyson's direction as if to say, "a nice shot, but you've got to do better than that to keep me down".

There were brief crisis moments for Tillis in each of the first six rounds, but each time Tyson failed to build on his foundation work, and the feeling was that he was conserving energy and was worried about punching himself out. Tyson scored heavily to the body in the sixth round and at one point referee Joe Cortez inquired whether Tillis wanted to continue, but be had too much pride to quit.

Tillis was less defensive in the last third of the fight, scoring well with jabs and right counters as Tyson tucked up behind his gloves just looking for an opening to land a finishing blow. It was this inactivity that brought boos from some sections of the crowd, although the more discerning spectators were impressed by Tyson's tight defence and the way he was pacing himself. All three judges scored the fight for Tyson, two giving him six rounds to four for Tillis and the third judge giving him a rather charitable eight rounds to two victory. "I knew I had the fight won and was looking to take him out with one punch," Tyson said later. "Tillis ran just like we knew he would. Anybody can look good running. He tried to fight back in the late stages but I was hurting him and there was no way be was going to beat me." Co-manager Jim Jacobs was delighted with Tyson's performance. "That was just the experience he needs at this stage of his career," be said. "Tillis presented him with problems he had not encountered before and he showed he is learning all the time by finding a way round them."

Fight No 21
v
Mitch Green
New York City
20. 5. 86
Won Pts 10

MITCH 'Blood' Green was a former New York street gang leader, and boxing legend has it that he was the inspiration for the explosively violent film *The Warriors* that centred on gang warfare in New York City. He certainly put up a fight *before* getting into the ring with Tyson, arguing right up until the day of the contest about how he felt he was getting a raw deal. Even at the weigh-in he was threatening to pull out of the fight because he was earning only $30,000 to the $200,000 being paid to Tyson. He later withdrew his threat, but not before demanding release from his contract with manager Karl (son of Don) King.

Green, anything but a jolly green giant at 6 foot 5 inches and weighing a pound over 16 stone (219 pounds), had won four consecutive New York Golden Gloves titles as an amateur and considered himself king of the Big Apple. He saw Tyson as a pretender to his throne and vowed: "I'll knock him out. If he tries to whip on me all he's going to do is get tired, and then I'll give *him* a good whipping." For Tyson, this was the most significant fight of his career so far. The fact that it was to be staged at Madison Square Garden gave it a magical meaning for the 19-year-old New Yorker who had been brought up on stories of the old historic Garden where all the greats of the fight game had fought in contests that Tyson had watched time and again on film. It was also the first of three fights in which he was to be featured by Home Box Office, the giant pay-TV network who have such a big say in word boxing.

The contrast between Tyson and Green could not been greater as they made their entrance into the Madison Square Garden ring. Green wore a flashy robe that could have come out of Michael Jackson's wardrobe and, when he removed it, he revealed long, white fringed trunks that had his 'Blood' nickname as if written in blood down the left leg of his shorts. As he skipped about the ring testing the ropes, crimson tassels danced on his high, white boxing boots. All the sockless Tyson wore was a pair of black trunks, old-fashioned black ankle-high boxing boots and a mean-looking snarl. He really looked a throwback to the old warriors of the Jack Dempsey era who used to thrill the fans at the original Madison Square Garden. Tyson was a big betting favourite despite the fact that Green had lost only one of his 18 previous fights, and that was a points loss to new WBC world heavyweight champion Trevor Berbick.

Right from the first bell, Tyson dictated the pace and the pattern of the fight. He bobbed, ducked and weaved inside Green's long left leads and banged away to the body with two-fisted assaults that forced the dreadlocked giant to hold on. All the bold talk from Green about knocking Tyson out disappeared within the first moments of the fight and it was quickly clear that he had abandoned all attacking notions in a bid to survive. As soon as Tyson got any sort of rhythm going with his punches, Green would trap his left arm in a clinch and referee Luis Rivera was kept busy breaking them apart. He was continually calling out to Green not to hold and deducted a point from him in the fourth round for persistent holding.

The fight lacked continuity and sparkle because of Green's bear-hugging tactics, but you could not help but be impressed by Tyson, who was showing a ring generalship and composure that suggested he was now developing into a complete fighter and was no longer just a knockout specialist. There was still thudding power in Tyson's punches and three times, in the second, third and tenth rounds, he knocked out Green's gumshield. When it happened in the third round, his left jab landed with such stunning force that Green lost not only his gumshield but also a piece of dental bridgework that was fitted with two new teeth. Green started to bleed from the mouth following this bizarre incident and he was spitting blood for the rest of the contest. The 'Blood' emblazoned on his trunks was soon crimson with the real stuff.

Every time Green tried to get into the fight by moving behind his long jab, Tyson would almost leap past his punch to land much more effective blows of his own. It soon became obvious to Green that he dare not open up the fight because he knew beyond argument that Tyson carried the heavier ammunition, and he was being punished each time he tried to take the initiative. He had his best moments in the eighth round, when his young rival appeared to be taking a breather, and a couple of solid left and right combinations to the head briefly stopped the tank-like Tyson in his tracks. But 'Iron Mike' was back in command in the closing moments of the round when a volley of punches to the head forced Green to hold on. Tyson was beating 29-year-old Green as much by speed as power. At times his hands were almost a blur as he drove three and four punches through Green's defence to the couple of ponderous replies from the bigger man.

Tyson was so intent on mastering Green – who had been the talk of the New York streets when he was just an impressionable kid – that he several times got careless with his head and was warned about it in the eight and ninth rounds. He also threw punches after the bell at the end of a couple of rounds and, all in all, gave the impression that Mitch Green was not exactly his best buddy. Tyson was unable to knock the former king of the New York street gangs off his feet but he certainly knocked him off his pedestal as the Big Apple's main man. All three judges scored it for Tyson – George DeGabriel by eight rounds to two and Pat Dolan and George Colon by nine rounds to one.

"I wasn't looking to knock him out," Tyson said in the after-fight interview. "Going ten rounds is fun. I was having a good time in there. It was my best fight ever. I don't want to sound egotistical, but I found it real easy to win the fight. I could have knocked him out if he had not held on like he did. "

Green was in no mood to give Tyson any credit. "He's a strong fighter but I didn't feel most of his punches," he said. "I just couldn't get myself motivated for the fight. I can't keep going into the ring with all this animosity, this nonsense over money. Every time I fight I get just a handful of dollars. If they were to pay me fair I'd be happy to get into the ring and give full value."

In the early hours of the morning, two years later, they resumed hostilities in a street brawl in Harlem. Tyson closed Green's left eye with one thumping right. The price Tyson paid was a broken bone in his hand. Green, who was continually insisting that Don King had short-changed him out of his purse money, demanded a return as payment for assault charges being dropped. But he was never able to get himself back in the ratings to warrant another official fight with Tyson.

Fight No 22

v

Reggie Gross

New York City

13. 6. 86

Won RSF 1

THERE was a distinct drop down in class and quality for Tyson's twenty-second fight. His opponent, 25-year-old Reggie Gross, of Baltimore, was considered little more than a trial horse against whom Tyson could keep sharp while waiting for much bigger and more lucrative assignments. Gross, 6 foot 2 inches tall but just a pound heavier than Tyson at 15 stone 9 pounds (218 pounds), had lost four of his 22 fights since starting out as a light-heavyweight in 1982. The Tyson-Gross fight was, on the Madison Square Garden card, an appetiser for the main event in which Hector 'Macho' Camacho just managed to retain his world lightweight title against fellow Puerto Rican, Edwin Rosario. It was Tyson who looked the part of the 'Macho Man' as he tore to a devastating victory over an opponent who, frankly, did not belong in the same arena as him, let alone the same ring. It was all over in two minutes 36 seconds.

After being taken a total of 20 rounds in his previous two fights, Tyson was back to his crash-bang-wallop style. He came charging after Gross, who surprised him with a right uppercut that convinced him he needed to get things over with as quickly as possible. A sweeping left hook sent Gross tumbling backwards to the canvas. He pulled himself up on shaky legs at six and referee Johnny Lobianco completed the mandatory eight count. Two more left hooks had Gross spread-eagled on the bottom rope. He was as brave as they come and complained when the referee rightly stopped it as he got up at eight. "You wanna fight on?" snapped Lobianco. "Youse can't even walk right now, let alone fight." He then compassionately led him back to his corner. "I was relieved when the referee stopped it," said Tyson. "I could have really hurt him. A lot of nonsense has been talked about me losing my power. Now people know different."

Fight No 23
v
William Hosea
Troy, NY
28. 6. 86
Won KO 1

THEY were keeping Tyson on the boil ready for his July showdown with Marvin Frazier, and William Hosea was brought in from Chicago to give him some public punching practice. Hosea, loser of five of his 22 fights, was out of his depth and folded under the first sustained attack of the opening round. A left hook to the body, followed by a stunning hook to the head, sent Hosea sinking to the canvas. He pulled himself up into a kneeling position and seemed to be in control of himself. But he mis-timed his rise and was still in a crouching position as referee Harry Papacharalambous spread his arms to signal a knockout. It was jokingly reported that the ring announcer had taken longer pronouncing the referee's name that it did for Tyson to win.

Hosea became more fighting mad than he had been during the actual contest when the referee waved that it was all over. He protested that he had beaten the count and the crowd booed as it was confirmed that he had been knocked out. It was Tyson's fourteenth first round victory – and his least satisfactory. "He seemed game enough to continue even though I'd caught him with a jolting punch, but the referee thought otherwise," said Tyson, who weighed in at a beefy 15 stone 9 pounds (219 pounds). "That was no knockout," said Hosea. "I had both gloves off the canvas and I was ready to fight on. I came here to give Tyson a fight. If Tyson's going to knock me out, then let him go ahead and try to do it. But that was no knockout. I admit I should have started getting up at eight and that I left it late, but it was obvious that I could have boxed on. We were into the last minute of the round. I would have recovered."

But the argument was academic. In the record books it will always read: Mike Tyson beat William Hosea, wko1. What Tyson didn't reveal until after his next fight was that, during the brief exchanges with Hosea, he had damaged his left hand.

Fight No 24

v

Lorenzo Boyd

Swan Lake, NY

11. 7. 86

Won KO 2

LORENZO Boyd came out of the same Oklahoma stable as James 'Quick' Tillis and so he had inside information on how best to fight Tyson. It didn't help him one little bit! He had his nose broken in the first round before being flattened in the second by the murderous-punching young gladiator from Brownsville. Boyd was conceding more than a stone to the 15 stones 9 pounds (219 pounds) Tyson, who kept secret the fact that his left hand was still sore following his one-round victory over William Hosea. They fought in Swan Lake, but the action belonged more in the bullring than the ballet. "I had decided that I would do all my attacking to the body to save damaging my hand any further," said Tyson. "But I could see from the pained look in his eyes that I was really hurting him and so I went head hunting to get it over quickly."

Boyd, a winner of 16 of 21 fights since turning professional under the guidance of Beau Williford in 1983, threw few punches in the first round. He was too busy covering up and trying to block Tyson's all-out attack to the body. A rare punch to the head from Tyson during this opening blitz flattened Boyd's nose, and a spurt of blood showed that it was broken. It would have been wise for Boyd to retire at the end of this painful first round, but he bravely came out for more punishment. Tyson duly obliged, digging in heavily to the body before throwing a perfectly timed right uppercut to the chin. Boyd crashed backwards to the canvas and referee Sid Rubenstein went through the formality of counting to eight before calling the ringside doctor in to treat the stretched-out Kentucky fighter.

"I've never been as hit as hard as that in my life," Boyd said later. "I was trying to guard my chin but his body punches made me bring my hands down." When told this, Tyson said with the cold smile of a professional hit man: "That was the general idea."

Fight No 25
v
Marvis Frazier
Glens Falls, NY
26. 7. 86
Won KO 1

MARVIS Frazier was famous more because of what his father had achieved than anything he had done in the ring. He was the son of Smokin' Joe Frazier, one of the greatest of all the modern heavyweight champions, who had been locked in an unforgettable series of fights with the one and only Muhammad Ali. Marvis, a likeable, God-fearing Christian who was a proper gentleman away from ring business, was finding it hard to escape his father's shadow. He saw a victory over Mike Tyson as a way to bring the spotlight on to himself so that he could be known as plain Marvis Frazier, rather than "Son of . . . "

Smokin' Joe encouraged him all the way, as he had when rushing him into a premature fight for the world heavyweight championship against Larry Holmes in 1983 after Marvis had fought just ten times as a professional. Holmes pounded him to defeat in one round. Marvis had won all of his other 16 fights and was fresh from a ten-rounds points victory over one James 'Bonecrusher' Smith after surviving a fifth-round knockdown. He had certainly been fighting in better company than Tyson, and Smokin' Joe reasoned: "We've jumped at the chance of taking this fight with Tyson. It's a great opportunity for Marvis. I have no doubt whatsoever that he can take Tyson because of his greater experience."

Marvis could give, as evidence of his staying power, points victories over Joe Bugner and James Broad as well as his win against the big-hitting Bonecrusher. "I've had a good hard look at Tyson," said Marvis. "With the greatest respect, he has been beating opponents from the second division. He is a good fighter and a good puncher. You don't win 24 fights without having a lot going for you. But I have set my heart on confounding everybody by beating him. I am totally confident that I can win, and then I will take his place in the world championship queue. I've still got my dream of following my Dad as heavyweight champion of the world." Smokin' Joe was talking a brave fight on his son's behalf. "Tyson is still a big baby," he said, " and he's gonna see a real man facing him in the ring. He's got a big shock coming."

Kevin Rooney winced when he heard what 'Old Man' Frazier was saying. "We'll see just who the baby is on 26 July," said Tyson's tough-talking trainer. "I just hope that Marvis Frazier is going to fight the way his father says that he's going to fight. I hope he comes hunting for a baby. He is going to find out that he is fighting a man and, by the time he realizes it, the fight will be all over and victory will be ours."

During the final build-up to the fight that had captured public imagination, Tyson said: "I can't understand how Joe Frazier can think his son is more experienced than me. I have had seven more fights and there's no way you can dismiss the likes of James Tillis and Mitch Green as nobodies. I'm twice the fighter now that I've got a couple of ten-rounders under my belt. I know how to pace myself if necessary, and my 14 wins in the first round prove that I also know how to punch. I certainly bang harder than Larry Holmes ever did. Marvis had better believe it!"

Tyson was favoured by most of the experts to win, but nobody could have predicted that he would finish the fight in quite such explosive fashion. Even by his scorching standards it was a phenomenally quick execution. Three inches shorter than the 6 foot 2 inch Frazier, Tyson, at 15 stone 7 pounds, had a weight advantage of just under half a stone. He came roaring out of his corner at the first bell obviously intent on making every ounce count. Frazier seemed shell-shocked, before a punch had landed, at the speed with which Tyson got to him. He just managed to duck under a right that could have finished it in the opening five seconds and was then forced back on to the ropes by a tattoo of left jabs. Tyson then threw two pulverising rights, one to the head and another to the rib cage. A dazed Frazier knew he had to get off the ropes and started to manoeuvre to his left and then to his right. But, no matter where he went, there was a faceful of leather coming his way from The Typhoon. He was cornered and, as he tried to duck under the fusillade of punches, Tyson brought his head jerking up with a devastating right uppercut. Marvis appeared out on his feet and only the force of another right uppercut stopped him from sinking to the canvas. Tyson's punches were travelling almost too quickly for the eye to see. A right cross, left hook and then another right came flashing through what was Frazier's now virtually nonexistent defence. He sagged slowly to the canvas like a puppet that has had its strings cut away. Referee Joe Cortez started to take up the count but quickly decided he was wasting everybody's time and he signalled that it was all over. "It was futile to carry on counting," Cortez said. "Frazier was conscious, but as far as the fight went he was out of it."

The ringside doctor was at Frazier's side within seconds of the finish and he was back on his feet and being consoled by Tyson after a couple of minutes' recovery time. For Marvis, it was all too reminiscent of his one-round destruction by Larry Holmes in Las Vegas in 1983. Then, he had lasted two minutes 57 seconds. This time it was all over in just 30 seconds of legalised mayhem. Tyson had wrecked his dream of following his father as world heavyweight champion.

Tyson won a lot of friends by not gloating in victory. "I honestly felt that I could win in the first round," he said. "My fight plan was to attack to the body and then concentrate on uppercuts, because Marvis has a tendency to dip down when punches are coming at him. I was going to wait before throwing the uppercut but the chance came early and it was too good to miss. I knew from the moment I landed with the first uppercut that I had him. There was nowhere for him to escape to."

Frazier, a true sportsman and a good advertisement for boxing with his politeness and pleasant personality, shook Mike's hand at the after-fight press conference and said: "Mike, I think you must have got into the ring with a sledgehammer! It certainly felt that way." Smokin' Joe talked like the old pro that he is. "That's the way a heavyweight fight should end," he said. "From what I've seen, Mike Tyson can go all the way to the championship because he goes out and does the job."

Now everybody watched and waited as Jim Jacobs and Bill Cayton sat down and started sifting through the possibilities. They had the choice of keeping out of the unification tournament and going for a big payday against either Larry Holmes or Gerry Cooney; or they could go for the WBC championship held by Trevor Berbick. With their deep sense of fight history, there could be only one choice – the world championship. They wanted to see Mike Tyson crowned as the youngest world heavyweight champion of all time.

Fight No 26
v
Jose Ribalta
Atlantic City
17. 8. 86
Won RSF 10

MIKE Tyson was by now within punching distance of a world title fight, and it would have been understandable if he had been put under wraps. But he kept up his training-by-fighting routine, and Cuban giant José Ribalta was lined up for his next test. Based in Miami Beach, 23-year-old old Ribalta had been boxing professionally since 1982 and had won 23 of his 27 fights. He was beaten on points over ten rounds by Marvis Frazier in Atlantic City in September 1985, but he insisted he could master Tyson. "He doesn't scare me," said Ribalta, who, at 6 foot 6 inches tall, did not look as if anything or anybody could frighten him. Asked how he could have any hope against Tyson after the way he bombed out Marvis Frazier in just 30 seconds, Ribalta shrugged and said: "No two fights and no two fighters are the same. Frazier stood around like a statue and let Tyson get to him. I just don't plan to be there when he comes looking for me."

True to his word, Ribalta kept on the move as Tyson came hunting him in their scheduled ten-round fight at the Trump Casino Hotel. He looked booked for an early exit when a right to the body, followed by a ripping right uppercut, dropped him for eight in the second round. But he got up and fought back gamely before returning to his safety-first, hit-and-hop-it tactics, frustrating Tyson with solid jabs and tying him up the moment the New Yorker bulldozed his way into close quarters. Referee Rudy Battle was continually telling Ribalta not to hold and warned him several times for forcing Tyson's head down in clinches. It was not a pretty sight, but at least the Cuban had found an effective, if illegal, way of breaking Tyson's momentum.

There was a lack of the old snap and sparkle in Tyson's work, and at times he was made to look almost pedestrian as he plodded after Ribalta throwing single punches rather than his usual dynamite combinations.

Just as Tyson and his supporters were beginning to get frustrated to the point almost of boredom, he produced a flash of his explosive power in the eighth round. A clubbing right sent Ribalta's gumshield spinning out of his mouth and over the top rope, and then a big left hook knocked him backwards into the ropes. Referee Battle interrupted Tyson's forward march and gave the Cuban a mandatory eight count. Ribalta looked ripe for the taking, but Tyson got himself tied up in a clinch and was unable to deliver his planned finishing punches. In round nine there were boos and jeers coming from some sections of the crowd who had clearly come hoping to see the usual fistic fireworks from Tyson. He tried hard to oblige them and produced a cracker of a left hook that made Ribalta buckle at the knees. It looked certain that the big man would topple, but he managed to clutch Tyson as he came forward trying to land the knockout blow from close range. They got tangled up, with Ribalta hanging on with a mixture of determination and desperation. By the time the referee had managed to part them, the Cuban's head had cleared and he was able to ride out the crisis.

Ribalta, with many of the neutrals in the audience now on his side, survived to the last round and, just as it seemed as if he was going to go the distance, Tyson put his foot hard down on the accelerator. A bombardment of punches to the body and hooks to the head had the Cuban flying distress signals in the opening minute of the tenth round. He fought back bravely and managed to sting Tyson with a left-right counter, but by opening up he left his chin exposed and a thundering left hook dropped him backwards to the canvas.

The referee seemed ready to stop it as Ribalta climbed back up before the mandatory count was completed, but the Cuban showed he was a man of courage and pride by demanding that he be allowed to continue. Tyson took the matter out of the referee's hands by forcing Ribalta back on the ropes and unleashing a torrent of punches that left Mr Battle with no alternative but to stop it with just 93 seconds to go to the final bell.

Tyson did not have to be told he had given a less than distinguished performance. "I had a bad night," he said. "But you have to learn that you can't knock everybody out. At least I showed I have stamina and that I can produce the big shots late in a fight. Ribalta was very brave and durable, but at times it was like fighting an octopus."

Fight No 27
v
Alonzo Ratliff
Las Vegas
6. 9. 86
Won RSF 2

THERE was enormous pressure on Tyson's wide, young shoulders as he climbed into the Las Vegas Hilton ring to fight former world cruiserweight champion Alfonzo Ratliff. He knew that a world title fight against Trevor Berbick had been virtually signed and sealed. But a defeat by Ratliff would have blown his ambitious title plans to pieces.

On his last trip to Vegas as an amateur two years earlier, he had wept with frustration and anger the night he was adjudged to have been outpointed by Henry Tillman, in a contest to decide who represented the United States in the 1984 Los Angeles Olympics. He was so outraged that he was spotted punching a tree with his hands and screaming into the night air in downtown Vegas long after the decision had gone against him. It's a scene often witnessed in Vegas, but it is losing gamblers who are doing the punching and screaming! Tyson was positive he had won the contest and was inconsolable after the judges' verdict had been announced. Tillman went on to win the Olympic gold medal that Tyson had been convinced would one day be his. Tyson went into the professional ranks, vowing to win the world heavyweight championship as consolation.

Now only Ratliff stood between him and his dream of trying to become the youngest world heavyweight titleholder in ring history. British fight fans had seen Ratliff in action just seven weeks earlier on the undercard of the Tim Witherspoon-Frank Bruno world title fight at Wembley. Standing a lanky 6 foot 5 inches and weighing 14 stone 7 pounds (203 pounds), he had been matched with fellow Chicagoan Stanley Ross in what developed into a monotonous bore of a contest. Ross fought a completely negative fight and hardly threw a heavy punch in anger. Ratliff won every round against an opponent who seemed content to play a walk-on part before retiring at the end of five rounds with what was announced as "a damaged arm". There was nothing in Ratliff's performance to suggest he had the armoury to worry Tyson, but he was confident he could end the New Yorker's winning run and detonate his world title plans. "Nobody's boxed him the way I will," he said at the Witherspoon training camp in Basildon, Essex. "I will move from side to side, not straight back like so many of his opponents have done. That's asking for trouble." But Tyson didn't give Ratliff a chance to show the boxing skill and style that had carried him to the world cruiserweight crown in 1985. In the first round Ratliff moved swiftly on the retreat, trying to make full use of his enormous 14-inch reach advantage. Tyson, weighing in at his heaviest at just three pounds inside 16 stone (224 pounds), stalked him with vicious intent in his eyes. He even gave a cold smile at the way Ratliff was moving away as if in fear of his life. "As Joe Louis used to say, 'He could run but he couldn't hide'," Tyson said later. Referee Davey Pearl was not amused and indicated to Ratliff that he should try to make a fight of it. As if in reply, Ratliff threw a wild right that Tyson ducked with ease, and the sneering look he gave simply encouraged his opponent to run away at an ever faster rate of knots.

The running stopped abruptly in the second round. Tyson connected with a vicious short left to the head and Ratliff bounced into the ropes as he went down. He was up at nine and stumbled and scrambled to the far side of the ring with Tyson in deadly pursuit. A flurry of punches pushed Ratliff to the edge of defeat and Tyson finally put him out of his misery with his favourite left to the ribs, left hook to the head combination. Ratliff went down on his knees as if bowing to his conqueror while referee Pearl signalled that it was all over without bothering to take up the count.

The fight was a supporting contest to the IBF world heavyweight championship contest in which Michael Spinks crushed Norwegian challenger Steffan Tangstad in four rounds. Most spectators at the ringside in Las Vegas must surely have been of the opinion that Tyson would have given Spinks a slightly harder time!

"Now bring on Berbick," said Tyson with a chilling confidence. "I'm good and ready for him." Who was arguing? Certainly not Ratliff. "He's unstoppable," was his verdict.

Fight No 28

v

Trevor Berbick

Las Vegas

22. 11. 86

Won RSF 2

JUDGEMENT Day had arrived for 'Iron Mike' Tyson. At 20 years, four months and 22 days of age he was being given the chance to make his dream come true of becoming the youngest world heavyweight champion of all time. Standing between him and ring history was Trevor Berbick, the Punching Preacher from Canada, via his homeland of Jamaica.

A professional since representing Jamaica in the 1976 Montreal Olympics, Berbick had won 31 of his 36 fights with 23 inside the distance victories. All the evidence was that he had a strong chin, although he had been caught cold in the first round by Colombian Bernardo Mercado in his twelfth fight and had been counted out for the only time in his career. He went the full 15 rounds with Larry Holmes before losing on points in a 1981 WBC title challenge. Leroy Caldwell had held him to a draw and his two other defeats were a ten rounds points loss to Renaldo Snipes in 1982 followed by a bizarre points setback against WBC cruiserweight champion S.T. Gordon in a desperately untidy maul after which Berbick claimed that he had been drugged.

Among the high points of his career were a points victory over a pathetically unrecognisable Muhammad Ali in 1981 (it was Ali's last stand before hanging up his gloves at least two years too late), a ninth round knockout of John Tate and a points victory against the highly touted Greg Page. His finest performance came in Las Vegas on 22 March 1986, when, against all the odds, he outpointed Pinklon Thomas to win the WBC world heavyweight title.

Berbick's preparation for his defence against Tyson was not exactly perfect. His concentration was continually ambushed by outside-the-ring pressures. At one stage he was threatening to pull out for a more lucrative date with Gerry Cooney, but this was sorted out after some bitter background bickering and bargaining with promoter Don King. Then, on the Tuesday before the contest, he was in court contesting a suit brought by a Texan promoter claiming a breach of a fight contract. The next day, he had sudden breathing problems and visited four doctors before he could get respiratory medication that met with the approval of the Nevada State Athletic Commission. He must have been in danger of a loss of breath again on the Thursday when a district court judge ruled that $495,000 should be held from his $2.1 million purse pending the outcome of his dispute with the Texan promoter.

On top of all this, Berbick had fallen out with his veteran trainer – the great strategist Eddie Futch – over how much Futch should be paid for his wise corner counselling. He found the best-possible substitute in former Muhammad Ali mentor Angelo Dundee, but Angelo was given less than a month in which to get his fight plan together. Futch, at 75 the most experienced cornerman in the business who had guided the likes of Joe Frazier and Larry Holmes, shrugged off Berbick's dismissal of his services and still gave his expert reading of how the fight could go. "Trevor has the nerve, the equipment and the ability to win," he said: "but it all depends on which Trevor Berbick gets into the ring. He is never the same fighter two contests in a row. You just never know how he will be. The important thing for him to remember is to stay off the ropes and out of the corners. He must dictate the fight from the middle of the ring, and keep backing Tyson up and not let him get to work at close quarters. I am deeply impressed by Tyson. He has got incredibly quick hands and can take your head off with his punches. But so far many of his opponents have been beaten before the first bell because they have felt so intimidated by him. They have just frozen and waited to be slaughtered. If the right Trevor Berbick gets into the ring, he won't be intimidated. We'll just have to wait to see what mood Trevor is in."

Angelo Dundee, a master of ring kidology who knows more strokes than the Oxford and Cambridge crews put together, quickly got to work with giving Berbick a confidence booster. "A lot of nonsense is being talked about Trevor being inconsistent and unpredictable," he said. "It's more than three years since he lost a fight, so that myth can be buried. Tyson is going to find Berbick a much tougher opposition than all those what I call 'strictly opponent' types that he has been knocking over. He won't be playing into Tyson's hands by running. He will be sliding this way and that, going from side to side and taking Tyson's momentum away. Then he will be looking to move back in and score with his excellent counter punches. Trevor is looking forward to having Tyson coming at him. He won't have to go looking for him. He will be a perfect target and I think he will stop Tyson late in the fight."

Meantime, Tyson was being hidden away from all the hype and hustling that always surround world heavyweight title fights. For the five weeks before the fight he lived in a private home in the wealthy suburb of Spanish Oaks, a mile west – and a world away – from the Las Vegas Strip. He made daily trips to Johnny Tocco's gym where only a handful of onlookers watched his work-outs. Trainer Kevin Rooney said: "We had planned to do most of our training at home in New York, but there was too much hassle there. We had to get away from all the distractions, and so we came here because we knew that Johnny Tocco would lock the door so that Mike could work in peace."

At the weigh-in, Tyson – three inches shorter than the 6 foot 2 inch Berbick – scaled a quarter of a pound over his heaviest-ever 15 stone 11 pounds (221 pounds). Berbick was three pounds lighter. "I've got a shock coming Tyson's way before I even throw a punch," he confided at the weigh-in. Angelo Dundee craftily went for a psychological advantage by demanding that the champion wear black, Tyson's favourite colour. It meant the challenger would have to wear white.

Berbick's "shock" for Tyson was revealed when he climbed into the ring. He was dressed in black from head to toe, including a floor-dusting full-length hooded robe and knee-high black socks that he had bought just hours before the fight. But Tyson didn't look the slightest bit perturbed because he, too, had a dress surprise. He had decided to risk a 'peanuts' fine and came into the ring wearing his customary all-black gear. It made for a funereal atmosphere . . . and it wasn't long before we discovered who was going to be buried.

Any fears Tyson's supporters might have had that the young challenger could be overawed by the occasion were quickly dismissed. He was the Great Dictator from the opening seconds, startling Berbick with a jarring left hook and then instantly following up with a cluster of heavy jabs and hooks from both hands. We all expected Berbick to box and move, but he stood his ground and tried to fight off the man he considered a pretender to his throne. Two big rights came winging over the top of Berbick's defence and he was forced to hold on. Referee Mills Lane ordered them to break, but they were soon back into a clinch after Tyson had piled in a procession of jabs and uppercuts. Midway through the round, a dynamite right jerked Berbick's head to one side, and then, in the closing seconds, a right had him wobbling and only the bell saved him from a visit to the canvas. He made a face at Tyson as the bell went as if to suggest he had not been hurt, but he was not kidding anybody. The first round had been so one-sided that it was difficult to believe that Tyson was the young untried and untested challenger. He was fighting like a man possessed and with the authority of a seasoned professional. "Now listen, Mike," said trainer Kevin Rooney as Tyson sat attentively in his corner. "You're doing too much head hunting. Get to his body first, then go for the head. Body. Head. Got it?" Tyson nodded grimly. It was Berbick who was going to get it.

Tyson head-hunted straight away with the first serious punch of the second round, a stunning right that turned Berbick flat-footed. Then another murderous right to the head sent Berbick reeling backwards as if a carpet had suddenly been pulled from beneath him. The champion should now have been running and hiding – slipping from side to side as Angelo Dundee had planned. But some macho impulse made him decide to try to stand and fight. It was suicide. Tyson beat a tattoo to his body and then threw a short right to the head that was so powerful that it turned Berbick around like a spinning top as he dropped to the floor. The champion, his senses scattered, scrambled up far too quickly with only three seconds of the mandatory count gone. He got in close to the challenger and covered up as he attempted to regain his composure. Tyson, remarkably cool, relaxed as he lay on inside conserving energy. Then he suddenly exploded into final action. A right to the kidneys made Berbick wince and a following right uppercut missed its intended target by a whisker. They were back together in mid ring like dancers in a disco and, as they bent towards each other, Tyson released a left hook to the temple that was absolutely perfect in its timing and delivery. There was a delayed effect as Berbick absorbed the punch. It appeared to have done no serious damage, but ever so slowly the champion dropped back like a parachutist leaving an aircraft. He landed with a thump and it was immediately obvious that it was all over bar the celebrations and commiserations, and the hundreds of action replays of Berbick's final seconds as champion. His instincts told him to get up, but his legs refused to obey his brain and he was stumbling round the ring like a newborn foal. Referee Lane caught hold of him as he staggered up at nine after a Chaplinesque circuit of the ring. "No more tonight," said Lane as he led the thoroughly confused champion back to the safe harbour of his corner. Mike Tyson was the youngest world heavyweight champion in boxing history.

He had beaten Floyd Patterson's record (set back in 1956 when he won the title vacated by Rocky Marciano) by a remarkable year and seven months, and for those people who pointed out that Patterson had been the undisputed champion there was still plenty of time for Tyson to put an end to all arguments. Patterson and Tyson had a common denominator in their rush to title-winning glory. Both were discovered and moulded by Cus D'Amato. "I dedicate this victory to the memory of Cus D'Amato," Tyson said after surprisingly low-key celebrations in his corner. It was almost an anticlimax, because they had been so sure that this young man of destiny would win. "This was as much Cus's dream as mine," said the new champion. "I was throwing hydrogen bombs out there. Every punch was delivered with murderous intentions and precision." He then added, not with arrogance but with chilling belief: "I am the youngest champion, and I shall be the oldest."

Trevor Berbick was in no mood to dispute that statement. "I made a silly mistake," he said. "I tried to prove my manhood. He hits so hard that anybody who stands with him like I did is going to be taken out. I still can't believe that I've lost. I was so sure that I could beat him, but I guess I fought the wrong fight." (Chillingly, within six years of losing his title Berbick was behind bars on a rape charge.)

Now all the talk was suddenly about the next target for Tyson – a showdown with the winner of the scheduled Tim Witherspoon-Tony Tubbs WBA heavyweight decider that was lined up for 12 December in Madison Square Garden. "I don't care which of them wins it," said the new WBC king. "If I am going to be great, then I am going to have to fight everybody." On this historic night for boxing, Tyson would not have believed it had he been told that "everybody" included a fighter by the name of Bonecrusher Smith.

Fight No 29
v
James Smith
Las Vegas
7. 3. 87
Won Pts 12

JAMES 'Bonecrusher' Smith came to his world championship showdown with Mike Tyson by way of the United States Army and the sort of hand of fate that was dealt to boxing's 'Cinderella Man' James J. Braddock back in the 1930s. Smith was training for a fairly meaningless match with Mitch 'Blood' Green when he got an SOS (Save Our Show) call from promoter Don King to substitute for Tony Tubbs, who had withdrawn from a WBA title fight with Tim Witherspoon because of an alleged shoulder injury. Witherspoon and King fell out over this late change and, after angry threats and verbal punch-ups, the fight only went ahead after the WBA had threatened to declare the title vacant.

At a pantomime of a press conference to announce that the Witherspoon-Smith fight was definitely on, an aggrieved – to put it mildly – Mitch Green stormed in and started screaming at Don King. "You done messed up my life for the last time," shouted the New York giant as he menacingly made in the direction of the equally huge promoter. "Six years you done took my money," Green accused, as reporters from all over the world looked on in open-mouthed wonder. This, they realised, was not the usual pre-fight hype. This was for real. "I'm gonna break your neck," snarled Green as a team of King's hefty helpers formed a protective shield round their boss. Amazingly, Green was finally brought under control and led out of the conference room by a girlfriend who was a good foot shorter and half his weight.

"This is getting to be a tough business," said King. They were sentiments sadly shared by Tim Witherspoon on fight night at Madison Square Garden on 12 December. He climbed almost reluctantly into the ring for his title defence against Smith and clearly had his mind a million miles away from the job in hand. Smith quickly recognised that Witherspoon was not his usual confident, belligerent self and seized the chance to snatch the championship in sensational style. Soundly outpointed by Witherspoon just 18 months earlier, Smith did not give the champion a single moment to compose himself. He roared after him from the first bell and a bemused and confused Witherspoon – who had never been off his feet in his career – was punched, or rather, clubbed to the canvas three times to force an automatic stoppage after just two minutes 12 seconds. Bonecrusher Smith was, incredibly, the new WBA champion and the first substitute ever to win the title.

"Witherspoon hurt me the first time we met and now I've paid him back," said 31-year-old Smith as the boxing world tried to get used to the fact that the WBA had a heavyweight champion who had lost five of his previous 23 fights. "Three of those defeats came in the 'down' period in my career after my world title fight with Larry Holmes," he said. "I had the wrong attitude and was thinking about giving up the game. But now my attitude is right and I am confident I can beat anybody. Yes, anybody."

During the one-round annihilation, Smith landed with a computer-counted 28 of 59 punches thrown. It was a torrent of punches that turned 'Terrible' Tim into 'Timid' Tim and he was on target with only seven of 11 punches as Smith ripped away from him not only his title but also a $1million purse for a unification battle with Tyson, who was among the ringside spectators.

"No doubt about it, Smith is a devastating puncher," Tyson said. "I can't wait to match my skills against him. He claims I've been fed a lot of soft touches. We'll see about that, won't we?"

Smith had no doubts that he could dish out the same quick-finish treatment to Tyson. "He has not met anybody who can hit like me," said the new champion. "It's going to be an early night for one of us and I think it's young Tyson who will be going to sleep!"

College graduate Smith was anything but a stereotyped heavyweight champion. He had never laced on a glove in his life until he was twenty-three. He concentrated on basketball while at high school and college in his hometown of Magnolia, North Carolina. He graduated from college with a degree in business management and then joined the US Army. It was while soldiering as a sergeant in West Germany that Smith started boxing for his company and he picked up his 'Bonecrusher' nickname after reeling off 25 knockout victories in 35 amateur contests. "I busted a few noses and broke a few ribs and the name 'Bonecrusher' just sort of stuck," recalled the immensely likeable, humorous and intelligent Smith, whose presence on the boxing scene brought a touch of class to a much-maligned sport.

After leaving the army, Smith became a guard at Raleigh maximum security jail and he started boxing professionally in 1982 to help feed his young family. He was not 100 per cent fit for his professional debut and was stopped in four rounds after coming in as late substitute against hot prospect James Broad. Smith was encouraged by his performance because he had given Broad a lot of trouble until – as he put it – "I ran out of steam because I had not trained properly." He wondered what he could achieve if he got himself into good shape. The answer was 13 successive victories, and the last nine inside the distance. His fifteenth professional fight was back in Europe where he had first started boxing, and waiting to face him in a ten-round international contest at Wembley was Britain's unbeaten heavyweight hope Frank Bruno. Smith was trailing on points going into the last round and looked booked for defeat, but then he knocked Bruno back on to the ropes with a left hook and bombarded him with a two-fisted barrage until big Frank toppled over on to his side to take the full ten-second count for the only time in his career.

The victory set Smith up as an international star and, six months later, he got a crack at world heavyweight champion Larry Holmes and gave him all the trouble he could handle before being stopped in 12 rounds. It looked as if Smith had 'peaked' and defeats by Tony Tubbs, Witherspoon and Marvis Frazier pushed him down the world ratings and apparently out of championship contention until he answered the SOS to tackle Witherspoon for the title. His stunning victory was his nineteenth win in 24 fights, with 13 of his victories coming inside the distance including a first round knockout over former world champion Mike Weaver.

Smith had enormous advantages in height, reach and weight against Tyson. He stood 6 foot 4 inches and, at 16 stone 9 pounds (224 pounds), he weighed a stone more than the New Yorker. But the ringside bookmakers were unimpressed and showed that they thought Tyson more than measured up to the task of becoming undisputed champion by making him an 8-1 favourite. There were few takers at these odds even in the gamblers' paradise of Las Vegas and most of the betting money changed hands on the naming of the round in which punters thought Tyson would win. Few dollars were laid on the fight going the distance.

Like so many before him, Bonecrusher Smith was unable to provide action to go with his warrior-like words. He had predicted somebody would be going to sleep early . . . and that it would be Tyson. What nobody realised is that it would have been the spectators. Due almost entirely to his spoiling tactics, a contest billed as 'The Superfight' became more of a 'stupor' fight. There was a definite (and understandable) fear factor in Smith's attitude and it seemed that he failed to take his own advice: "Don't be intimidated by Tyson's reputation." From the first bell, there was a climate of extreme caution cloaking and choking just about every move that Smith made. Tyson was never allowed to fight in anything but short spasms. The moment he threatened to get into something approaching a rhythm, Smith grabbed him and held on with limpet-like survival instincts. They were tactics that angered and aggravated Tyson to the point where he sometimes had less than total control of his temper and several times he risked disqualification by throwing punches after the bell. The stuttering action was often nasty and bad-tempered and rarely a good advertisement for world heavyweight championship boxing. The pattern and pace of the fight became predictable and monotonous. Tyson kept pressing forward, bobbing and weaving his way inside Smith's long reach and then, as he wound up to deliver his settle-it-all punches, he would find himself locked in a bear hug. Referee Mills Lane was often the busiest man in the ring, continually tugging the two fighters apart and giving Smith a string of verbal warnings for holding.

Smith was handicapped by a cut over his left eye from the second round, and so much grease was being slapped on it between rounds it looked as if he had a spoonful of lard on his eyebrow. When Mills Lane tried to wipe some of the grease off with his hand, Smith surely became the first heavyweight champion in history to protest: "Hey, ref, you're scratching my face!" That was nothing to what Tyson was trying to do to it but, every time he got through with telling punches, Smith would put him on hold. The referee twice gave Smith public cautions for holding and ordered the judges to deduct a point each time. At the midway point in a frustrating contest that never lived up to pre-fight hope or hype, Smith started to adopt strange walkabout tactics. He dropped his arms and walked round the ring mocking and taunting Tyson, who was clearly confused but just kept on Smith's trail with his hands held high determined not to offer Bonecrusher the chance to land a sneaky counter punch.

There were partly justifiable criticisms that Smith had exposed Tyson's limitations, because he rarely looked like stunning, let alone stopping, the man from Magnolia, but it takes two to tango and Bonecrusher rarely attempted to make it a two-man fight. The way Smith kept holding Tyson in the clinches, it was as if he was more interested in an old-fashioned waltz than a tango.

One question the fight answered is that Tyson certainly had no stamina problems. He entered unknown territory once the fight was past the tenth round but his pace and power were in no way diminished. He even managed to let a flash of humour slip through his iron mask in the twelfth and final round, when he suddenly stopped chasing after Smith and just stood and poked his tongue out at him like a kid in the playground. It was certainly one of the more unusual world heavyweight title fights. For reasons known only to himself, Smith suddenly cut loose with his one big attack of the fight in the last ten seconds and got through Tyson's defence with a fusillade of lefts and rights that drove the Iron Man back on to the ropes. He was not looking in any trouble but the question on everybody's mind was, "Why on earth didn't Smith open up earlier in the fight?"

There were jeers for Smith and cheers for Tyson at the final bell of a contest that quickly fell off the memory shelf. All three judges voted overwhelmingly for Tyson: 120-106, 119-107 and 119-107. It was one of the most convincing points victories in world championship history, but Tyson knew that a lot of people were disappointed with his performance. "This is show business and people expect a performance," he said. "But it was difficult to do what I wanted to do because Smith fought only to survive. He was not there to win."

Kevin Rooney was more to the point about Smith's performance. "Bonecrusher just came to stink the joint out," he said. Smith shrugged at the criticism of his tactics. "I kept grabbing him to try to break his concentration," he said. "Sure I fought to survive. Wouldn't you?"

Fight No 30
v
Pinklon Thomas
Las Vegas
30. 5. 87
Won RSF 6

THE memory of the monotonous maul against Bonecrusher Smith was wiped away with a devastating volley of punches as Mike Tyson tore gifted boxer Pinklon Thomas apart in six rounds at the Las Vegas Hilton. All the critics who said that the young champion had lost his power were made to eat their words . . . as Thomas was made to eat his punches. Tyson showed that any fighter who is prepared to open up against him – unlike Smith – is asking for trouble. Thomas must have been wondering if perhaps Bonecrusher had come up with the right tactics because at least he survived for twelve rounds without ever being in really serious trouble. But Thomas did not try to smother or hold, and paid the price when Tyson hit him so hard that he must have felt the roof had caved in on him.

Thomas had talked a good fight before his challenge for Tyson's World Boxing Council and World Boxing Association heavyweight titles. He gave assurances that he had no intention of 'doing a Bonecrusher' and running or holding for 12 rounds because, he claimed, he was not in any way intimidated by Tyson or his reputation. "I'm a grown man," he said, "and I have seen tougher streets and harder times than Tyson. If he wants to keep his title he'll have to fight his brains out. I give him this warning – if he tries his usual dirty tactics he will find that I can give better than I get. If he hits after the bell, then I'll do likewise. If he hits low, I'll hit low. If he uses the elbow and the head, I'll use the elbow and the head. I am in the best shape of my life, and Mike is going to know he's been in one helluva fight. I'm as confident as a man can be that I will win. I've been to hell and back, and I've known far more terrifying things than Mike Tyson. I ain't the slightest bit scared of him."

The "hell" that Thomas was referring to was his battle against heroin addiction. He had become hooked at the age of 12 in the tough backstreets of his hometown of Pontiac, Michigan, and he beat the habit by taking the cold turkey method of complete withdrawal.

A converted southpaw, he had taken the WBC title with a points victory over Tim Witherspoon in 1985 and had then knocked out Mike Weaver with a blockbuster of a right hand. He was talked of as the most accomplished heavyweight since Ali, but then inexplicably lost his title on a points decision against Trevor Berbick. It was his only defeat in 31 fights before facing 'Iron Mike'.

The challenger, acknowledged as one of the most skilful heavyweights in the world, showed he was not just a talker by making a strong recovery after taking a shellacking in the first round. For a while it seemed that he just might have the plan and the ability to take Tyson's titles. His wise old trainer Angelo Dundee had told him to work inside and then move away at speed behind one of the finest left jabs in the game. Thomas followed his instructions to the letter, and kept the bulldozing champion on the end of an educated left jab. Each of the three judges had Tyson ahead on points, but there were several astute ringside observers who considered Thomas at least level as he moved confidently into the sixth round after a delay to have a torn glove replaced. There had been no hint that he was about to walk into a storm.

It was a thunderous right uppercut that started the Thomas downfall. This was instantly followed by a left hook that sent the challenger staggering sideways. His arms were suddenly waving around in the air as if being pulled by invisible strings. Tyson then went after him with mounting ferocity. He crashed home an incredible volley of 16 punches without reply, and Thomas – who had never before been off his feet – fell backwards with blood spurting from cuts on his nose, mouth and cheekbone. Somehow he started to drag himself off the canvas but, before he could get off his haunches, Angelo Dundee had leapt into the ring and urged referee Carlos Padilla to stop the fight.

"When the kid got Pinklon in his sights, he was awesome," Dundee, said. "The kid just triggered and blew my man away."

"I was happy with the way I finished it," said Tyson, "but I was pretty disappointed with my performance up until then."

Thomas, who went to hospital for a check up, revealed that the force of one of the punches had dislocated his shoulder.

Fight No 31
v
Tony Tucker
Las Vegas
1. 8. 87
Won Pts 12

WITH typical understatement, promoter Don King billed the Las Vegas showdown between Mike Tyson and Tony Tucker as "Glory hallelujah". It was the fight that would unify the world heavyweight championship, and King trumpeted: "Not since the days of Muhammad Ali has there been just one king on the throne, one champion for the world to respect and admire as the greatest heavyweight on God's earth. Now we have cleaned up the mess of all those champions, just like I promised we would, and after this fight we will have just one man to whom we shall bow the knee. Glory hallelujah!"

King was conveniently forgetting to mention that undefeated Michael Spinks had remained aloof from the eliminating process to find one champion. Many considered that he was the best man around to challenge Tyson following his destruction of Gerry Cooney.

Against Tucker, Tyson defended his World Boxing Council and World Boxing Association titles, while Tucker put his International Boxing Federation version of the championship on the line. Few people considered Tucker powerful enough to stop Tyson's mopping-up operation. He had won the IBF crown on the Tyson-Thomas undercard when he stopped Buster Douglas in ten rounds, but he had not won public acclaim for his performance against an opponent who was giving as good as he got until suddenly running out of steam.

Tucker had been a highly rated amateur who won a World Cup gold medal at light heavyweight. He was also a Pan-American, national Golden Gloves and USA amateur champion, and he won all but six of 96 contests before turning professional as part of a stable of fighters labelled 'Tomorrow's Champions' and promoted by Bob Arum. It was an arrangement that ended in bitter dispute with Tucker's father, Bob –

a former fighter and his co-manager – protesting that his son had not been paid according to contract. Tucker appeared to be doing more fighting (of the legal variety) outside than inside the ring. He parted company with his original manager, Lou Duva, and was involved in courtroom arguments with another former manager, Dennis Rappaport, on the eve of his 'date with destiny' with Tyson.

The 28-year-old IBF champion had found the time away from the legal fisticuffs to put together an impressive record of 34 unbeaten contests, including ten first-round victories. There was also a 'no contest' on his record after he had twisted his knee during a fight with Danny Sutton. He won the rearranged fight. Born in Grand Rapids Michigan but based in Houston, Tucker had long spells in Emanuel Steward's famous Detroit Kronk gym where his all-round skills were sharpened. At 6 foot 5 inches and close to 16 stone, he was an imposing figure but he was lacking in crowd-pulling charisma and really explosive power.

The difference in the attitudes of Tyson and Tucker was glaringly obvious in their final press conference at the Las Vegas Hilton. Tucker said he was glad the referee stopped his bout with Buster Douglas because he did not want to hurt anyone; Tyson said he had hoped Pinklon Thomas would get up so that he could have knocked him down again. Tucker had to force himself to be ruthless in the ring. With Tyson, it came naturally. He freely acknowledged that he was in the business of hurting people.

After all the ballyhoo and drum-beating from Don King, the fight did not live up to expectations. There was the promise of a sensational start when Tucker staggered Tyson with a left uppercut in the opening seconds but, from then on, Iron Mike was firmly in control without really getting into his most brutal mood.

Tyson forced the pace for most of the 12 mainly uneventful rounds, while the taller, more mobile Tucker concentrated on counter punches that – opening seconds apart – did little to concern his bobbing and weaving opponent.

The previously unbeaten Tucker showed he had a strong jaw when Tyson found the target with some hefty left hooks and right handers. Each time he shook his head in an attempt to show he had not been hurt, but the spray flying from Tucker's long, matted hair as his head turned under the impact of the blows proved that he was acting.

Tyson concentrated much of his attack to the body in a bid to bring the mountainous Tucker down to his size, but he failed to put his combinations together with their usual zip and ferocity.

The judges were unanimous in their verdict that Tyson had won comfortably on points, although Tucker felt that he had done enough to steal victory. If he had been more adventurous, he might have closed the points gap, but he was too often in a defensive mode and unable to take full advantage of his ten-inch reach advantage. Even in the first round, when he shook Tyson to his boots, he failed to open up with all guns blazing, and the three judges awarded the round to Iron Mike.

Tyson said after the fight that Tucker had given him the hardest fight of his career. "I was in real pain at the end of that first round," he revealed. "It was nothing to do with Tony's punching, although he did shake me up pretty bad in the first minute. The pain was caused when he trod on my toe. It broke a toenail, and my right foot was throbbing throughout the fight."

He revealed that he knew he had the fight won at the halfway stage. "Round about the sixth or seventh round he stopped fighting," Tyson said. "He started moving and running. He knew he couldn't win and he decided to survive. He wanted to go the distance. He was taking chances at the beginning but he stopped. But I would say he is the best fighter I've fought. He gave me my toughest fight. He took some good shots and came back very well. There was one time he got cocky and gave me the Ali shuffle. That made me more determined to win the fight."

Tucker explained that he would have performed better if he had not damaged a hand early in the fight. "The world knows Tony Tucker's here and I'm for real," he said. "I thought I did enough with my jabbing to have won the fight. But I'm not complaining. I took Tyson's best shots and proved that I could hurt him. Next time I shall leave no doubt about who is the best."

There was now only one official champion, Michael Gerard Tyson. But it was generally accepted that the real unification fight would be Tyson against Michael Spinks, who watched with promoter Butch Lewis from the back row of the balcony. Lewis said: "If that's the best Tyson can do then he can kiss his titles bye-bye. He is made for Michael's left hand, and I can see him being in all sorts of trouble against my man's lethal right uppercut."

The hype for Tyson v Spinks had started.

Fight No 32
v
Tyrell Biggs
Atlantic City
16. 10. 87
Won RSF 7

GOOD fight judges expected Tyrell Biggs, the 1984 Olympic super-heavyweight gold medallist, to give Tyson one of his toughest tests. But he met a champion at his most menacing and merciless and was bombed to defeat in seven one-sided rounds. Biggs looked as if he had been run over by a truck at the end of his painful challenge. He suffered a cut over the left eye and a deep gash inside the lower lip after being floored twice by left hooks in the closing moments of the seventh round. Biggs finished his night's work propped up against the ring post in his own corner, looking a wreck of a man in stark contrast to when he had come bounding full of confidence into the ring just a little over 30 minutes earlier.

It had looked a good match on paper, but in the ring it proved to be a total mismatch. Biggs, a shade under 6 foot 5 inches and with a 12 pounds weight advantage, was completely overwhelmed, and the only surprise was that the 26-year-old challenger managed to get through to the seventh round before Tyson completed the execution.

This was Tyson at his most brutal, and he explained later: "I wanted to hurt him. He paid me no respect and showed no class when he was mouthing off about me before the fight. There was no need for some of the things he said. I wanted to make him pay with his health."

The background to this deep bitterness from Tyson could be traced to his last year in the amateurs when he sparred with Biggs in the US Olympic team headquarters. Biggs, born in Philadelphia and based in Los Angeles, had said that he had found Tyson easy to hit and suggested that he was all brawn and no brain. Tyson got his revenge in a savage style that was not for the squeamish. "I could have finished him off in the third round," he said. "But I wanted to prolong his agony. I was having fun in there. He should have paid me more respect."

Fight No 33

v

Larry Holmes

Atlantic City

22. 1. 88

Won RSF 4

LARRY Holmes made his professional debut in 1973 when seven-year-old Mike Tyson was just starting to run wild in the ghettos of New York City. Now, 15 years on, he was vowing to turn the clock back and regain the world title that he had lost, in controversial circumstances, to Michael Spinks in 1985.

In the build-up to the fight, Holmes and Tyson did not try to disguise their dislike for each other. It was not ticket-selling hype. It was genuine, naked hatred. Tyson was fuming over remarks 38-year-old Holmes had made after his victory over Tyrell Biggs. The old warrior had accused the champion of using dirty, gutter tactics. "He hits after the bell, butts with his head, uses his elbow and hits opponents when they are down," he said. "If he tries any of those tricks with me he will find I can be just as dirty."

Tyson publicly snubbed Holmes at the pre-fight press conference, refusing to shake the former champion's proffered hand. "I am going to beat the old man up," he said with chilling certainty in his voice. Holmes told the media that he had no respect for Tyson and that he disliked him more than any man he had ever fought in his 50 professional fights. He had been beaten only twice – both disputed points defeats by Michael Spinks.

Holmes revealed that he was so disgusted with the tactics that Tyson used in the ring that he had taken down the champion's photograph from the gallery at his gymnasium at Easton, Pennsylvania. "Tyson will not be fighting some kid like Biggs who didn't know how to cope with his bullying tactics," he said. "He will be facing a mature fighter who knows how to look after himself."

Holmes had been inactive for 21 months since losing back-to-back fights and his undefeated record to Spinks. He had quit the ring in disgust at the two decisions. Now he was back amid rumours that his vast $30 million fortune was melting away, but Holmes insisted he was not back for the money (a $3 million purse) but because he wanted the title back. "The layoff from boxing was just what I needed to recharge my batteries," said the father of four who has a baby grandson. "I feel like a new man. I can't wait to get into the ring with Tyson. His style is just made for me. He will be eating my jab, just wait and see."

When it was pointed out that Muhammad Ali had been a worn-out 38-year-old when he beat him in 1980, Holmes snapped: "I'm not Ali. My body has never felt better. I am good and ready to end the myth of Mike Tyson."

There had been a chorus of criticism over the decision to allow grandfather Holmes to challenge for the world crown after his long layoff. But the World Boxing Council and World Boxing Association both approved the fight because of his past greatness and exceptional ring record. The International Boxing Federation refused to recognise it as a title fight because the contest was scheduled for 12 and not 15 rounds.

As it turned out, Tyson needed less than four rounds to prove that he was too strong and too powerful for Holmes. The message on the challenger's dressing-gown – 'This Is It' – and the 'Shock The World' legend on the jackets of his cornermen, proved to have no basis in reality. Tyson stamped his authority on the fight from the first bell. He forced Holmes to the ropes with a right to the body and a left to the head and the veteran challenger had to clinch. This set the pattern of the fight: Tyson attacking, Holmes holding and smothering in a style reminiscent of Bonecrusher Smith's performance. He was cautioned for clinging on in the second round as Tyson relentlessly banged away to the body.

At his peak, Holmes had one of the most fearsome and accurate left jabs in the business, but he was pawing with it against Tyson who was walking through his punches with something approaching contempt. Only in the third round did Holmes have the satisfaction of opening up on Tyson. He landed with a sequence of right uppercuts. Tyson responded with a ferocious overhand right that rocked the challenger back on his heels. The bell rang to rescue Holmes before the champion could build a finishing attack.

Holmes came out for the fourth round on his toes and throwing his bop-bop-bop jab as in his golden days. But, just as it looked as if he had found the springtime of his form, winter arrived in the guise of a savage attack by Tyson. He whipped over a left hook that turned the veteran's legs to lead. He tried to pull Tyson into another clinch, but the champion was too quick for him and sent him falling sideways to the canvas with a thumping right. Holmes somehow pulled himself up at four, shaking his head as if he could not believe the power of the punches coming at him. Referee Joe Cortez gave him the rest of the mandatory eight count, then waved Tyson back in. Holmes tried to retreat across the ring on legs that were suddenly betraying him. Tyson roared after him and dropped the dazed challenger with a burst of punches that were not quite timed to perfection.

Once more Holmes was up at four, and indicated to the referee that he was fit to continue. But he was deluding himself. He stumbled back on to the ropes and, in a dazed condition, got his right glove tangled up in the middle strand as he attempted a counter punch. Tyson, one of the most ruthless finishers in boxing history, showed no mercy. He unloaded a full-blooded right to the head and Holmes fell straight backwards, out to the world before he hit the floor. The referee did not bother to take up the count, and waved it all over with five seconds of the round left. There was genuine concern that Holmes might have been seriously hurt, but he got to his feet after a few anxious minutes.

"I made it clear to Larry Holmes that his career is unquestionably over," said Tyson. "He was a great champion, but not any more. He's had his era. This is mine."

Holmes said: "My game plan was to tie him up and make him miss and then get in my own shots. But I made the mistake of waiting for him to tire. I fought Tyson not for money but because I was trying to get something back after being deprived of victory against Michael Spinks. I found out that Tyson is better than I thought. There is no question that he's the champion."

The biggest cheer of the evening from the 17,000 crowd in the Convention Centre was reserved for the one and only Muhammad Ali as, shuffling, he took his seat at ringside. Eight years earlier, he had been pummelled to a tenth-round defeat by Holmes. Now it was Larry's turn to be on the receiving end.

The cruel wheel of boxing fortune had made another turn.

Fight No 34
v
Tony Tubbs
Tokyo
21. 3. 88
Won RSF 2

TONY Tubbs meant it as a throwaway joke when he said at the pre-fight press conference: "I'm just here as a stepping stone. I've been brought in as the tune-up." But the laugh was on him when Mike Tyson blasted him to a second-round defeat to open the way to a mega-bucks date with Michael Spinks. Watched from the ringside by his new bride Robin Givens, Tyson allowed Tubbs a one-round honeymoon period during which the bloated-looking challenger impressed with fast footwork and flashy popping jabs. Then Tyson took over. Early in round two he made Tubbs wince with a right to his fat midriff followed instantly by a right to the jaw. Then a single punch finish – a whiplash left hook that brought a look of startled surprise that seemed frozen on the challenger's face. The man from Santa Monica via Cincinatti suddenly did not know whether he was in Tokyo or Timbuktu. There was a delayed, almost slow-motion reaction to the punch. He wobbled like a drunk suddenly hitting fresh air. The punch had ripped a gash on his eyebrow, and he pawed at his eye and then reached for the top rope to try to steady himself. But his legs were out of control and he looked as if he was break dancing before crash-landing in a neutral corner.

New York referee Arthur Mercante was about to take up the count, but waved proceedings over as he was joined alongside the stricken Tubbs by trainer Odell Hadley. It was announced that Tyson had won on a knockout after two minutes 54 seconds of round two, but in fact the count had hardly started. "He took a great shot and he went down," Tyson said afterwards. "But he came to fight – he didn't come just to pick up a payday. Now I want to get it on with Spinks."

Tyson was paid $10 million for his first professional fight on foreign territory. It was staged at midday Tokyo time to hit the HBO screens at peak time in the United States.

Fight No 35
v
Michael Spinks
Atlantic City
27. 6. 88
Won KO 1

MIKE Tyson had the troubles of the world on his shoulders as he climbed into the ring at Atlantic City's Convention Centre to defend his titles against unbeaten Michael Spinks. His marriage was in trouble, his influential co-manager Jim Jacobs had died and he was locked in dispute with his remaining manager, Bill Cayton. It was hardly the sort of pressure he needed as he prepared for what most people considered would be the toughest defence of his crowns but, Tyson being Tyson, he actually thrived on what was a boiling-point crisis in his life. He responded by producing what was, even by his explosive standards, an astonishing peak performance that had the most jaundiced of onlookers agreeing that he was quite awesome.

Spinks was the man most experts picked as the opponent best equipped to stop Tyson's winning march. He was unbeaten in 31 professional fights after an amateur career during which he won the 1976 Olympic middleweight gold medal. He had been the undisputed world light-heavyweight champion and had gone on to capture the IBF version of the heavyweight crown, twice getting disputed 15-round decisions over Larry Holmes. He had the extra incentive of following his brother, Leon, as undisputed champion.

Just before the bell rang, Spinks knelt in his corner and offered a brief prayer. It proved a last act before going to the scaffold where his executioner awaited him in the intimidating shape of Tyson at his most ferocious. The champion took just 91 seconds to end the argument as to who was the world's best heavyweight. There was a chilling inevitability about it all. From the moment the first bell rang, Tyson came at Spinks like an unstoppable tank. In the first seconds, Tyson connected with a right to the head and Spinks was visibly surprised by the heavy thud as he grabbed hold of his tormentor who was about to become the terminator. The challenger tried to meet Tyson with the looping right that he had nicknamed his 'jinx' punch, but it had no effect whatsoever. Tyson backed Spinks towards the ropes, and then let loose a left uppercut that jolted his head back. This was followed by a thumping right to the body and Spinks sank to his knees as if returning to the praying position. He stood up at two, but his face was clouded with doubt while Tyson's face had 'bad intentions' written all over it.

Spinks elected to go down firing. He wound up for a hopeful right, but Tyson walked inside it and from close range fired his own right to the point of the jaw. The challenger crashed backwards as if shot, and would have only heard in the misty distance referee Frank Cappuccino start to toll the ten second count. At around four he rolled over on to his side and then tried to rise, but his head moved as if it suddenly weighed a ton and as the count reached ten he tumbled face-first into the ropes. Standing in a neutral corner, Tyson made an unnerving sign to Spinks' voluble manager Butch Lewis. He ran his glove across his throat. The executioner had done his job.

"When I got into the ring I saw the fear in his eyes and I knew I could go for a quick knockout," Tyson said later. It was the fourth fastest finish in the history of the heavyweight championship. James J. Jeffries (v Jack Finnegan), Tommy Burns (v Jim Roche) and Michael Dokes (v Mike Weaver) provided the only quicker climaxes.

Tyson turned his attack on the media after his instant success. "I wasn't too appreciative of what you did to me," he said. "You tried to embarrass me, you tried to embarrass my family, tried to disgrace them. I don't mean all of you. Some of you are my friends, but some of you are assholes. All of my life has been chaos. It didn't get to me. Since I was 12 I was groomed for this. I knew what you would try to do to me. But my job has to be done regardless of what happens outside the ring. As far I know this could be my last fight."

He ended by saying what few would have disputed: "There's no fighter like me. I can beat any man in the world."

The 31-year-old Spinks was left to count his $7 million purse, while Tyson's take was around $22 million. "I came to fight like I promised I would," said Spinks. "I wasn't intimidated in any way. There's no man on this earth that I fear. I respect everybody. I have no excuses. I felt 100 per cent going in. I just got hit."

Fight No 36

v

Frank Bruno

Las Vegas

25. 2. 89

Won RSF 5

IT'S doubtful whether any challenger in the history of heavyweight boxing has been so messed about in the build-up to a championship contest as British hero Frank Bruno. There again, it is unlikely that a champion has ever had such a stormy, muddled and confused preparation for a title defence. The difference was that Tyson's troubles were self-inflicted, while Bruno was the innocent party on the receiving end.

When Tyson and Bruno finally got it together in the Las Vegas Hilton it was on the sixth date set for the fight in eight months. It had originally been scheduled for Wembley Stadium on 24 June 1988, but Tyson's personal and domestic problems kept getting in the way. Bruno received considerable financial compensation for having to switch his challenge to an American ring rather than at Wembley, where he would have fed on his fanatical home support.

To help him cope with the pressure, Bruno underwent daily hypnosis sessions while training in the United States. The objective was to try to ease the sort of tension that robbed him of so much strength and stamina in his first world title fight against Tim Witherspoon when he was stopped in the eleventh round after having the better of the first half of the contest.

Just 11 days before his title defence, Tyson flew down to the Dominican Republic to finalise his divorce from Robin Givens. Then he shrugged off a $10 million writ from his sacked trainer, Kevin Rooney, and got on with the business of preparing for the battle with Bruno, with whom he had sparred when he was just 16.

The champion came in ten pounds lighter than Bruno at 15 stone 8 pounds (218 pounds) to make nonsense of the rumours that he had not trained properly for this, his ninth world championship contest. He found the magnificently conditioned Bruno really fired up for the fight, and outstaring him as referee Richard Steele gave final instructions.

Bruno produced the performance of his life after a stunning start when he looked doomed to a Michael Spinks-speed defeat. Tyson went straight for Bruno from the bell. He was surprised to find Bruno, perhaps suicidally, meeting him head on. It was the challenger who came off the worse in the explosive exchange when a right hand struck him high on the head and sent him floundering towards the canvas. The fight was just 18 seconds old and a new record for the quickest knockout in the world heavyweight championship history looked a distinct possibility.

But fortunately for Bruno, it was only a glancing blow. He jumped up at three but had to take the mandatory eight second count. As Tyson came powering in towards him, Bruno took his leverage away from him by pushing his neck down with his left hand. The referee deducted a point for holding. The delay gave Bruno time to recover his senses, and, instead of running as so many of Tyson's opponents had, he came looking for the champion. The challenger had decided that attack was the best form of defence.

Tyson performed one of his kangaroo hop-and-hit movements, but missed with a left hook, and Bruno caught him with a thundering left hook of his own on the side of the jaw. The champion's legs wobbled and he hurled himself against Bruno to hang on while his head cleared. It was the closest in his career that Tyson had come to getting knocked out. There is no doubt that for several seconds he was out on his feet.

Bruno fatally hesitated in following up, If he could have landed another couple of head blows in those ten seconds after his left hook had landed, he might well have become the first man to beat Tyson. But his biggest chance had gone, and Tyson made him pay for the pain he had caused him.

Clearly ring rusty after his six months' layoff because of all his marital and managerial problems, Tyson started to get into his rhythm in the second round and began to unleash his big bombs. The challenger was knocked back on his heels by a volley of three punches, but got himself out of serious trouble by again clutching the champion's neck and forcing it down. At the end of the round, referee Steele told him: "The next time you're out."

Tyson gradually increased his bombardment, and Bruno was showing tremendous resilience under the sort of pressure that had proved too much for a procession of Tyson's opponents. But a sustained onslaught in the fifth round proved too much for the game challenger. Trapped on the ropes, Bruno was rocked by a left, a right, followed by a right uppercut, then another jolting uppercut followed by a short right.

Only the ropes were holding Bruno up and, as Tyson prepared to unload another barrage of punches, Bruno's caring manager, Terry Lawless, was running along the ring apron with his towel in his hand. A ringside spectator held the towel, but Lawless jerked it away and threw it into the ring just as the referee stepped in between the boxers. Tyson let one more punch go as Bruno jackknifed forward into Steele's arms.

Bruno did not take long to recover. His pal, Harry Carpenter, glasses awry, leapt into the ring for an interview and Bruno obliged in the gentlemanly manner that has won him so many followers in Britain. "I'm sorry I've let everybody down at home," he said, not aware that a hero's welcome was waiting for him on his return. It added to the legend that the British love a good loser.

"I was more embarrassed than hurt when Tyson put me down in the opening seconds," Bruno said later. " 'Please God,' I said in silent prayer, 'don't let me go out in the first.' I couldn't understand why the referee kept on at me. He shouted: 'Watch the rabbit punching, Bruno,' but he ignored all the rough stuff we've come to expect from Tyson. I knew I had badly hurt Tyson with my left hook because he was really body-popping. I did not willingly let him off the hook. He fell against me and I could not get my arms out to get in a punch to the head. By the time the referee had pulled us apart, Tyson had cleared his head. He went on to give me a good hiding, but not before I had let him know that I could dish out some tasty punishment of my own. I would love another crack at him, particularly in front of my own supporters in Britain where this fight should have taken place. I would really fancy my chance at home."

Tyson was impressed by Bruno's performance, but had a moan about his holding tactics. "He was pulling my head so hard that I thought it would come off," Tyson said. "He hit me with some hard punches, the hardest I've been hit. But this is the hurt business. From the third round I knew I would break him. How dare they challenge me with their somewhat primitive skills? They're as good as dead."

Fight No 37

v

Carl Williams

Atlantic City

21. 7. 89

Won RSF 1

CARL 'The Truth' Williams was convinced that he was the man with the ability to end Mike Tyson's reign of terror. He recalled that, six years earlier, he had continually got the better of Tyson in gymnasium sparring sessions. "Oh boy, did I give him some lessons," he said. "I couldn't miss him with my left jab." That was not the way Tyson remembered it, but at least the 29-year-old challenger's confidence was boosted by his recollections. He had won all but two of his 22 professional fights since a distinguished amateur career during which he won a World Cup championship, and he was recognized as one of the more skilful boxers on the heavyweight circuit. His first defeat was a disputed points loss to Larry Holmes in a title fight in 1985. Heavy-hitting Mike Weaver stopped him in two rounds, and raised doubts about his ability to absorb a really heavy punch. He claimed that his suspect chin had been considerably strengthened by the fitting of a specially designed gumshield.

But Williams folded under the first serious attack from a determined champion, and was sat on the seat of his pants by a devastating left hook. With one hand on the bottom rope, he managed to pull himself up at a count of eight. He looked in a position to defend himself, but referee Randy Neumann stared into his eyes and decided he was not in a condition to continue. Williams protested in the ring for much longer than the 93 seconds that the fight lasted.

"I was standing upright and in complete control of myself," said Williams. "I've been down before and have got up to win. I deserved the chance to carry on. This was a world title fight, and I had worked my butt off to get in the best possible shape."

"That's the way it goes," said Tyson. "The referee was a bit quick, but it proves again that when I hit 'em they have to go."

Fight No 38

v

James Douglas

Tokyo

11. 2. 90

Lost KO 10

IT read like a script from *Rocky*: a going-nowhere fighter gets a shot at the world heavyweight title because he is considered to have no chance of upsetting the champion then a mega-bucks match with the number one contender. His beloved mother has just died; the mother of his own son is suffering from a severe kidney ailment. He has been taking pain-killing penicillin shots for a nagging infection. And now, watched from the ringside by his 11-year-old son, he must step into the ring against a man who has destroyed every opponent with ferocious power. The odds against the Rocky character winning are so high that most bookmakers take bets only on the round in which the champion will stop him.

But the plucky hero surprises – no, amazes – everyone by carrying the fight for the first seven rounds. Then, in the eighth, he is knocked down by a vicious uppercut and staggers to his feet at the end of a count that lasts 12 seconds. The bell saves him from a pounding, and he comes back strongly in the ninth to rock the champion continually with long left jabs and follow-through rights. Then, in the tenth round, he knocks the previously unbeaten champion to the canvas for the first time in his professional career. He is so dazed that he scrabbles around on the canvas trying to put his gumshield back in his mouth as the referee counts him out. 'Rocky' is the winner and new heavyweight champion of the world!

But this was not a Hollywood script. This was for real. James 'Buster' Douglas, 29-year-old 'no hoper', sensationally ended Mike Tyson's four year reign with a tenth-round knockout victory in Tokyo. It blew away the $32 million showdown between Tyson and Evander Holyfield that had been arranged for June. Don King tried to hang on to the title by demanding that the fight be declared null and void because of the long count in the eighth round. But the boxing commissions dropped their charade and acknowledged what every onlooker knew: Douglas had won the fight fair and square. He could not be blamed because the referee, Octavio Meyran, had failed to pick up the count and was trailing three seconds behind the timekeeper. Amazingly, one of the Japanese judges had Tyson ahead on points at the end. Most neutral spectators were scoring Douglas ahead by at least three rounds.

"I don't want anybody to stick me with the Rocky image," Douglas said through victory tears. But the former basketball player from Columbus, Ohio, had to accept that his story had a real Rocky feel to it. His father, Bill, was a good-class middleweight who filled Buster with dreams of boxing glory. Another inspirational character appeared in the shape of Buster's manager, John Johnson, who helped steer his fighter through recent family tragedies – especially the death of his mother, Lula, while he was training for the title challenge.

Everything about Buster's victory over Tyson was remarkable. He was considered only a fair puncher, stopping just 19 opponents in his 29 winning fights. Three stoppages – by David Bey, Mike White and Tony Tucker – suggested his chin was suspect, and there seemed little chance of his being able to withstand the sort of sledgehammer attacks that had made Tyson the most feared fighter in the world.

But the Tyson he fought in Tokyo was a stranger to anybody who had followed the champion's career. He fought as if his mind was elsewhere, and his torso looked unusually fleshy and less than well prepared. Apart from his eighth round uppercut he never looked capable of worrying the 6 foot 4 inch Douglas, who made full use of his massive 84-inch reach. He continually battered Tyson with ramrod left jabs and rocked his head back with heavy, telegraphed rights that Tyson would usually have slipped with ease. He was clearly missing the corner motivation of the sacked Kevin Rooney. His seconds seemed in awe of him, and were unable to get a spark out of him when it was obvious his title was slipping from his grasp.

When news was relayed to Douglas's manager, John Johnson, that Don King was trying to get the result rubbed out, he exploded: "It's sickening to see Don King trying to manipulate the WBC and WBA. Buster kicked Tyson's ass. It's as simple as that. These guys can go to hell." It could have been a line straight out of *Rocky*.

Fight No 39
v
Henry Tillman
Las Vegas
16. 6. 90
Won RSF 1

FORMER champion Mike Tyson's return to the ring was billed as 'The Road Back', and co-promoters Don King and Bob Arum dipped back into his past to find him a passable opponent. Coming out of the opposite corner was Henry Tillman, the man who had shattered his Olympic dream in 1984. Tyson had twice been outpointed by the Californian in the US Olympic trials, and it was Tillman who went on to win golden glory in the LA Games.

Tillman was really only a blown-up cruiserweight, and had moved up into the heavyweight division after being stopped in seven rounds when challenging Evander Holyfield for the IBF title in 1987. He had lost four of his 20 professional contests, and was noted more for his smart jab-and-move boxing skill than his power. He was an ideal opponent for Tyson's first outing since his devastating defeat by Buster Douglas.

When he climbed back into the Las Vegas ring, it was immediately obvious that Tyson was in much better shape than in Tokyo. He had his old muscle definition back, and he was making those snake-like movements with his wide neck that is a sign that he is in his most menacing mood. Tillman quickly found out that Tyson was back to his brutal best. He came roaring out of his corner and virtually chased Tillman around the ring. The Californian boxed constantly on the retreat, and looked to be almost running scared. At one stage, he nearly tripped over his own feet in his desperate bid to avoid the punches winging his way. Tyson was so keen to get to him that he pushed referee Richard Steele out of his way. A right to the head stunned Tillman and he tried to clinch, but Tyson wrestled him off and then threw another right that landed high on the side of the head. Tillman crashed down and out. Michael Gerard Tyson was on the road back.

Fight No 40
v
Alex Stewart
Atlantic City
8. 12. 90
Won RSF 1

ANY doubts about the depth of the desire and seriousness of Mike Tyson to regain his place as the world's number one heavyweight were dispelled by the ruthless way he dispatched Alex Stewart. The London-born Jamaican was left in a stunned heap on the canvas after two minutes 27 seconds of the first round at Atlantic City's Convention Centre. Stewart, who had maintained that he would not be intimidated by Tyson, had lost only one of 27 previous fights. His one setback was an eighth-round cut eye stoppage against Evander Holyfield, and he had only once been briefly off his feet. He was expected to give Tyson a hard fight, but was completely overwhelmed by the former champion's devastating opening attack.

Within ten seconds he was on the floor from two rights. He was up very quickly to take a standing count, but was clearly in a state of shock and was hammered to the canvas three more times as Tyson swarmed all over him. Many of Tyson's punches were wildly aimed, but even the glancing blows had Stewart in trouble. Referee Frank Cappuccino, forgetting that the three-knockdown rule was in operation, counted over him on his fourth trip to the canvas, but then waved the fight off when he realised Stewart's distressed condition.

A distraught Stewart could only keep repeating afterwards: "I just got caught. I just got caught. I didn't expect it. I just got caught early. I tried my best to hit him but could not find the target."

Tyson said: "I was a little untidy but I wanted to explode on him. I knew as soon as I hit him he'd go. If I hit anyone they go. Too bad it had to happen to Alex. He's a nice guy. I would now like to fight Razor Ruddock. They keep saying how dangerous he is, but I'm ready for him whenever he wants. Let's get it on."

Fight No 41
v
Donovan Ruddock
Las Vegas
18. 3. 91
Won RSF 7

THERE was a free-for-all fight in the ring after Mike Tyson had scored a controversial seventh-round stoppage over Donovan 'Razor' Ruddock at the outdoor Mirage arena. Referee Richard Steele ruled that Ruddock was in no position to defend himself after he had been knocked backwards into the ropes. As the decision was announced, supporters of both fighters started swapping punches in the ring.

Unlike so many of Tyson's opponents, Ruddock was not intimidated by the ex-champion. He had waited 18 months for this fight after Tyson had pulled out of a scheduled title defence, and he was more than willing to swap punches with the New Yorker. He was prepared to mix it all the way down the line, and when Tyson hit him after the bell at the end of the fourth round, he retaliated with a blow of his own.

Ruddock also proved he had courage and staying power. He survived two knock-downs, in the second and third rounds, and was still firing back after absorbing a ferocious body attack. Tyson was always the more aggressive, but many of his punches were wild and badly timed. The 6 foot 3 inch Ruddock clutched Tyson at close quarters and refused to let him work, but gradually the superior power of the stocky American began to tell. Tyson came out with renewed determination for the seventh and landed with a powerful right hook. A cluster of clubbing blows sent the Canadian-based Jamaican reeling and, as he slumped back onto the ropes, Mr Steele stepped in and stopped it.

Ruddock was standing upright and looked in control of his senses. It seemed a premature stoppage, and immediately sparked a near riot. Ruddock's camp had made an official protest about the appointment of Steele as referee because of what they claimed was a close association with promoter Don King. The only way to end the arguments was to organize a rematch.

Fight No 42

v

Donovan Ruddock

Las Vegas

28. 6. 91

Won Pts 12

WHAT proved to be Mike Tyson's final fight before his imprisonment was one of the most unsatisfactory of his career. He scored an emphatic 12-rounds points victory in the return match against Razor Ruddock, but there was little sign of the punching power and precision that had made him the most feared heavyweight in the world.

Tyson laboured for much of the fight, particularly from the halfway stage when Ruddock began to score freely with sweeping left hooks and right uppercuts. It was a vicious, unattractive slugging match, and Ruddock paid heavily for his courageous bid to gain a revenge win. At the end of the fight, he was taken to hospital for an x-ray on a suspected broken jaw and urgent dental treatment.

As in their first meeting, Ruddock got off the canvas in the second and fourth rounds to stage a spirited fight back. The old Tyson would never have let him off the hook, but the former champion was sluggish and seemed to be fighting without enthusiasm. It was just as well that he had built up a commanding points lead by round five because Ruddock at least shared the honours in the second half of the fight as Tyson visibly tired.

There were boos and jeers from the crowd as the two fighters mauled their way through the closing stages. Tyson had two points deducted for low blows, but had clinched his victory thanks to his positive start, during which he showed just flashes of the fire that had once scorched the best heavyweights in the world.

This was Tyson's hardest battle since his defeat by Buster Douglas. "Ruddock really made me dig deep," he said, holding an ice pack to a puffy left eye and bruised cheek. "I guess we'll have to go through it all again. He deserves another shot at me."

But it was handcuffs rather than boxing gloves waiting for Tyson.

APPENDIX

History of the Heavyweights

from John L. Sullivan to
Oliver 'Atomic Bull' McCall.
A complete breakdown of all
world heavyweight title-holders
for the past 100 years,
including a computer rating
of both ancient and
modern champions.

Compiled by Norman and Michael Giller

JOHN L. SULLIVAN 1882-1892

Born Roxbury, Massachusetts, 15 October 1858.
Died Abington, Massachusetts, 2 February 1918.
Ht: 5ft 10in Wt: 13st 6lb (188lbs)
Reach: 74in Chest: 43-48in Fist: 14in
Nickname: The Boston Strong Boy. Career span: 1878-1905.
Record: 42 fights, 38 wins (33 KOs*), 3 draws, 1 loss (KO'd 1).
Rounds boxed: 258. Age at which title was won: 26 (35th fight).
**KOs as in stoppages as well as count-outs.*

THERE was no greater hero in American sport than John L. (for Lawrence) Sullivan, the last of the bare-knuckle champions. He was a larger-than-life character who earned his 'Boston Strong Boy' nickname by astonishing feats of strength. When he was just 16, he lifted a streetcar back on its rails, and he could hoist a full barrel of beer above his head like a weightlifter. Mind you, he usually first preferred to drink the barrel dry. Modesty never became him and he used to swagger into bar-rooms and shout: "I'll fight any man in the house." There were never any takers! He had an enormous capacity for drink until in his later years, when he travelled the United States as an Evangelist preaching against the evils of alcohol. Sullivan won the bare-knuckle version of the world heavyweight title in 1882 when he battered Tipperary's Paddy Ryan into submission in nine rounds in Mississippi City. When they met in a return wearing gloves in New York City three years later, police clambered into the ring and stopped the fight in the first round to save Ryan from annihilation. Sullivan was crowned Queensberry world heavyweight champion when he beat Dominick McCaffrey over six rounds in Cincinnati on 29 August 1885. His most famous victory came when he knocked out Irishman Jake Kilrain in the seventy-fifth round of a brutal battle to retain his bare-knuckle title in 1889. It was the last fight staged under London Prize Ring Rules. Grown men cried when a potbellied, out-of-condition Sullivan was knocked out by James J. Corbett in the twenty-first round in New Orleans on 9 July 1892. Both men wore five-ounce boxing gloves. It was Sullivan's only defeat in 42 fights. He retired after a couple of exhibition bouts, toured as an actor and remained an idol until his death at the age of 59.

JAMES J. CORBETT 1892-1897

Born San Francisco, 1 September 1866.
Died Bayside, Long Island, 18 February 1933.
Ht: 6ft 1in Wt: 13st (182lbs)
Reach: 73in Chest: 38-42in Fist: 12.75in
Nickname: Gentleman Jim. Career span: 1884-1903.
Record: 19 fights, 11 wins (7 KOs), 2 draws, 4 losses (KO'd 3), 2 DNC.
Rounds boxed: 215. Age at which title was won: 26 (13th fight).

JAMES J. Corbett was one of the pioneers of scientific boxing who believed that the sport should be as much about avoiding punches as landing them. He was never a devastating puncher, but a master tactician who nullified the work of his opponents by clever footwork and smart defensive strategy. It was a long time before the American public warmed to this former bank clerk after he had beaten their hero for all seasons, John L. Sullivan, who was used to fighting toe-to-toe sluggers and was out-boxed by the elusive and fitter challenger. Like Sullivan, Corbett was the son of an Irishman but he was the complete opposite to the Bostonian braggart, both with his style inside the ring and his behaviour outside. He was a dandy dresser, articulate and quietly spoken. His good manners earned him the nickname Gentleman Jim, which was the title of the biographical film in which Errol Flynn portrayed Corbett. He earned a crack at the title by fighting a draw over 61 rounds with Peter Jackson, the black West Indian Sullivan had refused to fight "on grounds of colour". In his first defence of the title, Corbett knocked out Englishman Charlie Mitchell in three rounds at Jacksonville on 25 January 1894. This was the one and only time Corbett lost his temper in the ring. Mitchell hurled a volley of verbal abuse at him as the referee was giving his final centre-of-the-ring instructions. Mitchell had deliberately set out to goad Corbett in the hope that it would affect his concentration, but the insults only served to turn the master of defence into a demon of attack and he gave Mitchell a terrible hiding before he was counted out in round three. After losing to Bob Fitzsimmons in his third defence following a three-year layoff, Corbett made two attempts to win back the championship against James J. Jeffries, but was each time bulldozed to defeat by his stronger, harder-punching opponent.

BOB FITZSIMMONS 1897-1899

Born Helston, Cornwall, 4 June 1862. Died Chicago, 22 October 1917.
Ht: 5ft 11.75in Wt: 11st 8lb Reach: 71.75in Chest: 41-44in Fist: 12.5in
Nicknames: Freckled Bob, Ruby Robert. Career span: 1880-1914.
Record: 62 fights, 40 wins (32 KOs), 11 losses (KO'd 8) 10 ND, 1 DNC.
Rounds boxed: 290. Age at which title was won: 35 (45th fight).

PRE-LENNOX Lewis claims that Bob Fitzsimmons was the 'only British boxer' to win the world heavyweight championship are on weak ground. He was still a child when taken by his Cornish parents to New Zealand where his father opened a blacksmith's business in Timaru. From his schooldays, Bob helped his father in the forge and developed an immense, heavily-muscled upper body that looked somehow out of place on what were spindly, freckled legs. He never weighed more than a middleweight and, with his prematurely balding, ginger hair, he gave the appearance of being a physical freak. But he was a phenomenal puncher who could take any many out with a single hit. The Americans didn't take him seriously when he arrived in California at the age of 28 to continue a career that started in Australia. He silenced the sneerers by knocking out Jack 'The Nonpareil' Dempsey to win the world middleweight title in 13 rounds in 1891. Fitz had already applied for US citizenship when he climbed into the ring against James J. Corbett at Carson City, Nevada, on St Patrick's Day 1897. At 35, Fitz was four years older and 20 pounds lighter than the champion, and he was very much the betting underdog. He was taking a battering from Corbett until he followed the ringside advice of his wife, Rose, who shouted: "Hit him in the slats, Bob." This referred to the rib area, and in the fourteenth round Fitz invented what became known as the 'solar-plexus' punch. He switched suddenly to southpaw and threw a straight left that corkscrewed deep into Corbett's stomach and knocked the breath out of him. The champion sank to the canvas fighting for air as the referee counted him out. Fitz lost the title to James J. Jeffries in his first defence, breaking the knuckles on both his hands against the granite-hard challenger who outweighed him by 64 pounds. He was knocked out in the eleventh round, and survived until the thirteenth in a return match. At the age of 41, he became the first man to win three world titles when he captured the light-heavyweight crown.

JAMES J. JEFFRIES 1899-1905

Born Caroll, Ohio, 15 April 1875.
Died Burbank, California, 3 March 1953.
Ht: 6ft 2.5in Wt: 15st 7lb (217lbs) Reach: 76.5in Chest: 43-48in Fist: 13.5in
Nickname: The Boilermaker, Californian Grizzly Bear.
Career span: 1896-1910.
Record: 21 fights, 18 wins (15 KOs), 1 loss, 2 draws.
Rounds boxed: 209. Age at which title was won: 24 (13th fight).

James J. Jeffries started his boxing career as a sparring partner for James J. Corbett. Gentleman Jim acted in something less than a gentlemanly manner and each day in training used to give the strongly-built boilermaker from California via Ohio a painful hiding. After taking the world heavyweight crown from outweighed and outgunned Bob Fitzsimmons in 1899, Jeffries gave Corbett two chances to regain the championship. Each time, he gained revenge for all the punishment he had taken in training, although he looked on the verge of defeat in their first meeting at Coney Island in 1900. Corbett outboxed and outfoxed him for 23 rounds before being caught by a right that stretched him flat out as he came bouncing off the ropes. In the return in San Francisco in 1903, the old champion ran out of steam after building up an early lead and Jeffries knocked him out in the tenth round. Trained by former world middleweight champion Tommy Ryan, Jeffries was taught to fight out of a crouch and his tucked-up style made him a difficult man to pin with any telling punches. The 'Jeffries Crouch' was copied by many fighters of his era, but few could match the champion's success with it. He defended the title against Tom Sharkey (wpts25), Gus Ruhlin (wret5) and Jack Munroe (wko2) before announcing his retirement as undefeated champion in 1905. He had won 20 and drawn two of his 22 professional contests. Five years into his retirement, Jeffries allowed himself to be talked back into the ring for a showdown with Jack Johnson, who was despised by many white American fight fans unable to come to terms with a black man holding the championship. Jeffries, as they say in the fight trade, 'Shoulda stood in bed.' At 35 and no longer a magnificent physical specimen, he was outclassed by the immensely talented Johnson who battered him to a standstill in 15 rounds.

MARVIN HART 1905-1906

Born Jefferson County, Kentucky, 16 September 1876.
Died Fern Creek, Kentucky, September 17 1931.
Ht: 5ft 11in Wt: 13st 5lb (190lbs) Reach: 74in Chest: 45-47in Fist: 14in
Nickname: Punching Plumber. Career span: 1899-1910.
Record: 47 fights, 32 wins (19 KOs), 9 losses, 6 draws.
Rounds boxed: 395. Age at which title was won: 29 (35th fight).

OF all the world heavyweight title holders, Marvin Hart has made least impact on the public consciousness, mainly because his was something of a paper crown; but if only for the fact that he was once given a points verdict over the mighty Jack Johnson – 'given' being the operative word – he merits his place in this parade of world heavyweight champions. Hart became world champion in dubious circumstances. When James J. Jeffries retired undefeated in 1905, the title became vacant. There were two contenders who stood out: Jack Johnson and Sam Langford, but both were ruled out by the boxing establishment because they were black. There was no sport that could quite match boxing for exposing the cancer of bigotry. On 28 May 1905, Hart met Johnson in a non-title contest over 20 rounds and was adjudged to have won on points. One ringside boxing reporter summed up the result memorably with the line: "Hart could only have got the decision owing to the fact that in the excitement the referee pointed to the wrong man." Hart outgunned former world light-heavyweight champion, Jack Root, at Reno on 7 July 1905, in a fight that the idolised Jeffries was persuaded to describe as for "my vacant title". Jeffries was the referee and stopped the fight in Hart's favour in the twelfth round. The son of a family with roots deep in Germany, Hart slipped quickly from the world stage when he lost his title in his first defence against Canadian Tommy Burns in Los Angeles on 23 February 1906. Again, Jim Jeffries was the referee. Hart retired to a red-shuttered cottage on a small farm in Fern Creek, where he combined farming with plumbing. He also became a prominent referee in both wrestling as well as boxing rings. Hart was an affable man who used to laugh a lot when questioned about his boxing career. "All the championship earned me was ten thousand dollars," he said. "I guess I was born 20 years too soon."

TOMMY BURNS 1906-1908

Born Chesley, Ontario, 17 June 1881.
Died Vancouver, 10 May 1955.
Ht: 5ft 7in Wt: 12st 5lb (173lbs)
Reach: 74.5in Chest: 40-44in Fist: 12in
Career span: 1900-1920.
Record: 60 fights, 46 wins (36 KOs), 8 draws, 5 losses (KO'd 1), 1 ND.
Total rounds boxed: 516.
Age at which title was won: 25 (42nd fight).

TOMMY Burns, at 5 foot 7 inches, was the shortest man ever to win the world heavyweight title, and was never more than a light-heavyweight. But he beat a procession of much bigger and more powerful men by nimble footwork, stunningly accurate counter punching and enormous willpower. Burns (real name, Noah Brusso) had an extraordinarily long reach for such a short man and he used to draw opponents in like a spider luring a fly and then knock them senseless with pinpointed punches to the most vulnerable parts of the body. Self-managed Burns, the thinking man's fighter, became champion in 1906 by winning on points over pretender to the throne Marvin Hart. Burns, an astute businessman, then set about earning as much money as possible while keeping ahead of the feared Johnson, who trailed him around the world throwing out challenges. He successfully defended the title 11 times (including a 20 rounds draw and then a 20 rounds points victory over Philadelphia Jack O'Brien) before Johnson finally caught up with him in Sydney, Australia, after chasing him through Europe. Burns knew he had little chance against the 'Galveston Giant' and demanded, and got, a record $30,000 purse to put his title on the line on Boxing Day, 1908. Johnson made him earn every cent, toying with the champion and hitting him with a stream of insulting words as well as injurious punches before police jumped into the ring and stopped the one-sided savagery in the fourteenth round. Burns had six more contests before retiring after a seventh-round defeat by Britain's Joe Beckett in London in 1920. Burns later became an ordained minister, and said: "Boxing is vicious and full of hatred. My only purpose in life now is to spread universal love. I'm through hurting people."

JACK JOHNSON 1908-1915

Born Galveston, Texas, 31 March 1878. Died North Carolina, 10 June 1946.
Ht: 6ft 13st 10lb (192lbs) Reach: 74in Chest: 38-43in Fist: 14in
Nicknames: Li'l Artha, The Galveston Giant. Career span: 1897-1928.
Record: 113 fights, 79 wins (45 KOs), 12 draws, 8 losses (KO'd 5), 14 ND.
Rounds boxed: 977. Age at which title was won: 30 (79th fight).

IT took Jack Johnson ten frustrating years to reach the status of number one challenger for the world heavyweight title in an era when the colour of your skin rather than your ability dictated matters. For at least five years, Johnson was the best heavyweight fighter in the world, but most of the leading white heavyweights dodged him by drawing what was known as the 'colour line'. He chased Tommy Burns halfway around the world before finally catching up with him and relieving him of the title in Australia. Johnson's victory, coupled with his arrogant manner and controversial lifestyle, made him one of the most unpopular figures in the United States and a massive hunt was launched for a 'white hope' who could dethrone him. World middleweight champion Stanley Ketchel, the 'Michigan Assassin', was persuaded to try his luck and finished with two of his teeth embedded in Johnson's right glove after he had been knocked cold in the twelfth round following a punch that briefly put Johnson on the canvas. Then James J. Jeffries was brought out of retirement and was pounded to a fifteenth round defeat. Johnson was the greatest defensive boxer ever seen, and a master at picking off punches with open gloves and then throwing cutting counters. He stopped 'Fireman' Jim Flynn in nine rounds in Las Vegas and then became exiled in Europe for three years after being accused of "transporting a white woman for immoral purposes". Johnson jumped bail and had three fights in Paris before being talked into defending his title against giant Jess Willard in the open air in Havana in 1915. He was well ahead on points until reaching the edge of exhaustion under the boiling sun and was knocked out in the twenty-sixth round. Johnson later claimed that he had deliberately thrown the fight, but the *Big Fights Inc.* film of the contest supports Willard's case that he won fair and square. Johnson carried on fighting until he was past 50, and right up until his death in a car crash at 68 he was still giving exhibitions.

JESS WILLARD 1915-1919

Born Pottawatomie County, Kansas, 29 December 1881.
Died Los Angeles, 15 December 1968.
Ht: 6ft 6.25in Wt: 17st 8lb (246lbs)
Reach: 83in Chest: 46-49.5in Fist: 14in
Nickname: The Pottawatomie Giant. Career span: 1911-1923.
Record: 35 fights, 24 wins (21 KOs), 1 draw, 6 losses (KO'd 3), 4 ND.
Rounds boxed: 273. Age at which title was won: 33 (31st fight).

JUST about everything was taken away from Jess Willard, the fighting cowboy. The glory he should have earned winning the world title was tarnished by Jack Johnson's claims that he had thrown the fight. Then his championship was ripped away by a two-fisted tornado called Dempsey, and unscrupulous managers fleeced him of his hard-earned money. They even tried to take away his lasting place in the record books. It was always believed that, at 6 foot 6.25 inches, Willard stood tallest of all the champions, but a Harvard University professor claimed, long after Willard was dead, that he could scientifically prove that Willard was in fact a full inch shorter than the promoters had always claimed. He was a manufactured fighter who did not take up boxing until he was 28. What he lacked in skill he made up for in strength and stamina, and he used to wear down rather than outclass his opponents. His colossal reach of 83 inches meant he was able to keep his opponents away merely by sticking out a ramrod left jab. Willard was manoeuvred into a fight with Jack Johnson because promoter Jack Curley believed it would take a strong rather than a skilful man to beat the 37-year-old champion. The fight was deliberately made over 45 rounds to handicap the veteran Johnson. After his twenty-sixth-round knockout victory, Willard became a hero to white America and he cashed in on his popularity by making a coast-to-coast tour as the main attraction with a travelling circus. He made a solitary defence, getting the best of Frank Moran in a ten-rounds no decision contest in 1916. Three years later Willard was coaxed into at last climbing into the ring to defend the title against Dempsey, who stopped the giant cowboy in three rounds of legalised brutality. Willard retired, and then in 1923 made a comeback against Luis Angel Firpo, who hammered him to an eighth-round defeat.

JACK DEMPSEY 1919-1926

Born Manassa, Colorado, 24 June 1895. Died New York, 31 May 1983.
Ht: 6ft1in Wt: 13st 4lb (186lbs)
Reach: 77in Chest: 42-46in Fist: 11.25in
Nicknames: Manassa Mauler, Idol of Fistiana.
Career span: 1914-1940.
Record: 81 fights, 60 wins (49 KOs), 8 draws, 7 losses (KO'd 1), 6 ND
Rounds boxed: 450. Age at which title was won: 24 (73rd fight).

THERE has been no more exciting and explosive heavyweight champion than William Harrison Dempsey, who took his ring name from a former middleweight ring hero. Dempsey, who had great charisma to go with his devastating power, rose from bar-room brawler and hobo to become one of the most famous and fêted sportsmen in history. After a string of unrecorded fights under the name of 'Kid Blackie', Dempsey teamed up with manager and publicist Jack 'Doc' Kearns. With Kearns beating the publicity drum and Dempsey beating all the opposition, the Manassa Mauler forced himself into championship contention and tore the title away from Jess Willard in three rounds. Kearns was so confident that Dempsey would crush Willard that he bet the entire $27,500 purse at odds of 10-1 that he would win in the first round. Dempsey dropped the hulking cowboy seven times, but the bell saved Willard and so Dempsey didn't earn a cent. But six successful title defences turned him into a millionaire before he lost the title to Gene Tunney in 1926. Dempsey was the first fighter to attract a million-dollar gate when he knocked out gallant Frenchman Georges Carpentier in four rounds in 1921, and his second title battle with Gene Tunney in 1927 drew the first two-million-dollar gate. Dempsey's championship clash with Argentinian Luis Angel Firpo was labelled the most thrilling fight of all time – and it was all over within two rounds. Firpo was flattened seven times in the opening round and then somehow found the strength to knock Dempsey through the ropes and out of the ring. The champion was pushed back in by pressmen just before the bell. Dempsey tamed the 'Wild Bull of the Pampas' by knocking him out in the second round. He was weighed down with worries of lawsuits and domestic problems when he lost his world title in his next defence against Tunney.

GENE TUNNEY 1926-1928

Born New York City, 25 May 1898.
Died Greenwich, Connecticut, 7 November 1978.
Ht: 6ft 1in Wt: 13st 5lb (187lbs)
Reach: 77in Chest: 42-45in Fist: 11.25in
Nickname: The Fighting Marine. Career span: 1915-1928.
Record: 77 fights, 57 wins (42 KOs), 1 draw, 1 loss, 17 ND, 1 DNC.
Total rounds boxed: 535. Age at which title was won: 28 (75th fight).

GENE Tunney was the most calculating of all the heavyweight champions. Everybody was convinced that Dempsey was unbeatable, but Tunney knew he could be mastered with the right tactics. He considered boxing the Noble Art, perfected and polished his skills in the gymnasium and always made a close study of his opponents. It was in the US Marines during the First World War that he first came to prominence as an outstanding ring technician while boxing as a light-heavyweight. Shakespeare-quoting Tunney out-thought all his opponents, and after reversing his one and only defeat by Harry 'Smash and Grab' Greb, he campaigned to challenge for Dempsey's crown. They finally met in a rainstorm in Philadelphia on 23 September 1926, and Tunney cleverly boxed on the retreat to win an undisputed points victory. Tunney gave Dempsey a revenge chance a year later in Chicago and came perilously close to losing the title in the famous 'Battle of the Long Count'. Dempsey dropped Tunney in the seventh round and hovered over the dazed champion, ignoring the referee's instructions to go to a neutral corner. By the time Tunney was back on his unsteady feet, 14 seconds had ticked away. Tunney danced away from further trouble and repeated his ten-round points victory. Tunney always maintained that he could have got up before the ten seconds count if it had been necessary, and the referee said that Dempsey had only himself to blame for not immediately abiding by the new rules and going to a neutral corner. Tunney successfully defended the title once more against New Zealander Tom Heeney in New York City on 23 July 1928. The fight did not capture the public imagination and promoter Tex Rickard lost $150,000. After stopping Heeney in 11 rounds, Tunney married a wealthy heiress and retired from the ring with his hero status undiminished.

MAX SCHMELING 1930-1932

Born Klein Luckaw, Brandenburg, Germany, 28 September 1905.
Ht: 6ft 1in Wt: 13st 4lb (186lbs)
Reach: 76in Chest: 43-47in Fist: 12in
Nickname: Black Uhlan. Career span: 1924-1948.
Record: 70 fights, 56 wins (38 KOs), 4 draws, 10 losses (KO'd 5).
Rounds boxed: 475. Age at which title was won: 24 (50th fight).

MAX Schmeling became the only champion to win the world heavyweight title while on the canvas. He was put there by a low punch from Jack Sharkey in the fourth round of a 1930 championship contest to find a successor to the throne vacated by Gene Tunney. Within seconds, Schmeling's voluble manager, Joe Jacobs, was up on the ring apron demanding that the referee disqualify Sharkey. Eventually the referee, Jim Crowley, reluctantly agreed to the demands of Jacobs after consulting the two ringside judges – much to the disgust and anger of the near-80,000 crowd at the Yankee Stadium in New York. This did not make Schmeling the most popular of champions, particularly as he became the first fighter to take the heavyweight crown away from North America (Bob Fitzsimmons adopted American citizenship). Schmeling proved his ability a year later by stopping the highly rated Young Stribling – 'The Pride of Georgia' – in the last seconds of a 15-round title defence. The champion was then pressed into giving Sharkey a return at Long Island on 21 June 1932, and lost a narrow points verdict and the title. The beetle-browed German had his most famous victory to come. Promoter Mike Jacobs fed Schmeling to the up-and-coming Joe Louis, who had been a winner of all his 27 fights. Schmeling, now a cagey veteran of 31, grounded the 'Brown Bomber' with his favourite straight right in the fourth round and finally knocked him out in the twelfth. This victory by Schmeling was later avenged by Louis with a devastating first-round knockout in a fight in which racial hatred poisoned the atmosphere because of Hitler's doctrine. During the war, Schmeling served as a paratrooper and was wounded at the Battle of Crete. He made a brief comeback in 1947 and then retired to run a mink farm, and he also had the lucrative franchise to distribute Coca-Cola in Germany. Max was still a fitness fanatic well into his eighties.

JACK SHARKEY 1932-1933

Born Binghampton, New York, 6 October 1902.
Died Epping, New Hampshire, 21 August 1994.
Ht: 6ft Wt: 14st 6lb
Reach: 74.5in Chest: 40.5-45.5in Fist: 12.75in
Nicknames: Boston Gob, Sobbing Sailor. Career span: 1924-1936.
Record: 55 fights, 38 wins (14 KOs), 3 draws, 13 losses (KO'd 4), 1 ND.
Total rounds boxed: 462. Age at which title was won: 29 (47th fight).

LOW blows played a prominent part in the career of Jack Sharkey, a Lithuanian-blooded fighter whose real name was Joseph Zukauskas. He won the right to meet Max Schmeling for the vacant world championship by beating British champion Phil Scott in an eliminator with a punch that was unquestionably below the belt. Sharkey, who had been in the US Navy, started his professional career while still a seaman. He made such rapid progress that he was matched with Jack Dempsey as a warm-up for the Manassa Mauler's second fight with Gene Tunney. In most of his previous contests, Sharkey had managed to tie up his opponents with clever use of the ring, but Dempsey knocked him cold in the seventh round. Ironically, the knockout blow landed while Sharkey was turning towards the referee to protest about an alleged low blow. After being disqualified for a low punch in his first fight with Schmeling, Sharkey earned another crack at the new champion by outpointing giant Italian, Primo Carnera. He won the return bout against Schmeling on a split points decision over 15 rounds to become world champion. His first title defence was against Carnera at Long Island on 29 June 1933. Even Carnera seemed surprised when a right uppercut dropped Sharkey to the canvas for the full count in round six. It was a 'mystery' punch, to rival that of the Muhammad Ali blow that knocked out Sonny Liston nearly 30 years later. Few at the ringside saw the punch and the claims of Sharkey's handlers that Carnera had a weight hidden in his glove were laughed off. During a comeback campaign three years later, Sharkey was talked into testing the young Joe Louis. The former sailor was all at sea against the Brown Bomber and was knocked out in the third round. He retired to become a champion fly-cast fisherman, and lived to the ripe old age of 91.

PRIMO CARNERA 1933-1934

Born Sequals, Italy, 26 October 1906. Died Sequals, 29 June 1967.
Ht: 6ft 5.75in Wt: 18st 6lb (258lbs)
Reach: 85.5in Chest: 48-54in Fist: 14.75in
Nickname: The Ambling Alp. Career span: 1928-1945.
Record: 103 fights, 88 wins (69 KOs), 14 losses (KO'd 5), 1 DNC.
Rounds boxed: 406. Age at which title was won: 26 (82nd fight).

PRIMO Carnera, a former circus strongman, had the saddest career of any world heavyweight champion. Because of his gigantic size, he was paraded around the boxing rings of the world as some sort of freak by managers who fleeced him and left him wrecked and destitute. In the days when he was being looked after properly, he came to Britain in 1930 and was trained by the famous Gutteridge Twins for a fight against British champion Reggie Meen that he won by a second-round knockout. It was when he moved to America that the leeches moved in and bled him dry. After beating a string of carefully chosen opponents, he became a box office attraction and emerged as a contender for the world title by stopping Ernie Schaaf in 13 rounds. Tragically, Schaaf died after the contest and Carnera had to face a commission before he was exonerated. The simple but likeable Italian challenged Jack Sharkey for the title at Long Island on 29 June 1933, and won the crown with a sixth-round knockout blow that became known as one of the phantom punches of boxing because few saw it. Despite his clumsy, lumbering style that earned him his 'Ambling Alp' nickname, Carnera was an accomplished boxer with a solid left jab and a ponderous but damaging right cross. He made successful title defences against Paolino Uzcudun and Tommy Loughran before losing the championship to Max Baer in the eleventh round of their 1934 title fight. Like so many of his contemporaries, Carnera was battered by the superior Joe Louis and disappeared from the title picture. Once his days as a meal ticket were over, all the hangers-on left him. He later found self respect and money that he could hang on to by becoming a successful professional wrestler. After his retirement, he ran (and tried to drink dry) a liquor store in Los Angeles before returning to his birthplace of Sequals for the last months of his life. He was given a national hero's funeral.

MAX BAER — 1934-1935

Born Omaha, Nebraska, 11 February 1909.
Died Hollywood, 21 November 1959.
Ht: 6ft 2.5in Wt: 15st (210lbs) Reach: 81in Chest: 44-47in Fist: 12in
Nicknames: The Livermore Larruper, Madcap Maxie.
Career span: 1929-1941.
Record: 83 fights, 70 wins (52 KOs), 13 losses (KO'd 3).
Rounds boxed: 406. Age at which title was won: 25 (47th fight).

MAX Baer could, and would, have been one of the greatest champions of the 1930s if only he had been able to take boxing – and life – more seriously. The thing Baer lacked was dedication. He was an unashamed playboy ("Give me broads before boxing any day") and was continually clowning, both in and out of the ring. During the first round of his rough-and-tumble title fight with Primo Carnera, champion and challenger fell to the canvas in an untidy heap. Baer patted a bewildered Carnera on the backside and said: "Last one up's a sissy." Poor old Primo wasn't laughing in the eleventh round when the referee stopped the fight after he had been down for the eleventh time in a farcical brawl that did little for the status of world heavyweight championship boxing. Baer lost the title a year later, on 13 June, 1935, to 10-1 underdog James J. Braddock. Few people gave Braddock a chance, but the casual, complacent Baer completely underestimated him and hardly bothered to train for the contest. He laughed and shrugged off his stunning points defeat: "Jimmy's only borrowed the title – I'll get it back," he said. But three months later, his hopes of recapturing the title were exploded when he became the latest slaughter victim for Joe Louis, who knocked him out in four rounds, despite the corner advice that Max was getting from former champion Jack Dempsey. His younger brother, Buddy, twice tried to regain the championship for the Baer family, but was each time destroyed by the lethal Louis. Clowning Max, one of the hardest right-hand punchers of all time, then had a losing and a winning fight against Britain's Tommy Farr and boxed on until joining the US Army in 1942. He later followed a career as an actor and entertainer in Hollywood where he died of a heart attack at the age of 50.

JAMES J. BRADDOCK 1935-1937

Born New York City, 6 December 1905.
Died New Jersey, 29 November 1974.
Ht: 6ft 2in Wt: 13st 8lb (190lbs) Reach: 75in Chest: 41-44in Fist: 11.5in
Nickname: Cinderella Man. Career span: 1926-1938.
Record: 86 fights, 46 wins (27 KOs), 4 draws, 23 losses (KO'd 2), 11 ND, 2 DNC.
Total rounds boxed: 695. Age at which title was won: 29 (84th fight).

JAMES J. Braddock became affectionately known as the 'Cinderella Man' because he arrived so late for the brawl. A 29-year-old dockworker, he had been on the breadline in the Depression years and was in semi-retirement when he got his world championship chance and astonished everybody by taking the title from Max Baer at Long Island on 13 June 1935. Suddenly the disbelieving world had a heavyweight champion who had won only 46 of his previous 83 contests. Braddock, who had boxed mainly as a middle and light-heavyweight, had failed in a bid for the light-heavy title in 1929 when he was outpointed over 15 rounds by Tommy Loughran. He was a smart, orthodox boxer, but lacked the punching power to make a really big impact in the heavyweight division – that is, until he got his opportunity against Baer. With the champion less than fully committed to the fight, Braddock produced the performance of a lifetime to outbox and outgeneral the lacklustre Livermore Larruper. He boxed on the retreat and never gave Baer the chance to set himself for his big right hand punch. At the end of 15 rounds he was voted a unanimous points winner and the new king of the world heavyweights. He should have met Max Schmeling in his first defence but was bribed into putting his title on the line against Joe Louis by being guaranteed ten per cent of his challenger's future purses as titleholder if the championship changed hands. Despite briefly flooring Louis for a two count in the first round, Braddock was no match for his young challenger who blasted him to defeat in eight rounds. Braddock had one more winning fight – a points victory over Tommy Farr – and then retired. His money was wisely invested and he became a wealthy businessman – a far cry from when he queued up for handouts to help feed his wife and three children.

JOE LOUIS 1937-1949

Born Lafayette, Alabama, 13 May 1914. Died Las Vegas, 12 April 1981.
Ht: 6ft 1.5in Wt: 14st 2lb Reach: 76in Chest: 42-45in Fist: 11.75in
Nickname: Brown Bomber. Career span: 1934-1951.
Record: 70 fights, 67 wins (53 KOs), 3 losses (KO'd 2).
Rounds boxed: 452. Age at which title was won: 23 (36th fight).

JOE Louis was the *complete* champion. He was a composed and clever boxer, carried a knockout punch in either hand and had strength and courage. The only opponent he could never beat was the tax man, and he finished up broke at the end of a career in which his ring earnings totalled $5 million. There was only one scar on the Louis's record when he captured the championship by knocking out James J. Braddock in eight rounds in Chicago on 22 June 1937. But he soon reversed this one setback by smashing Max Schmeling to a sensational one-round defeat a year to the day after becoming champion. Louis survived a close call against brave Welshman Tommy Farr on the way to a record 25 successful title defences. He was champion – a great champion – for 12 years, overcoming all challengers during what became famous as his 'Bum a Month' campaign. After winning two memorable battles with Jersey Joe Walcott, Louis announced his retirement from the ring in March 1949. The Brown Bomber was grounding himself as undefeated champion. Sadly, his story does not end there. His tax troubles ran so deep that he was forced into making a comeback within two years and failed in a bid to regain the title from the skilled and strong Ezzard Charles. Though a shuffling shadow of his former self, he was allowed to be put up for slaughter against a rising young hurricane of a heavyweight called Rocky Marciano. The fight produced one of the saddest sights in sporting history, Louis being pounded through the ropes and stopped in eight one-sided rounds. "I couldn't bring myself to count Joe out, so I stopped the fight," said referee Ruby Goldstein, capturing the supreme status that Louis had in boxing. Joe always carried himself with great dignity, both inside and outside the ring, and there has never been a more respected champion in sporting history. In later years, he had drug-habit and domestic problems, but this was not allowed to damage his standing as a hero for all seasons.

EZZARD CHARLES 1949-1951

Born Lawrenceville, Georgia, 7 July 1921. Died Chicago, 27 May 1970.
Ht: 6ft Wt: 13st (182lbs) Reach: 74in Chest: 39-42in Fist: 12in
Nickname: Cincinnati Cobra. Career span: 1940-1959.
Record: 122 fights, 96 wins (58 KOs), 1 draw, 17 losses (KO'd 7).
Rounds boxed: 968. Age at which title was won: 29 (74th fight).

EZZARD Charles was never the most popular of champions, mainly because he did the unforgivable thing of beating the legend that was Joe Louis. Charles had turned professional at 18 in 1940 after winning all of his 42 amateur contests, including the Golden Gloves final. He first of all campaigned as a light-heavyweight, beating Archie Moore and Joey Maxim three times each, and then moved up to the heavyweight division and captured the title relinquished by Louis in 1949 by outpointing Jersey Joe Walcott. The Brown Bomber, weighed down by financial problems, changed his mind about retiring and challenged Charles for the title that the public still considered Joe's property. The fight was staged on 27 September 1950 in New York, and Charles scored a points victory over a man who was just a shambling shadow of a once-great fighter. Charles, a stylish fighter with fast fists and a solid defence, successfully defended the title eight times in two years before running into a classic left hook in the seventh round of a third title clash with Walcott. He was outpointed by his old adversary Walcott when he tried to regain the championship and, in 1954, lost two bruising title battles with Rocky Marciano. Ezzard, who never scaled more than a few pounds above the light-heavyweight limit, was skilful enough to take Marciano 15 rounds in their first meeting but was knocked out in the eighth round of their return, after inflicting a serious nose injury on Rocky that was to hurry Marciano's retirement from boxing. In all, Charles took part in 13 world title contests yet somehow managed to wind up broke and bitter, hanging up his gloves at the age of 38 when he started being beaten by opponents who would not have been able to hit his shadow when he was at his peak. He finished up in a wheelchair suffering from a form of multiple sclerosis. Ezzard is remembered as a fine all-round ring technician, who was unlucky to live in the shadow of Joe Louis and to have stood in the path of Rocky Marciano.

JERSEY JOE WALCOTT 1951-1952

Born Merchantville, New Jersey, 31 January 1914.
Died Camden, New Jersey, 25 February 1994.
Ht: 6ft Wt: 13st 8lb (190lbs)
Reach: 74in Chest: 40-43in Fist: 12in
Nickname: Jersey Joe. Career span: 1930-1953.
Record: 69 fights, 50 wins (30 KOs), 1 draw, 18 losses (KO'd 6).
Rounds boxed: 475. Age at which title was won: 37 (66th fight).

JERSEY Joe Walcott became, at 37 years, six months, the oldest man to win the world heavyweight title (until the second coming of George Foreman) when he knocked out Ezzard Charles with a cracking left hook in the seventh round of their 1951 title fight. It had been a long, hard haul to the top of the mountain for Walcott, who had started out in life as Arnold Cream. He borrowed his ring name from a famous former world welterweight champion. Jersey Joe, a God-fearing man who always carried a Bible with him outside the ring, had been a hungry fighter in the truest sense. He had a wife and six children to feed. He had lied about his age so that he could launch his professional career at barely 15, and he had been swindled so many times by unscrupulous managers and promoters that he kept giving up boxing in disgust. His hungriest years were between 1938 and 1945, when he had just seven fights and he went on the dole to pay the food bills. One freezing cold evening in the winter of 1945, Walcott was visited at his Jersey home by a boxing manager called Felix Bocchicchio, who wanted Joe to sign with him. Walcott pointed to an empty coal-bin in the corner of his living-room and said: "Mister, if you can keep that bin full for me I will fight for you." Over the next eight years, Walcott earned enough to buy a coal-mine. He took part in eight world title fights, including two with Joe Louis and four with Ezzard Charles. He was a crafty and shifty box-fighter, bewildering opponents with clever footwork and feints, and he had the punching power to finish fights with one well-executed blow and was particularly successful with his potent left hook. His brief reign as world champion ended when he came up against a human destroyer by the name of Rocky Marciano. Gentle and genial outside the ring, he later became a referee – remembered for getting flummoxed during the second Ali-Liston title fight.

ROCKY MARCIANO 1952-1955

Born Brockton, Massachusetts, 1 September 1923.
Died in an air crash Newton, Iowa, 31 August 1969.
Ht: 5ft 10.25in Wt: 13st 2lb (184lbs)
Reach: 68in Chest: 39-42in Fist: 11.5in
Nickname: Brockton Blockbuster. Career span: 1947-1955.
Record: 49 fights, 49 wins (43 KOs).
Rounds boxed: 240. Age at which title was won: 29 (43rd fight).

MIKE Tyson is the nearest thing there has been to 'another' Rocky Marciano. Like Tyson, Rocky used his fists as if they were sledgehammers and he launched his clubbing attacks in such a brutal manner that he was called the 'Twentieth-Century Caveman'. Marciano's rise to fame and fortune was like something out of a Hollywood movie. Come to think of it, they could have called his life story *Rocky*! He was born Rocco Marchegiano in Brockton, Massachusetts, the eldest of six children of immigrant Italian parents who lived on the poverty line. After a brief amateur career, Rocky hitchhiked to New York for a gymnasium trial under the all-knowing gaze of Madison Square Garden matchmaker Al Weill, who noted Rocky's raw power and had the vision to realize he could be moulded into a fearsome force. He put him under the wing of trainer Charley Goldman, an old-time bantamweight who knew every boxing trick in the book and a few that never quite got into print. Rocky did not have the ideal build. His fists were small and his reach at 68 inches was the shortest of any world champion. But the tale of the tape doesn't give the overall picture of a man who simply oozed menace. Neither does it record that Rocky had the physical strength of a weightlifter and a granite-tough jaw. Rocky was totally dedicated to his training and there has rarely been a fitter fighting machine. After battering an aged, over-the-hill Joe Louis to an eight-round defeat, he tore the world title away from Jersey Joe Walcott with a thirteenth round knockout victory in his forty-third fight on 23 September 1952. He knocked Walcott spark out in the first round in a return match and successfully defended his crown against Roland LaStarza, Ezzard Charles (twice), Britain's Don Cockell (crudely clubbed to a ninth-round defeat) and Archie Moore, before retiring as the only undefeated world heavyweight champion in history. He tragically died in an air crash the day before his forty-seventh birthday.

FLOYD PATTERSON 1956-1961

Born Waco, North Carolina, 4 January 1935.
Ht: 5ft 11in Wt: 13st 2lb (184lbs)
Reach: 71in Chest: 40-42in Fist: 12.75in
Nickname: Freudian Floyd. Career span: 1952-1972.
Record: 64 fights, 55 wins (KOs 40), 1 draw, 8 losses (KO'd 5).
Rounds boxed: 418. Age at which title was first won: 21 (32nd fight).

FLOYD Patterson is the fighter in whose path Tyson tornadoed. Guided by Cus D'Amato, Floyd followed Rocky Marciano as world heavyweight champion when he knocked out 'Ageless' Archie Moore in five rounds in a fight for the vacant title on 30 November 1956. At 21 years, 11 months, he was then the youngest heavyweight champion of all time. He had fast fists and a distinctive style, launching sudden two-handed attacks from behind a high guard that became known as his 'peek-a-boo' method. He did not have the best of physiques for what was to become the era of the super-heavyweights, and he adopted risky attacking tactics in a bid to make up for his lack of weight and reach. He would lunge forward with both feet off the ground in an effort to get maximum power into his punches, but it meant he often left himself open to counter blows and in seven of his 13 title bouts he was knocked down 16 times. The cautious D'Amato rarely allowed Patterson into the ring with legitimate contenders, and he steered Floyd through successful defences against Tommy Jackson, Pete Rademacher (the 1956 Olympic champion making his professional debut), Roy Harris and Britain's Brian London, who hardly made an aggressive move before being knocked out in the eleventh round. Then Floyd's world was turned upside down when he underestimated European champion Ingemar Johansson and was stopped in three rounds. Patterson created history by becoming the first heavyweight champion to regain the title, but his 'bogeyman' was waiting around the corner for him in the menacing shape of Sonny Liston. After twice being shattered inside a round by Liston, Patterson made unsuccessful bids to regain the title for a second time against first Muhammad Ali and then Jimmy Ellis. Freudian Floyd ironed out his psychological problems after retiring, and gave a lot back to the game he served with such distinction as a New York boxing commissioner. He also managed his adopted son Tracy.

INGEMAR JOHANSSON 1959-1960

Born Gothenburg, Sweden, 22 September 1932.
Ht: 6ft 0.5in Wt: 14st (196lbs) Reach: 72.5in Chest: 43-45in Fist: 13.5in
Nickname (his right-hand punch): Ingo's Bingo. Career span: 1952-1963.
Record: 28 fights, 26 wins (KOs 17), 2 losses (KO'd 2).
Rounds boxed: 173. Age at which title was won: 26 (22nd fight).

THERE has never been a world heavyweight champion quite like Ingemar Johansson. He was a handsome man with a big dimple in his chin and he had a winning smile. Nothing was ever allowed to stop him enjoying the good life, and he led a playboy existence even when training for major fights. It was the norm for him to go nightclubbing and dancing into the early hours during the build-up for title fights, and his beautiful 'secretary' Birgit – later his wife – used to stay with him at his training camps. Ingo cleverly exaggerated his playboy image while in the United States preparing for his title shot against Floyd Patterson, and he duped the press and Patterson into thinking he was more interested in fun than fighting. He didn't look a class fighter in the ring, but there were a procession of battered heavyweights in Europe – including Henry Cooper and Joe Erskine – who could vouch for the fact that he was much better than he looked. They had all felt the weight of 'Ingo's Bingo' – his 'goodnight right' that could put anybody to sleep. His left jab seemed nothing more than a pawing punch, but in actual fact it was an important range finder for what he called his 'Hammer of Thor', a right hand punch that was absolutely lethal. Johansson exploded the punch on Patterson's jaw in the third round of their title fight in New York on 26 June 1959, and Floyd was up and down like a yo-yo seven times before he was finally rescued by referee Ruby Goldstein. Patterson beat Ingo in two more fights over the following two years when they tied up the world championship, much to the anger of a string of contenders. Johansson, who had been disqualified in the 1952 Olympic final for allegedly not giving of his best, beat Joe Bygraves, Dick Richardson and Brian London in a brief comeback, but he was saved from a knockout defeat by the final bell against London and he decided there and then to pack in his distinguished career, during which he was beaten only by Patterson. He ran the New York marathon with Floyd in 1982, and became a successful hotelier in Florida.

SONNY LISTON 1962-1964

Born Arkansas, 8 May 1932. Died Las Vegas, 30 December 1970.
Ht: 6ft 1in Wt: 15st 3lb (213lbs) Reach: 84in Chest: 44-46.5in Fist: 15in
Nickname: Old Stone Face. Career span: 1953-1970.
Record: 54 fights, 50 wins (39 KOs), 4 losses (KO'd 3).
Rounds boxed: 270. Age at which title was won: 30 (35th fight).

CHARLES (Sonny) Liston was the meanest, moodiest and also the most mysterious world heavyweight champion of all time. And, in the end, he finished up as the most tragic of all the champions. Liston started life right at the bottom of the heap. He was one of 25 children fathered during two marriages by Tobe Liston, a poverty-stricken Arkansas farmer. Liston ran away from home when he was 13 and started a life on the wrong side of the law. He was continually in trouble with the police and it was while serving a five-year prison sentence for robbery that he began to take an interest in boxing. He was paroled in 1952 and, after winning a Golden Gloves title, he turned professional in 1953. He won 14 of his first 15 fights and his career was just taking off in a big way when he got involved in an argument with a policeman over a parking ticket. The policeman finished up in hospital with a broken leg. Liston finished up back in prison. He made his comeback after 20 months out of the ring on 29 January 1958 and took his winning streak to 33 out of 34 fights. There were several investigations into Liston's gangster connections and it was with some reluctance that he was given the go-ahead to challenge Floyd Patterson for the world title in Chicago in 1962. A powerhouse of a fighter, Liston flattened Floyd inside one round and gave a repeat performance when they met again the following year. Liston looked just about unbeatable but then tamely surrendered the championship to chatterboxer Cassius Clay, retiring at the end of six rounds with a mystery shoulder injury. There was an even deeper mystery 15 months later, when Clay knocked him out with a phantom punch in the first round. Liston won 14 out of 15 fights over the next five years, but was then found dead in his Las Vegas apartment on New Year's Eve, 1970. He was said to have died of natural causes, but there were strong rumours that mystery man Liston had been 'eliminated' by gangster associates. Sad Sonny took his secrets with him to the grave.

MUHAMMAD ALI 1964-67, 74-78

Born Louisville, Kentucky, 17 January 1942.
Ht: 6ft 3in Wt: 15st 10lb (220lbs)
Reach: 82in Chest: 43-45.5in Fist: 12.5in
Nicknames: Louisville Lip, The Greatest. Career span: 1960-1981.
Record: 61 fights, 56 wins (37 KOs), 5 losses (stopped once).
Rounds boxed: 551. Age at which title was first won: 22 (20th fight).

BOXING has always attracted colourful, controversial and entertaining characters, but they would all have to bow the knee to Muhammad Ali as the greatest sporting showman of the twentieth century. He transcended sport and his face – and voice – became just about the best-known in the world. The descendant of a slave and the son of a Kentucky signwriter, he had three boxing careers in one. First there was the brash, flash, gaseous Cassius Clay who, after winning the Olympic light-heavyweight gold medal, was launched as a professional and was dubbed the 'Louisville Lip' as he drummed up box-office business with a tongue that was even quicker than his fast fists. He survived a fourth-round knockdown against Henry Cooper on the way to 19 victories and a title challenge against 'big, bad' Sonny Liston. Following two dramatic victories over Liston, he dropped his slave name of Clay and started the second phase of his career with the Muslim name Muhammad Ali. He made ten winning title defences before being stripped of the title in 1967 for refusing to join the US Army on religious grounds. The third stage of his extraordinary career came after a three-and-a-half year layoff and he regained his title with an incredible eighth-round knockout victory over George Foreman in Zaire in 1974. He again defended the title ten times before losing it to Leon Spinks, whom he outpointed in a return to become the first man in history to win the heavyweight crown three times. Ali went to the well once too often and was stopped for the only time when he retired at the end of ten rounds against Larry Holmes in 1980. He avenged three of the five defeats in his 21-year career (by Joe Frazier, Ken Norton and Spinks) and his setbacks against Holmes and Trevor Berbick came long after he should have dropped the curtain on perhaps the greatest boxing career of all time. Sadly, he was afflicted by Parkinson's Disease in retirement, and became a shadow of the man who had been the Great Entertainer.

JOE FRAZIER 1968-1973

Born Beaufort, South Carolina, 12 January 1944.
Ht: 5ft 11.5in Wt: 14st 7lb (203lbs)
Reach: 73.5in Chest: 42-44in Fist: 13in
Nickname: Smokin' Joe. Career span: 1965-1981.
Record: 37 fights, 32 wins (27 KOs), 1 draw, 4 losses (KO'd 3).
Rounds boxed: 214. Age at which title was won: 24 (20th fight).

JOE Frazier became champion in Muhammad Ali's enforced absence, but those who disputed his right to the title were silenced when he beat Ali on points in a magnificent battle in New York in 1971. Like so many fighters before him, Frazier had used the boxing ring to escape the poverty trap. He was the seventh son in a family of 13 and worked on his father's rundown vegetable plantation from the age of seven. He followed his elder brothers to Philadelphia and got himself a job in what was, perhaps fittingly, a slaughterhouse. Joe won 38 of his 40 amateur contests, his two defeats both being at the massive hands of Grand Rapids giant Buster Mathis. The second setback came in the US Olympic trials, but the victory cost the luckless Mathis a broken thumb and it was Frazier who went to Tokyo in his place and won the Olympic gold medal. Joe fought like a black Marciano with a perpetual motion two-fisted style that earned him the nickname 'Smokin' Joe'. In his first 28 months as a professional he hurried through 19 straight victories and then, in 1968, he was matched with his old rival Buster Mathis in a fight that was billed for the heavyweight title vacated by Ali. Frazier gave Mathis quite a mauling before the referee stopped the fight in the eleventh round. He eventually beat Jimmy Ellis for the undisputed championship and then, after outpointing comeback man Ali, he had easy-pickings fights against Terry Daniels and Ron Stander before running into the formidable fists of George Foreman. Frazier was never the same force after his two-round demolition by Foreman. He lost two storming fights with Ali and then in 1976 tried again to get the better of Foreman, but was hammered to defeat in five rounds. At his peak, Smokin' Joe was one of the great champions, but his style of fighting left him too exposed to punches and he was tailor-made for a big hitter like Foreman.

GEORGE FOREMAN 1973-1974, 94-

Born Marshall, Texas, 10 January 1948.
Ht: 6ft 4in Wt: 15st 17st Reach: 82in Chest: 42-44.5in Fist: 12in
Nickname: The Punchin' Preacher.
Career span: 1969-1977. 1987-
Record: 77 fights, 73 wins (68 KOs), 4 losses (KO'd 1).
Age at which title was won: 25 (38th fight) and 45 (77th fight).

WHETHER the reign of George I or George II is taken into consideration, the astonishing George Foreman has assured himself a lasting place in the boxing hall of fame. He stirred up the world punchbowl with his 'second coming' after a ten-year retirement, and at the age of 45 took over from Jersey Joe Walcott as the oldest champion in heavyweight history when he blasted southpaw Michael Moorer to a tenth-round knockout defeat in Las Vegas on 5 November 1994. Foreman had achieved enough the first time around to earn himself a rating in the 'great' category. Boxing followers were first alerted to his power when he won the gold medal in the 1968 Olympics in Mexico. The fifth of seven children of a railroad construction worker, he used the boxing ring to save himself from a life of crime. In his first four years as a professional he knocked out all but three of his 37 opponents, clubbing them to defeat in a brutal fashion that owed little to the boxing textbook. There was an almost novice-like rawness about his style that persuaded world champion Joe Frazier that he could handle him in what was intended as a warm-up fight for a rematch with Muhammad Ali. They met in Kingston, Jamaica on 22 January 1973 – Foreman's twenty-fifth birthday. It is now history that Frazier made the biggest misjudgement in boxing history, and was parted from his championship and a promised fortune in two rounds of unbridled savagery. Frazier was blitzed to the canvas six times before the referee, Arthur Mercante, saved him from the ignominy of a count out. In almost any other era, the magnificently sculptured Foreman could have looked forward to a long reign, but the one and only Muhammad Ali was waiting in the wings for *his* 'second coming'. After destroying Joe Roman in 1973 and Ken Norton in 1974, Foreman was talked into putting his title on the line against Ali in the 'Rumble in the Jungle' in Zaire on 30 October

1974. It was Don King's first world heavyweight championship promotion. Ali psyched Foreman out of the fight and his championship. The eighth-round knockout defeat ended Foreman's unbeaten run of 40 fights. Foreman was so shattered by the defeat that he confesses that he lost his way in life, going back to his bad old ways as the fortune he had made in the ring ran away from him like water through a gold prospector's fingers. He returned to the ring for a gimmick night in Toronto when he took on five different fighters one after the other and knocked them all out. Then victories over Ron Lyle and Joe Frazier put him back in the title picture before an inexplicable points defeat by Jimmy Young in San Juan on 17 March 1977 was followed by the shock announcement that he was quitting the ring to become a preacher. He claimed that he had a religious experience in the dressing-room after the loss to Young. "I found God," explained Foreman. "There I was floundering back into a life of sin when I was given the sense and the strength to save myself. I decided there and then to devote the rest of my life to the word of the Lord." For ten years, Foreman pounded the Bible and set up a charity to help wayward youngsters in Texas where he had often been tempted to cross the wrong line of the law. Then, shortly before his fortieth birthday, he stunned the boxing world again by announcing his comeback. Few took him seriously at first, as he thumped his way to slow-motion victories over a procession of cruiserweights and unrated heavies, but there was no doubting that all his old power was still packed into his fists. He was more than 30 pounds heavier than in his championship days, and his shaven head gave him a menacing appearance that was totally alien to the image he had fashioned outside the ring as a preacher spreading the word of God. He gave Evander Holyfield all the trouble he could handle, before going down to a twelve rounds points defeat in a title challenge in 1991. He refused to retire, even after losing a WBO title fight on points against Tommy Morrison. Ol' George was rewarded for his persistence when he grabbed the WBA and IBF titles from Moorer with a right-hand punch pulled up from his memory when way behind on points. He has sunk much of his fortune into his church in the small town of Humble in Texas where he is the pastor of the Church of the Lord Jesus Christ. Five times married Foreman has nine children, four of whom are called George! There has never been a fighter or a man quite like him.

LARRY HOLMES 1978-1985

Born Cuthbert, Georgia, 3 November 1949.
Ht: 6ft 4in Wt: 15st 3lbs (215lbs) Reach: 81in Chest: 45-48in Fist: 13.5in
Nicknames: Black Cloud, Easton Assassin. Career span: 1973-1986. 1991-
Age at which title was won: 28 (28th fight).

LARRY Holmes found himself haunted by a living legend, Muhammad Ali, and a dead hero, Rocky Marciano, during a three-tier career in which he made a not-quite-accepted bid to be recognized as one of the greatest of all heavyweight champions. Like George Foreman, he decided to make a comeback as a 40-something fighting grandfather out to prove that the modern young contenders were just pretenders. He was convinced they were not in the same class as he had been when he ruled the world heavyweights for seven years, while a fleet of Alphabet Boys sank out of sight like torpedoed ships in the night. His comeback started in 1991 and, by the spring of 1995, he had manouevred himself into a title fight against Oliver McCall. Holmes had ascended to the WBC heavyweight throne on 10 June 1978, by narrowly outpointing Ken Norton in a classic 15 rounds contest. During this first phase of his career, Holmes was never able to exorcise the ghost of his phenomenally popular predecessor Muhammad Ali, whose performances and personality continually cast a giant shadow over just about every move that Holmes made. Even Holmes idolized Ali, for whom he used to work as a young sparring partner. It was one of the saddest days of his life when he forced Ali – dangerously weakened by shedding too much weight too quickly – to retire at the end of ten rounds in a title fight at Las Vegas in 1980. The only way Holmes might have closed the gap on Ali in the never-ending 'Who's the greatest?' debate was to equal or beat Rocky Marciano's record of 49 unbeaten fights. He was one away from drawing level when he dropped a bitterly disputed points decision to light-heavyweight champion Michael Spinks in Las Vegas on 21 September 1985, and then lost the return match in Las Vegas seven months later. Two years later, he staged the first of two comebacks when, aged 38, he challenged for Mike Tyson's world crown. Even his $5 million purse seemed small consolation for the humiliation and pain he suffered at the hands of a peak-power Tyson, who knocked him out in four rounds.

THE ALPHABET BOYS

THE world heavyweight scene has become clouded in confusion by the proliferation of so-called world governing bodies recognizing a queue of different title holders. There was the World Boxing Association (WBA), the World Boxing Council (WBC), the International Boxing Federation (IBF) and, later, the World Boxing Organization (WBO), all of whom were dishing out championships to a parade of boxers who have become known as 'The Alphabet Boys'. There have also been others trying to make an initial impact, for instance the IBO, WBF, IBC and WBU. It is all in danger of diluting the value of what has always been considered the number one prize in sport. This, in processional order, is how the main Alphabet Boys won and lost their paper crowns.

ERNIE TERRELL, WBA titleholder 1965-1967

Ernie Terrell, born on 4 April 1939, was the first of the pretenders to the heavyweight throne. The WBA stripped Ali of his championship because he entered into a return-match agreement with Sonny Liston. Terrell, a 6 foot 6 inch giant from Chicago via Mississippi, was nominated to fight veteran Eddie Machen and outpointed him on 5 March 1965. He outpointed George Chuvalo and Doug Jones in title defences before a summit showdown with Ali in Houston on 6 February 1967. Ali handed out a humiliating hiding over 15 rounds, during which he repeatedly demanded that Terrell should call him by his new name instead of Cassius Clay. Terrell, the human skyscraper, was never the same force after his hammering by Ali.

JIMMY ELLIS, WBA titleholder 1968-1970

Jimmy Ellis, born on 24 February 1940, came from the same Louisville background as Muhammad Ali, and was one of Ali's best friends as well as his chief sparring partner. He outpointed Jerry Quarry on 27 April 1968, to win the WBA version of the title after Ali had been forced to surrender the crown because of his refusal to join the United States Army. Ellis successfully defended the title with a controversial points win against Floyd Patterson in Sweden on 14 September 1968, before being matched with Joe Frazier for the undisputed championship in New York on 16 February 1970. 'Smokin' Joe' floored Ellis at the end of the fourth round with a devastating left hook. He was saved by the bell, but was in no condition to come out for the fifth round. A stylish, upright boxer, Ellis continued to tour as a sparring partner with his Louisville pal Ali, but dropped out of championship contention because of eye problems.

LEON SPINKS, Undisputed titleholder 1978
Leon and Michael Spinks created ring history by becoming the first brothers to win Olympic titles, in the 1976 Games in Montreal. Leon, the light-heavyweight champion, was then rushed with indecent haste into a title fight with Muhammad Ali after only seven professional fights, six of which he won with one drawn. Born in St Louis on 11 July 1953, Leon caused one of the boxing shocks of the century by outpointing Ali at Las Vegas on 15 February 1978, but he only had the title on loan. Ali outpointed him in the return in New Orleans seven months later to win the crown for a record third time. These were peak performances by ex-Marine Spinks, who was never able to cope with the pressures and fame that come hand in hand with the world title. He had problems with drugs and seemed doomed to disappear back into the ghetto from which boxing had briefly released him. His attempt at a comeback turned into sad farce when he was knocked out in the first round by an opponent making his professional debut.

KEN NORTON, WBC titleholder 1978
Ken Norton, born in Jacksonville, Illinois, on 9 August 1945, was a 'paper' champion, the title being handed to him by the WBC after Leon Spinks had refused to defend against him because of his return match with Ali. Norton was named champion on account of a title eliminator victory over Jimmy Young in Las Vegas on 25 November 1977, but he, more than any of the other Alphabet Boys, deserves his place in this trip through the history of the world heavyweight champions because of his three marvellous battles with Ali. He broke Ali's jaw and outpointed him in their first contest in San Diego on 31 March 1973, and many spectators considered him unlucky to be judged a points loser in their two other meetings on 10 September 1973, and 28 September 1976. Norton had a magnificent physique and good boxing skills, but his reign was brief. Larry Holmes edged him out in a tremendous battle

in Las Vegas on 9 June 1978. His promising Hollywood acting career was finished by a car crash that left him partly crippled. His son, Ken Jnr, is a heralded American Football star and has created history by being on the winning side in three successive Superbowls.

JOHN TATE, WBA titleholder 1979-80

John Tate, born in Marion City, Arkansas, on 29 January 1955, became one of the biggest of all heavyweight champions when he outpointed South African Gerrie Coetzee for the vacant WBA title in Pretoria on 20 October 1979. Standing 6 foot 4 inches and weighing 17 stone 2 pounds (240 pounds), he captured the championship in his twentieth contest. He lost the title in dramatic fashion in his first defence on 31 March 1980, when Mike Weaver produced an explosive punch to knock his man-mountain opponent down and out in the last minute of their 15-round battle. Tate had turned professional after being hammered to a first-round defeat by Teofilo Stevenson in the 1976 Olympic semifinals. Following his knockout by Weaver, his hopes of getting back into the title reckoning were shattered when Trevor Berbick beat him in nine rounds in Montreal on 20 June 1980. His career was then wrecked by an addiction to drugs and alcohol, and he was given a three-year prison term for breaking a man's jaw while robbing him of $14.

MIKE WEAVER, WBA titleholder 1980-1982

Mike Weaver, born in Gatesville, Texas, on 14 June 1952, was always a dangerous opponent provided he could get past the first round! A mighty-muscled black Adonis of a fighter, he had a string of first-round knockout defeats in a seesawing career. His greatest moments were knocking out John Tate in the final minute to win the WBA title in Knoxville on 31 March 1980, and then defending it with a knockout win over Gerrie Coetzee in Bophuthatswana on 25 October 1980, and a points victory over James 'Quick' Tillis on 3 October 1981. But then his world came apart when Mike Dokes stopped him in 63 seconds of his third defence in Las Vegas on 10 December 1982. Weaver claimed he could have continued and screamed for a return. He came within a whisker of regaining the title, drawing with Dokes over 15 gruelling rounds. His career continued late into his thirties, but he was never able to recapture the form of his peak years.

MIKE DOKES, WBA titleholder 1982-1983

Mike Dokes, born in Akron, Ohio, on 10 August 1958, messed up what could have been one of the great careers in heavyweight boxing by getting involved in the drugs scene that is a black cloud over the American fight game. He was undefeated when he grabbed the WBA version of the world title from Mike Weaver in 1982, with a sensational 63 seconds victory that caused an uproar of controversy. 'Dynamite' Dokes had rocked Weaver with a big left hook, but most spectators thought the referee was too hasty in stopping the fight. Dokes clung on to the title by drawing with Weaver, but then suffered the first defeat of his career when he was clubbed to a tenth round defeat by Gerrie Coetzee at Richfield on 23 September 1983. His arrest on a drugs charge suddenly wrecked his comeback campaign. After rehabilitation treatment, he returned to the ring, but stoppages by Razor Ruddock and Evander Holyfield, followed by a return to his drug habit, pushed him out of championship contention.

GERRIE COETZEE, WBA titleholder 1983-84

Gerrie Coetzee, born in Boksburg, South Africa, on 4 August 1955, was known as the 'Bionic Man' because of surgery on his feared right hand, which prolonged his career. He was a devastating puncher, as he proved when stopping Leon Spinks in one round in Monte Carlo in 1979. Because of the politics of his country, Coetzee found it difficult to get top contenders into the ring with him but, when he finally got his title chance in 1983, he proved too powerful for Mike Dokes, stopping him in the tenth round to become the first South African to win the world heavyweight crown. He lost the WBA title in controversial circumstances, getting stopped by Greg Page in an eighth round that ran into overtime in Sun City on 1 December 1984. Coetzee's chances of getting back on to the title bandwagon ended with a shattering first round knockout defeat by British heavyweight hope Frank Bruno at Wembley in 1986.

TIM WITHERSPOON,
WBC titleholder 1984; WBA titleholder 1985-1986

Tim Witherspoon, born on 27 December 1957, was nicknamed 'Terrible Tim' by Muhammad Ali in the days when he hired the young

Philadelphian as his sparring partner. Witherspoon thought he had won the WBC title in his sixteenth professional fight but a disputed points decision went to Larry Holmes. When Holmes switched to the newly-founded International Boxing Federation (IBF), Witherspoon outpointed Greg Page for the vacant WBC crown on 9 March 1984. His reign was brief, Pinklon Thomas taking the title from him with a points win five months later. Witherspoon became only the third champion to regain the title when he outpointed Tony Tubbs in 1986, this time for the WBA version of the championship. He beat a drugs habit and, after a successful title defence against Frank Bruno at Wembley Stadium on 19 July 1986, he looked set for a big-money showdown with Mike Tyson. But then he was bombed to a stunning first round defeat by 'Bonecrusher' Smith in New York on 12 December 1986, after which he became frozen out of the title scene following a bitter legal battle with promoter Don King. He kept battling into the 1990s, but could never force his way back into the title picture.

GREG PAGE, WBA titleholder 1984-85

Greg Page, born on 25 October 1958, was out of the same Louisville, Kentucky, territory as Muhammad Ali and Jimmy Ellis. After a brilliant amateur career, he chalked up 23 successive wins as a professional to earn a fight with Tim Witherspoon for the vacant WBC title on 9 March 1984. Witherspoon outpointed him but, within nine months, Page had helped himself to a title by stopping Gerrie Coetzee in the eighth round of an eventful WBA championship contest in Sun City. A timekeeping error meant the round ran into extra time and it was in the closing moments that Page pounded Coetzee to defeat when by rights the South African should have been sitting on his stool. But the musical chairs with the title continued when Page was outpointed by Tony Tubbs at Buffalo, New York, on 29 April 1985. Page never really lived up to his early potential, and drifted out of the ratings.

PINKLON THOMAS, WBC titleholder 1984-1986

Pinklon Thomas, born in Pontiac, Michigan, on 10 February 1957, appeared to be the best of the new crop of 'dreadnought' heavyweights and realized his potential when outpointing Tim Witherspoon to win the WBC championship in Las Vegas on 31 August 1984. He looked set for a long reign and an eighth-round knockout defeat of Mike Weaver on 15 June 1985 seemed to confirm that he was a class above most other contenders. It was one of the biggest shocks of the decade when he lost his unbeaten record, and his title, to Trevor Berbick at Las Vegas on 22 March 1986. He started a comeback eight months later with a victory over William Hosea, but he went on the slide after taking a hammering from Mike Tyson in a world championship contest at Las Vegas on 30 May 1987. Like so many of the other Alphabet Boys, he got mixed up with drugs but he managed to beat the habit, and then became a trial horse opponent for up-and-coming prospects with much less talent than he showed in the early stages of his career.

TONY TUBBS, WBA titleholder 1985-1986

Tony Tubbs, born in Cincinnati, Ohio, on 15 February 1959, was nicknamed 'TNT', but he was not an explosive puncher, relying on skill to emerge as a title challenger. Tubbs is surprisingly light on his feet and a slick boxer considering his enormous 230-pound bulk. He won the WBA title by smartly outpointing Greg Page in what was tagged as 'The Buffalo Blockbuster' on 29 April 1985, but was then outmauled by Tim Witherspoon in his first defence on 17 January 1986. It was announced after the fight that Witherspoon had failed a drugs test and he was ordered to give Tubbs a return, but he took step-aside money so that Tim could defend against Frank Bruno – a fight that Witherspoon won in the eleventh round. After being blasted to a second-round defeat by Mike Tyson in Tokyo on 21 March 1988, Tubbs admitted to being hooked on cocaine. When he hit the comeback trail in 1991, he dropped a disputed points decision to the rising young prospect Riddick Bowe. In March 1992, he was tested positive for cocaine in Las Vegas, and was ordered to do 100 hours community service after being suspended by the Nevada Boxing Commission.

MICHAEL SPINKS, IBF titleholder 1985-1988

Michael Spinks, born in St Louis on 13 July 1956, was the 1976 Olympic middleweight gold medallist and, after an unbeaten four-year reign as world professional light-heavyweight champion, he challenged Larry Holmes for the IBF heavyweight crown at Las Vegas on 21 September 1985. Inspired by the wonderfully eccentric and dynamic manager-promoter Butch Lewis, he put on more than 20 pounds and the performance of a lifetime to outpoint the previously undefeated Holmes and to follow his brother, Leon, as heavyweight king. Just to show it was no fluke, he outpointed Holmes in the return match. Both decisions were angrily disputed by Holmes. An easy victory by Spinks over Norway's European champion Steffan Tangstadon 6 September 1986, set him up for a championship showdown with Mike Tyson in Atlantic City on 27 June 1988. Spinks folded in just 91 seconds against 'Iron Mike', and cried all the way to the bank as he announced his retirement after this first defeat as a professional.

TREVOR BERBICK, WBC titleholder 1986

Trevor Berbick, born in Port Anthony, Jamaica, on 1 August 1953, caused a major upset when he outpointed Pinklon Thomas to win the WBC version of the title in Las Vegas on 22 March 1986. It was his second bid for the title, having been outpointed by Larry Holmes five years earlier. He was Muhammad Ali's last opponent and scored a ten-rounds points victory in 1981 that at last convinced the great old champ that he should hang up his gloves. It was Berbick who stood between Mike Tyson and history in Las Vegas on 22 November 1986. But he did not stand for long, getting knocked down and stopped in two explosive rounds as Tyson became the youngest champion of them all. Berbick has since run into difficulties both inside and outside the ring. At one stage, the man who used to be a preacher had charges ranging against him that included theft, mortgage fraud, rape and assault, and – like his old rival Tyson – he was sent to prison. He resumed boxing on his release as Israel T. Berbick, and in his eighth comeback fight at the age of 40 was outpointed by Jimmy Thunder for the obscure Continental Americas title.

JAMES SMITH, WBA titleholder 1986

James 'Bonecrusher' Smith, born in Magnolia, North Carolina, on 3 April 1955, came in as a late substitute for the allegedly injured Tony Tubbs against Tim Witherspoon in New York on 12 December 1986, and snatched the WBA title away with a sensational smash-and-grab, first-round victory. Witherspoon, who held a points decision over Smith, was battered to the canvas three times and stopped on the three-knockdown rule. The victory made Bonecrusher the 'Cinderella Man' of the 1980s. He had not started boxing until 23 while serving as a sergeant in the US Army. After coming from behind to hand Frank Bruno his first defeat at Wembley on 13 May 1984, he failed in a bid for the IBF title held by Larry Holmes, who stopped him in 12 rounds on 9 November 1984. Smith was outpointed by Mike Tyson in an uninspiring fight for the undisputed title on 7 March 1987, and during a comeback campaign, was beaten by Razor Ruddock and then, after a long sequence of victories, surprisingly dropped a points decision to Levi Billups on 4 November 1991.

TONY TUCKER, IBF titleholder 1987

Tony Tucker, born in Grand Rapids, Michigan, on 28 December 1958, was shaping up as the best of the Alphabet Boys until he ran into the iron fists of Mike Tyson. He won the IBF title on 30 May 1987, by stopping James 'Buster' Douglas in ten rounds. Three months later, he took a pounding from Tyson, but managed to survive the full 12 rounds. He went off the rails after his points defeat and got involved in the drugs scene. Tucker looked to the disciplines demanded of boxing to help him beat the habit, and shaped well enough in a comeback campaign to earn a title shot against London-born Lennox Lewis in a WBC championship contest in Las Vegas on 8 May 1993. He climbed off the canvas to give Lewis a tough battle before losing the 12-rounds decision on points.

FRANCESCO DAMIANI, WBO titleholder 1989-1991

Francesco Damiani, born in Kavenna, Italy, on 4 October 1958, had an amateur career, the highlight of which was a victory over triple Olympic champion Teofilo Stevenson. He was the silver medallist at the Los Angeles Olympics in 1984, losing on points to Tyrell Biggs in the final. After winning the European title as a professional, Damiani became the first holder of yet another confusing version of the world heavyweight championship as the title became further devalued. He knocked out South African Johnny Duplooy in three rounds on 6 May 1989, to win the WBO crown. He successfully defended the title against Daniel Netto in 1990 before being knocked out by Ray Mercer in the ninth round in Atlantic City on 11 January 1991.

RAY MERCER, WBO titleholder 1991

Ray Mercer was a US Army sergeant when he won the 1988 Olympic heavyweight gold medal. He made rapid progress as a professional and, after outpointing Bert Cooper in a war in 1990, he knocked out Damiani in nine rounds to win the WBO title in 1991. After blasting out 'White Hope' Tommy Morrison in five rounds, he was stripped of the WBO title for agreeing to a match against the veteran Larry Holmes at Atlantic City on February 7, 1992. He was soundly outpointed and his championship value dropped several points. Mercer got involved in a bribery scandal when he was alleged to have offered his opponent, Jesse Ferguson, money to lose. He was said to have made the offer during the fight that could have earned him another crack at the title.

MICHAEL MOORER,
WBO titleholder 1992; WBA, IBF titleholder 1994

Michael Moorer, a product of the Detroit Kronk Gym, became the first southpaw heavyweight champion of the century when he twice got off the canvas to stop Bert Cooper in the fifth round of a fight for the vacant WBO title in Atlantic City on 15 May 1992. He surrendered the title to pursue more lucrative prizes and on 22 April 1994 – inspired by Tyson's former trainer Teddy Atlas – he stunned Evander Holyfield by outpointing him over 12 frantic rounds. But before the year was out, he had walked into the mighty right hand of George Foreman and was an ex-champion.

LENNOX LEWIS, WBC titleholder 1993-1994

Lennox Lewis became the first British-born world heavyweight champion since Bob Fitzsimmons when he was awarded the WBC belt after Riddick Bowe had relinquished it (by throwing it in a dustbin!). Lewis was rated champion on account of his sensational two-round stoppage of Razor Ruddock in a final eliminator at Earls Court on 31 October 1992. Standing 6 foot 5 inches and weighing around 16.5 stone (231 pounds), Lewis had looked the brightest of all the heavyweights chasing titles after launching his professional career under the management of Frank Maloney in London, where he was born on 2 September 1965. He had first come to world prominence when stopping Riddick Bowe in two rounds to win the super-heavyweight gold medal for his adopted country of Canada in the 1988 Seoul Olympics. In Britain, he was continually being compared to Frank Bruno, and the two great rivals met in a bitter showdown in Cardiff on 1 October 1993. Bruno was giving a good account of himself until walking into a left hook in the seventh round. He was forced back on to the ropes, and the referee had to rescue him as Lewis unloaded a barrage of punches on his defenceless opponent. Lewis underlined that he had power to go with his boxing skill when he stopped Phil Jackson in eight rounds, and then met Oliver McCall at Wembley on 24 September 1994 for what most people expected would be a comfortable defence of his crown. McCall, Mike Tyson's former sparring partner, produced an explosive right out of the blue in the second round and dropped Lewis for the first time in his career. He was up at the count of nine, but his legs were shaky and the referee decided that he was not in a fit state to continue. Lewis protested, but later shrugged off the disappointment of this first defeat in 26 fights, and he vowed to get back on the championship trail. He hired master motivator Emanuel Steward as his new trainer as he set out to re-establish himself as the heavyweight king. The first hurdle he had to clear was in the formidable shape of hard-hitting American, Lionel Butler.

TOMMY MORRISON, WBO titleholder 1993

Tommy Morrison was being billed as the new great American 'White Hope' until he was comprehensively beaten by Ray Mercer when challenging for the WBO title in Atlantic City on 18 October 1991. The publicity drums had been beating hard for Morrison, who was related to Hollywood hero John Wayne. He was given a starring role opposite Sylvester Stallone in *Rocky V*, but the script went wrong for him in the real ring when Mercer trapped him on the ropes in the fifth round and knocked him cold with a volley of punches to the jaw. They picked Morrison up and put him together again and, in Las Vegas on 7 June 1993, he had too much stamina and steam for old George Foreman, and outpointed him over twelve laborious rounds. In his first defence, Morrison stopped the obscure Tim Tomashek, who had been brought out of the audience at the last minute when the original opponent withdrew. The WBO later withdrew recognition of the sham as a title fight. Morrison then put his championship on the line against Michael Bentt in Tulsa on 29 October 1993. Few experts gave Bentt a hope of winning. Morrison clearly thought he had an easy job on his hands and came rushing across the ring in search of a quick knockout and soon had Bentt on the ropes under an all-out attack. He forgot about defence and was wide open as Bentt threw a counter punch that landed on his suspect jaw, and the referee stopped the fight with Morrison floundering and in trouble. It was as if the Indians had upped and massacred John Wayne.

MICHAEL BENTT, WBO titleholder 1993-1994

Michael Bentt, born in London and raised in America, took one of the quickest routes of all time to a world heavyweight title. He was knocked out in his debut and, just 11 fights later, was hailed as the WBO champion after his shock victory over Tommy Morrison. He then came to London to defend the championship against Herbie Hide at the Millwall Football Club ground on 19 March 1994. The publicity hype for the fight got out of control, and they were both fined by the British Boxing Board for scrapping in front of photographers in the street. Hide was always in command in the official fight against Bentt, who seemed listless, weak and unsteady from the opening exchanges. Bentt was taken to hospital after being knocked out in the seventh round and there were brain-damage scares. His career had ended on a sad note.

HERBIE HIDE, WBO titleholder 1994

Herbie Hide, born in Nigeria on 27 August 1971 and raised in Norfolk, captured the WBO title in his twenty-sixth professional fight. He had won all but one of his contests inside the distance. Few of his opponents were of any real quality, and in March 1995, he took an enormous step up in class when putting his title on the line against Riddick Bowe who was too big and strong for him and knocked him out in the sixth round. Hide, a flashy boxer with fast fists and solid punching power, stopped Conroy Nelson in two rounds in front of his hometown fans in Norwich on 21 January 1992 to win the vacant WBC international title. Just over a year, later he added the vacant British title to his collection when stopping Michael Murray in five rounds at Dagenham. He relinquished the British crown to concentrate on his world title ambitions, and gave a flawless performance against Michael Bentt, who never once troubled him and looked as if he should not have been allowed into the ring with the confident Hide. But Bowe was a bridge too far.

OLIVER McCALL, WBC titleholder 1994

Oliver McCall was more famous as Mike Tyson's sparring partner than as a world title contender until he exploded his right fist on the jaw of Lennox Lewis at Wembley on 24 September 1994. One of the first people McCall telephoned after his shock victory, was his pal Tyson in prison. "When you come out, Mike, we can get it together," he told him. Success had come late for McCall. He was approaching 30 when he stopped Lewis but, with five children to feed, he was a hungry fighter and ready to take on all-comers. Larry Holmes was the next in line for him, with Frank Bruno waiting in the wings. Bruno had often hired McCall as a sparring partner, and that was the way he was looked on in the boxing world – as somebody to help the big earners prepare for battle. McCall – nicknamed the 'Atomic Bull' – had put together a record of only 29 fights in his nine years as a professional, preferring to do most of his earning in the gymnasium. At 6 foot 2 inches, McCall conceded three inches in height to Lewis, but prepared himself to throw right hand bombs over the sometimes lazy Lewis left lead. His plan worked to perfection, and when he detonated his right it flattened Lewis, stunned the Wembley crowd and cheered up Prisoner 922335 in his cell in Indiana.

RIDDICK BOWE,
WBA, IBF titleholder (He relinquished the WBC crown)

Riddick Bowe was briefly undisputed champion of the world until tossing the WBC belt into a dustbin rather than defend it against his old foe Lennox Lewis. Like Mike Tyson, Bowe was born and brought up in Brooklyn and used boxing as his springboard out of the ghetto. Lennox Lewis had raised doubts about his ability to absorb a punch when he stopped him in two rounds in the1988 Olympic super-heavyweight final, but there has been no sign of weakness under pressure throughout his professional career. His peak performance came when he challenged Evander Holyfield for the three main titles at Las Vegas on 13 November 1992, surviving an early crisis to to win an epic battle on points. He successfully defended the WBA and IBF titles against Michael Dokes and Jesse Ferguson before losing them back to Holyfield in another war in Las Vegas on 6 November 1993. He was back as a champion in March 1995 when he knocked out Herbie Hide in six rounds to win the WBO title. He then visited Mike Tyson in prison to offer him a title shot.

JAMES DOUGLAS 1990

Born Columbus, Ohio, 7 April 1960.
Ht: 6ft 4in Wt: 16st 8lbs (232lbs) Reach: 84in Chest: 44-48in Fist: 13.5in
Career span: 1981-1990.
Record: 37 fights, 30 wins (KOs 19), 7 losses (KO'd 2).
Age at which title was won: 29 (36th fight).

JAMES 'Buster' Douglas had two universally recognized world title fights, during which he managed to cause first the biggest shock and then one of the biggest stinks in boxing history. His knockout defeat of Mike Tyson in 1990 was a performance of a lifetime in which he fought like a lion. Eight months later, he went out like a lamb. He surrendered the crown so tamely to Evander Holyfield that it was almost impossible to believe that this was the same fighter who had vanquished the 'unbeatable' Tyson. Douglas was taught to box at an early age by his father Billy Douglas, who had been a highly-rated middleweight. Douglas Senior had the last fight of his long career only ten months before his son turned professional. Nicknamed 'Buster', Douglas Junior preferred basketball to boxing and won a two-year scholarship to a college in Kansas where his 6 foot 4 inch height and his 84-inch reach made him a formidable force on the basketball court. It was after winning a junior Olympics boxing title that he decided to follow in his father's footsteps, but the way his weight seesawed between 220 pounds and a massive 245 pounds suggested that he was not totally dedicated to his chosen profession. Despite his great bulk, he had rarely looked a big puncher and had stopped only 18 of his opponents. He fought Tony Tucker for the paper IBF crown on 30 May 1987, and suddenly ran out of steam and ambition on his way to a painful tenth-round defeat. It was one of six losses in a 35-fight career before he stepped into the Tokyo Dome ring on Sunday, 11 February 1990, for what everybody thought would be a ritual slaughter. But Tyson made the mistake of completely underestimating his challenger and paid the price with a tenth-round knockout defeat. He seemed to be lacking condition and enthusiasm when he defended the title against Evander Holyfield eight months later and went down and out in the third round to the first heavy blow of the fight. In 1995 he started trying to shed weight for a comeback and a hoped-for return with Tyson.

EVANDER HOLYFIELD 1990-92, 93-94

Born Atmore, Alabama, October 19 1962.
Ht: 6ft 2in Wt: 15st 2lbs (212lbs) Reach: 77in Chest: 43-46in Fist: 13in
Nickname: The Real Deal. Career span: 1984-
Record: 31 fights, 29 wins (KOs 24), 2 losses.
Rounds boxed: 201. Age at which title was won: 28 (25th fight).

EVANDER Holyfield rose to the top like cream, with a procession of impressive victories, winning his fights with style and precision in contrast to Tyson's bludgeoning ferocity. He launched his professional career as a cruiserweight after a disqualification cost him almost certain gold medal success in the 1984 Olympics. In only his twelfth contest in Atlanta on 12 July 1986, he took the world WBA title from Dwight Muhammad Qawi and defended the title four times before pumping pounds on to his frame with a special diet and fitness programme. He made his debut in the heavyweight ranks as a solid, 210-pounds force in 1988 with a fifth round victory over James 'Quick' Tillis. Holyfield hammered out spectacular victories over Pinklon Thomas, Michael Dokes, Adilson Rodrigues and Alex Stewart to set up what he thought would be a get-rich-quick confrontation with Mike Tyson. He had the consolation of taking the title from Tyson's conqueror, 'Buster' Douglas, with an easy third-round knockout victory. The new champion had to dig deep down into his boots before pounding out a points victory over the old champion George Foreman and, after his showdown with Tyson had been called off, he struggled before stopping Bert Cooper in seven rounds. A laboured points victory over Larry Holmes on 18 June 1992 did little to boost his reputation, and five months later he lost a points verdict and his titles to Riddick Bowe. This was when Holyfield showed his great character, beating Bowe on points in a return fight interrupted by a parachuting skydiver invading the ring. Only in America! After having his title taken away from him by Michael Moorer in a brawling battle on 22 April 1994, Holyfield was diagnosed as having a heart condition. He announced his retirement, but then revealed that he had been cured after visiting a faith healer and set about making plans for another assault on the world championship. Mike Tyson and a share of $50 million was his target.

MIKE TYSON 1986-1990

Born Brooklyn, New York, 30 June 1966.
Ht: 5ft 11in Wt: 16st (224lbs) Reach: 71in Chest: 43-45in Fist: 13in
Nicknames: Iron Mike, Mighty Mike. Career span: 1985-
Record: 42 fights, 41 wins (36 KOs), 1 loss (KO'd).
Total rounds boxed: 157. Age at which title was won: 20 (28th fight).

THIS book has been all about Mike Tyson, the man and the fighter. But just for the record he became the world's youngest world heavyweight champion at 20 years, four months and 22 days, when he bombed out Trevor Berbick in two rounds on 22 November 1986. In nine title fights after defeating Berbick, Tyson beat 'Bonecrusher' Smith (points, twelfth round, 1987), Pinklon Thomas (stopped, sixth round, 1987), Tony Tucker (points, twelfth round, 1987), Tyrell Biggs (stopped, seventh round, 1987), Larry Holmes (stopped, fourth round, 1988), Tony Tubbs (stopped, second round, 1988), Michael Spinks (knockout, first round, 1988), Frank Bruno (stopped, fifth round, 1989) and Carl Williams (stopped, first round, 1989). Tyson appeared to be cracking under all the well-chronicled, self-inflicted pressure, but the boxing world was still astonished when he lost his title to James 'Buster' Douglas in Tokyo on 11 February 1990, in what was expected to be just a routine defence. Frank Bruno had showed that Tyson could be hit and hurt by staggering him in the first round of their world title fight, and that should have sounded alarm bells. Too many of his opponents had frozen with fear because of the hype that surrounded Iron Mike, but Douglas realized that he was only human and took the fight to him. There were loud and angry complaints from the Tyson camp over a slow count that allowed Douglas to escape a possible knockout in the eighth round, but most observers agreed that Buster thoroughly deserved his startling victory. Tyson licked his wounds and was back in dynamic action four months later, winning in one round against Henry Tillman, the opponent who had beaten him in the 1984 US Olympic trials. On December 8, 1990, he knocked out Alex Stewart in one round in Atlantic City. Then in 1991 he had two wars with Razor Ruddock in Las Vegas, winning both of them, but with performances that made critics wonder if his best was behind him. He had even bigger battles to face outside the ring.

MIKE TYSON: A Chronology

1966: Born at Bedford-Stuyvesant, Brooklyn, on 30 June 1966.

1979: Arrested for purse snatching as a 12-year-old in New York. Sent to Tryon School for Boys.

1980: Bobby Stewart, a social worker and boxing instructor at Tryon, brings Tyson to Cus D'Amato's attention. Tyson moves to D'Amato's home in Catskill. Teddy Atlas trains him under the eye of D'Amato.

1982: Expelled from Catskill High School for a series of transgressions, including threatening a teacher. Lorna, Tyson's mother, dies of cancer. Atlas is reported to have held a gun to Tyson's head and warned him about his behaviour after he makes a lewd suggestion to a 12-year-old girl. Atlas is sacked and Kevin Rooney takes over as trainer.

1983: Tyson reaches the final of the National Golden Gloves tournament in which he is outpointed by Craig Payne.

1984: D'Amato becomes Tyson's legal guardian, Camille Ewald his surrogate mother. Tyson is beaten by Henry Tillman in the US Olympic trials. He cries and punches a tree in frustration. Decides to turn professional with Jim Jacobs and Bill Cayton as co-managers.

1985: Makes professional debut on 6 March with a first round stoppage of Hector Mercedes. D'Amato dies of pneumonia on 4 November. Nine days later Tyson wins his twelfth professional fight.

1986: Tyson is accused on 20 February of sexually propositioning a female sales clerk in an Albany shopping mall and of becoming violent and abusive when she rebuffs him. Later the same night, he is ejected from an Albany movie theatre following a similar incident. On 22 November he knocks out Trevor Berbick in the second round in Las Vegas to win the World Boxing Council heavyweight title. At 20 years, four months and 22 days, he becomes the youngest heavyweight champion in history.

1987: Outpoints James 'Bonecrusher' Smith in Las Vegas to win the World Boxing Association heavyweight title on 7 March. Stops Pinklon Thomas in the sixth round in Las Vegas to retain WBA-WBC heavyweight titles. Parking lot attendant alleges Tyson tried to kiss a female employee and then struck him when he intervened. Charged with misdemeanour assault and battery. Jim Jacobs pays $105,000 to settle case out of court. Outpoints Tony Tucker in Las Vegas to retain WBA-WBC heavyweight titles and to win the International Boxing Federation heavyweight title on 1 August. Stops Tyrell Biggs in the seventh round in Atlantic City to retain world heavyweight title on 16 October.

1988: Knocks out Larry Holmes in the fourth round in Atlantic City, to retain world heavyweight title on 22 January. Marries Robin Givens in Chicago on 7 February. Knocks out Tony Tubbs in the second round in Tokyo to retain world heavyweight title on 21 March. Jim Jacobs is buried in Los Angeles on 25 March following his death from leukaemia. Robin Givens and her mother, Ruth Roper, demand access to a trust fund set up for Tyson. Robin Givens and family go public with tales of beatings by Tyson on 17 June. Knocks out Michael Spinks in 91 seconds in Atlantic City, to retain world heavyweight title on 27 June. Robin says in a nationally televised interview on 30 September that Tyson is a manic depressive and their marriage is a living hell. Tyson sits meekly next to her. Two days later, police are called to the Bernardsville, NJ, home after Tyson hurls furniture out the window and forces Givens and her mother to flee the house. Police dismiss the incident as 'a domestic disturbance'. Givens files for divorce on 7 October. Tyson countersues Givens for divorce and annulment six days later. Tyson announces that he is becoming a partner with Don King. Fires trainer Kevin Rooney. Sandra Miller of Queens, NY, sues Tyson on 12 December for allegedly grabbing her, propositioning her and insulting her at a Manhattan nightclub. Three days later, Lori Davis of Bay Shore, NY, sues Tyson for allegedly grabbing her buttocks while she was dancing at the same nightclub, on the same night as the incident with Miller.

1989: Flies to Dominican Republic to finalize his divorce on Valentine's Day. Eleven days, later stops Frank Bruno in the fifth round in Las Vegas to retain his world heavyweight title. Stops Carl 'The Truth' Williams in the first round in Atlantic City to retain world heavyweight title on 21 July.

1990: Tyson is knocked out by James 'Buster' Douglas in the tenth round in Tokyo and loses his world heavyweight title on 11 February. Knocks out Henry Tillman in the first round of a non-title fight in Las Vegas on 16 June. Phyllis Polaner, former aid to Givens, announces on 17 August that she is suing Tyson for alleged sexual assault and harassment. A New York City civil jury finds Tyson committed battery in the Sandra Miller case. She is awarded just $100 in damages because the jury decides Tyson's behaviour was "not outrageous". Knocks out Alex Stewart in the first round of a non-title fight in Atlantic City on 8 December.

1991: After a guest celebrity appearance at a black beauty pageant in Indianapolis in July, Tyson is accused of rape by 18-year-old contestant Desiree Washington. In October, Tyson injures cartilage in left rib cage while training for fight with heavyweight champion, Evander Holyfield. The fight is called off after Marion Superior Court Judge Patricia J. Gifford denies motion to postpone the rape trial.

1992: The rape trial begins with jury selection in Marion Superior Court on 27 January. Following nine hours of deliberation by the jury, Tyson is found guilty on one count of rape and two counts of deviate sexual conduct. The three counts carry a maximum penalty of 60 years in prison. On 26 March Judge Patricia Gifford sentences Tyson to six years in prison, denies him bail and orders him to serve the term immediately.

1995: Tyson is released from jail on 25 March, and plans a comeback to the ring. Don King (with the powerful support of the *Showtime* TV company) is the promoter favourite to launch his return, but Butch Lewis, the Duva brothers and a queue of promoters are jostling for his services. Riddick Bowe, like Tyson, born in a Brooklyn ghetto, visits him in prison after taking the WBO heavyweight title from Britain's Herbie Hide. Bowe's manager, Rock Newman, outlines to Tyson how he can generate $100,000 from just one fight against his man. George Foreman, stripped of the WBA title for refusing to defend against a rated opponent, is also looking in Tyson's direction, along with Oliver McCall, Frank Bruno, Buster Douglas and every heavyweight dreaming of picking up millions of dollars for the dubious privelege of being punched by the former champion. Hundreds of reporters, photographers and televiosion crews descend on Indiana for Mike Tyson's farewell to prison. They are all there to record *The Release of Power*.

MIKE TYSON: The amateur

It has been continually mis-reported that Mike Tyson had 26 amateur contests before turning professional. Thanks to the considerable help of ABC Television fight statistician Bob Yalen, we have been able to trace 35 contests. He had another 19 unrecorded 'learning experience' bouts on unofficial 'smoker' shows.

	1981	
	Region I Junior Olympics at Queens, New York	
May	A.N.Other	WRSC1
	National Junior Olympics at Colorado Springs	
June	Jesus Esparza	WRSC1
June	Randy Wesley	WRSC1
June 27	Joe Cortez	WRSC1
	1982	
	Junior Olympics Regionals at Syracuse	
April	Tito Llanes	WRSC1
	National Junior Olympics at Colorado Springs	
June	Jonathan Littles	WRSC2
June	Dan Cozad	WRSC1
June 26	Kelton Brown	WRet1
	Region I USA/ABF Tournament at Boston	
November 19	Kilbert Pierce	WPts3
	US Amateur Championships at Indianapolis	
December 12	Al Evans	LRSC3
	1983	
	Western Massachusetts Golden Gloves at Holyoke	
February	Jimmy Johnson	WKO 1
	New England Golden Gloves at Lowell	
February 16	Jim Rayborn	WPts3
	New York State Golden Gloves at Utica	
		Walkover in finals
	National Golden Gloves Championships at St. Louis	
March	Ronald Williams	WRSC1
March	Andrew Stokes	WRSC3

March	Mike Bardwell	WRSC1
March	Warren Thompson	WPts3
March	Craig Payne	LPts3
	Ohio State Fair at Columbus	
August	Jeff Goff	WKO1
August	Olian Alexander	Walkover
	US Junior Amateur Championships at Colorado Springs	
August	David Yonko	WRSC1
August	Mark Scott	WRSC1
	USA v West Germany at Lake Placid	
September 16	Peter Geier	WRet1
	New England Amateur Championships at Lake Placid	
October 22	Results unrecorded	
	US Amateur Championships at Colorado Springs	
November	Kimmuel Odom	LDis2
	1984	
	National Golden Gloves Championships at St. Louis	
April	Roger Pepel	WON
April	Derek Isaman	WON
April	Johnny Williams	WRSC1
April	Richard Johnson	WRSC3
April 21	Jonathan Littles	WRSC1
	US Olympic Trials at Fort Worth	
June	A.N.Other	WPts3
June	Henry Milligan	WRSC2
June 10	Henry Tillman	LPts3
	US Olympic Box-Offs at Las Vegas	
July 7	Henry Tillman	LPts3
	Empire State Games at Syracuse	
August 18	Winston Bent	WRSC
	US Junior Amateur Championships at Lake Placid	
August 23	Kelton Brown	WRSC1
	International Tournamen in Tampere, Finland	
September	Hakan Brock	WON

MIKE TYSON: The Professional

1985

March 6	Hector Mercedes	WRSF1	Albany, NY
April 4	Trent Singleton	WRSF1	Albany, NY
May 23	Don Halpin	WKO4	Albany, NY
June 20	Ricardo Spain	WRSF1	Atlantic City
July 11	John Alderson	WRet2	Atlantic City
July 19	Larry Sims	WRSF3	Ploughkeepsie
August 15	Lorenzo Canady	WRSF1	Atlantic City
September 5	Michael Johnson	WRSF1	Atlantic City
October 9	Donnie Long	WRSF1	Atlantic City
October 25	Robert Colay	WRSF1	Atlantic City
November 1	Sterling Benjamin	WKO1	Latham, NY
November 13	Eddie Richardson	WKO1	Houston, Texas
November 22	Conroy Nelson	WKO2	Latham, NY
December 6	Sammy Scaff	WKO1	Felt Forum, NY
December 27	Mark Young	WRSF1	Latham, NY

1986

January 11	Dave Jaco	WRSF1	Albany, NY
January 24	Mike Jameson	WRSF5	Atlantic City
February 21	Jesse Ferguson	WRSF6	Troy, NY
March 10	Steve Zouski	WRSF3	Uniondale, NY
May 3	James Tillis	WPts10	Glens Falls, NY
May 20	Mitch Green	WPts10	New York City
June 13	Reggie Gross	WRSF1	New York City
June 28	William Hosea	WKO1	Troy, NY
July 11	Lorenzo Boyd	WKO2	Swan Lake, NY
July 26	Marvis Frazier	WKO1	Glens Fall, NY
August 17	Jose Ribalta	WRSF10	Atlantic City
September 6	Alfonzo Ratliff	WRSF2	Las Vegas
November 22	Trevor Berbick	WRSF2	Las Vegas

(Won WBC title)

1987

March 7	James Smith	WPts12	Las Vegas
	(Retained WBC title, won WBA title)		
May 30	Pinklon Thomas	WRSF6	Las Vegas
	(Retained WBC/WBA titles)		
August 1	Tony Tucker	WPts12	Las Vegas
	(Unified heavyweight title)		
October 16	Tyrell Biggs	WRSF7	Atlantic City
	(Retained unified title)		
	1988		
January 22	Larry Holmes	WRSF4	Atlantic City
	(Retained unified title)		
March 21	Tony Tubbs	WRSF2	Tokyo
	(Retained unified title)		
June 27	Michael Spinks	WKO1	Atlantic City
	(Retained unified title)		
	1989		
February 25	Frank Bruno	WRSF5	Las Vegas
	(Retained unified title)		
July 21	Carl Williams	WRSF1	Atlantic City
	(Retained unified title)		
	1990		
February 11	James Douglas	LKO10	Tokyo
	(Lost unified title)		
June 16	Henry Tillman	WKO1	Las Vegas
December 8	Alex Stewart	WRSF1	Atlantic City
	1991		
March 18	Donovan Ruddock	WRSF7	Las Vegas
June 28	Donovan Ruddock	WPts12	Las Vegas

Record: 42 fights, 41 wins (36 stoppages), 1 loss

FOR THE RECORD

WORLD HEAVYWEIGHT TITLE FIGHTS

James J. Corbett wko21 John L. Sullivan, New Orleans 9.7.1892
James J. Corbett wko3 Charlie Mitchell, Jacksonville 25.1.94
Bob Fitzsimmons wko14 James J. Corbett, Carson City 17.3.97
James J. Jeffries wko11 Bob Fitzsimmons, Coney Island 9.6.99
James J. Jeffries wpts25 Tom Sharkey, Coney Island 3.11.99
James J. Jeffries wko23 Corbett, Coney Island 11.5.1900
James J. Jeffries wret5 Gus Ruhlin, San Francisco 15.11.01
James J. Jeffries wko8 Bob Fitzsimmons, San Francisco 25.7.02
James J. Jeffries wko10 James J. Corbett, San Francisco 14.8.03
James J. Jeffries wko2 Jack Munroe, San Francisco 26.8.04
Jeffries announced his retirement as undefeated champion
Marvin Hart wrsf12 Jack Root, Reno 3.7.05
Tommy Burns wpts20 Marvin Hart, Los Angeles 23.2.06
Tommy Burns wko15 Jim Flynn, Los Angeles 2.10.06
Tommy Burns drew 20 Phil Jack O'Brian, Los Angeles 28.11.06
Tommy Burns wpts20 Phil Jack O'Brian, Los Angeles 8.5.07
Tommy Burns wko1 Bill Squires, California 4.7.07
Tommy Burns wko10 Gunner Moir, London 2.12.07
Tommy Burns wko4 Jack Palmer, London 10.2.08
Tommy Burns wko1 Jem Roche, Dublin 17.3.08
Tommy Burns wko5 Jewey Smith, Paris 18.4.08
Tommy Burns wko13 Bill Squires, Paris 13.6.08
Tommy Burns wko13 Bill Squires, Sydney 24.8.08
Tommy Burns wko6 Bill Lang, Melbourne 2.9.08
Jack Johnson wrsf14 Tommy Burns, Sydney 26.12.08
Jack Johnson wko12 Stanley Ketchel, California 16.10.09
Jack Johnson wrsf15 James J. Jeffries, Reno 4.7.10
Jack Johnson wrsf9 Jim Flynn, Las Vegas 4.7.12
Jack Johnson wko2 Andre Spoul, Paris 28.11.13
Jack Johnson drew10 Jim Johnson, Paris 19.12.13
Jack Johnson wpts20 Frank Moran, Paris 27.6.14

Jess Willard wko26 Jack Johnson, Havana 5.4.15
Jess Willard nd10 Frank Moran, New York 25.3.16
Jack Dempsey wret3 Jess Willard, Toledo 4.7.19
Jack Dempsey wko3 Billy Miske, Benton Harbour 6.9.20
Jack Dempsey wko12 Bill Brennan, New York 14.12.20
Jack Dempsey wko4 Georges Carpentier, Jersey City 2.7.21
Jack Dempsey wpts15 Tom Gibbons, Montana 4.7.23
Jack Dempsey wko2 Luis Angel Firpo, New York 14.9.23
Gene Tunney wpts10 Jack Dempsey, Philadelphia 23.9.26
Gene Tunney wpts10 Jack Dempsey, Chicago 22.9.27
Gene Tunney wrsf11 Tom Heeney, New York 23.7.28
Tunney announced his retirement as undefeated champion
Max Schmeling wdis4 Jack Sharkey, New York 12.6.30
Max Schmeling wrsf15 Young Stribling, Cleveland 3.7.31
Jack Sharkey wpts15 Max Schmeling, Long Island NY 21.6.32
Primo Carnera wko6 Jack Sharkey, Long Island NY 29.6.33
Primo Carnera wpts15 Paulino Uzcudun, Rome 22.10.33
Primo Carnera wpts15 Tommy Loughran, Miami 1.3.34
Max Baer wrsf11 Primo Carnera, Long Island NY 14.6.34
James J. Braddock wpts15 Max Baer, Long Island NY 13.6.35
Joe Louis wko8 James J. Braddock, Chicago 22.6.37
Joe Louis wpts15 Tommy Farr, New York 30.8.37
Joe Louis wko3 Nathan Mann, New York 23.2.38
Joe Louis wko5 Harry Thomas, Chicago 1.4.38
Joe Louis wko1 Max Schmeling, New York 22.6.38
Joe Louis wrsf1 John Henry Lewis, New York 25.1.39
Joe Louis wko1 Jack Roper, Los Angeles 17.4.39
Joe Louis wrsf4 Tony Galento, New York 28.6.39
Joe Louis wko11 Bob Pastor, Detroit 20.9.39
Joe Louis wpts15 Arturo Godoy, New York 9.2.40
Joe Louis wrsf2 Johnny Paychek, New York 29.3.40
Joe Louis wrsf8 Arturo Godoy, New York 20.6.40
Joe Louis wret6 Al McCoy, Boston 16.12.40
Joe Louis wko5 Red Burman New York, 31.1.41
Joe Louis wko2 Gus Dorazio, Philadelphia 17.2.41
Joe Louis wrsf13 Abe Simon, Detroit 21.3.41
Joe Louis wrsf9 Tony Musto, St Louis 8.4.41

Joe Louis wdis7 Buddy Baer, Washington 23.5.41
Joe Louis wko13 Billy Conn, New York 18.6.41
Joe Louis wrsf6 Lou Nova, New York 29.9.41
Joe Louis wko1 Buddy Baer, New York 9.1.42
Joe Louis wko6 Abe Simon, New York 27.3.42
Joe Louis wko8 Billy Conn, New York 19.6.46
Joe Louis wko1 Tami Mauriello, New York 18.9.46
Joe Louis wpts15 Jersey Joe Walcott, New York 5.12.47
Joe Louis wko11 Jersey Joe Walcott, New York 25.6.48
Louis announced his retirement as undefeated champion
Ezzard Charles wpts15 Jersey Joe Walcott, Chicago 22.6.49
(NBA title)
Ezzard Charles wrsf7 Gus Lesnevich, New York 10.8.49
Ezzard Charles wko8 Pat Valentino, San Francisco 14.10.49
Ezzard Charles wrsf14 Freddy Beshore, Buffalo 15.8.50
Ezzard Charles wpts15 Joe Louis, New York 27.9.50
(Undisputed title)
Ezzard Charles wko11 Nick Barone, Cincinnati 5.12.50
Ezzard Charles wrsf10 Lee Oma, New York 12.1.51
Ezzard Charles wpts15 Jersey Joe Walcott, Detroit 7.3.51
Ezzard Charles wpts15 Joey Maxim, Chicago 30.5.51
Jersey Joe Walcott wko7 Ezzard Charles, Pittsburgh 18.7.51
Jersey Joe Walcott wpts15 Ezzard Charles, Philadelphia 5.6.52
Rocky Marciano wko13 Jersey Joe Walcott, Philadelphia 23.9.52
Rocky Marciano wko1 Jersey Joe Walcott, Chicago 15.5.53
Rocky Marciano wrsf11 Roland LaStarza, New York 24.9.53
Rocky Marciano wpts15 Ezzard Charles, New York 17.6.54
Rocky Marciano wko8 Ezzard Charles, New York 17.9.54
Rocky Marciano wrsf9 Don Cockell, San Francisco 16.5.55
Rocky Marciano wko9 Archie Moore, New York 21.9.55
Marciano announced his retirement as undefeated champion
Floyd Patterson wko5 Archie Moore, Chicago 30.11.56
Floyd Patterson wrsf10 Tommy Jackson, New York 29.7.57
Floyd Patterson wko6 Pete Rademacher, Seattle 22.8.57
Floyd Patterson wret12 Roy Harris, Los Angeles 18.8.58
Floyd Patterson wko11 Brian London, Indianapolis 1.5.59
Ingemar Johansson wrsf3 Floyd Patterson, New York 26.6.59

Floyd Patterson wko5 Ingemar Johansson, New York 20.6.60
Floyd Patterson wko6 Ingemar Johansson, Miami 13.3.61
Floyd Patterson wko4 Tom McNeeley, Toronto 4.12.61
Sonny Liston wko1 Floyd Patterson, Chicago 25.9.62
Sonny Liston wko1 Floyd Patterson, Las Vegas 22.7.63
Cassius Clay wret6 Sonny Liston, Miami 25.2.64
Clay changed his name to Muhammad Ali. He was stripped of WBA title because he signed for return bout with Liston, 14.9.64
Ernie Terrell wpts15 Eddie Machen, Chicago 5.3.65
(*Vacant WBA title)*
Muhammad Ali wko1 Sonny Liston, Maine 25.5.65
Ernie Terrell wpts15 George Chulavo, Toronto 1.11.65
(*WBA title*)
Muhammad Ali wrsf12 Floyd Patterson, Las Vegas 22.11.65
Muhammad Ali wpts15 George Chuvalo, Toronto 29.3.66
Muhammad Ali wrsf6 Henry Cooper, London 21.5.66
Ernie Terrell wpts15 Doug Jones, Houston 28.6.66
(*WBA title)*
Muhammad Ali wko3 Brian London, London 6.8.66
Muhammad Ali wrsf12 Karl Mildenberger, Frankfurt 10.9.66
Muhammad Ali wrsf3 Cleveland Williams, Houston 14.11.66
Muhammad Ali wpts15 Ernie Terrell, Houston 6.2.67
(*Undisputed title)*
Muhammad Ali wko7 Zora Folley, New York 22.3.67
Ali stripped of both titles for refusing to join US Army, 28.4.67
Joe Frazier wrsf11 Buster Matthis, New York 4.3.68
(*New York State version of vacant title)*
Jimmy Ellis wpts15 Jerry Quarry, Oakland 27.4.68
(WBA version of vacant title)
Joe Frazier wret2 Manuel Ramos, New York 24.6.68
(New York State title)
Jimmy Ellis wpts15 Floyd Patterson, Stockholm 14.9.68
(WBA title)
Joe Frazier wpts15 Oscar Bonavena, Philadelphia 10.12.68
(New York State title)
Joe Frazier wko1 Dave Zyglewicz, Houston 22.4.69
(*New York State title)*

Joe Frazier wrsf7 Jerry Quarry, New York 26.6.69
(New York State title)
Joe Frazier wret4 Jimmy Ellis, New York 16.2.70
(Undisputed title)
Joe Frazier wko2 Bob Foster, Detroit 18.11.70
Joe Frazier wpts15 Muhammad Ali, New York 8.3.71
Joe Frazier wrsf4 Terry Daniels, New Orleans 15.1.72
Joe Frazier wrsf4 Ron Stander, Omaha 25.5.72
George Foreman wrsf2 Joe Frazier, Kingston Jamaica 22.1.73
George Foreman wko1 Joe Roman, Tokyo 1.9.73
George Foreman wrsf2 Ken Norton, Caracas 26.3.74
Muhammad Ali wko8 George Foreman, Kinshasa 30.10.74
Muhammad Ali wrsf15 Chuck Wepner, Cleveland 24.3.75
Muhammad Ali wrsf11 Ron Lyle, Las Vegas 16.5.75
Muhammad Ali wpts15 Joe Bugner, Kuala Lumpur 1.7.75
Muhammad Ali wret14 Joe Frazier, Manila 1.10.75
Muhammad Ali wko5 Jean-Pierre Coopman, Puerto Rico 10.2.76
Muhammad Ali wpts15 Jimmy Young, Maryland 30.4.76
Muhammad Ali wrsf5 Richard Dunn, Munich 25.5.76
Muhammad Ali wpts15 Ken Norton, New York 28.9.76
Muhammad Ali wpts15 Alfredo Evangelista, Maryland 16.5.77
Muhammad Ali wpts15 Earnie Shavers, New York 29.9.77
Leon Spinks wpts15 Muhammad Ali, Las Vegas 15.2.78
*Spinks was stripped of the WBC version for failure to defend against **Ken Norton**, who was proclaimed WBC champion*
Larry Holmes wpts15 Ken Norton, Las Vegas 10.6.78
(WBC title)
Muhammad Ali wpts15 Leon Spinks, New Orleans 15.9.78
(WBA title)
Larry Holmes wko7 Alfredo Evangelista, Las Vegas 10.11.78
(WBC title)
Larry Holmes wrsf7 Osvaldo Ocasio, Las Vegas 24.3.79
Larry Holmes wrsf12 Mike Weaver, New York 22.6.79
Larry Holmes wrsf11 Earnie Shavers, Las Vegas 28.9.79
Ali announced his retirement as WBA champion, September 1979
John Tate wpts15 Gerrie Coetzee, Johannesburg 20.10.79
(Vacant WBA title)

Larry Holmes wko6 Lorenzo Zanon, Las Vegas 3.2.80
Larry Holmes wrsf8 Leroy Jones, Las Vegas 31.3.80
Mike Weaver wko15 John Tate, Knoxville 31.3.80
(WBA title)
Larry Holmes wrsf7 Scott Le Doux, Bloomington 7.7.80
Larry Holmes wret10 Muhammad Ali, Las Vegas 2.10.80
Mike Weaver wko13 Gerrie Coetzee, Sun City 25.10.80
(WBA title)
Larry Holmes wpts15 Trevor Berbick, Las Vegas 14.4.81
Larry Holmes wrsf3 Leon Spinks, Detroit 12.6.81
Mike Weaver wpts15 James Tillis, Rosemount 3.10.81
(WBA title)
Larry Holmes wrsf11 Renaldo Snipes, Pittsburgh 6.11.81
Larry Holmes wdis13 Gerry Cooney, Las Vegas 11.6.82
Larry Holmes wpts15 Randy Cobb, Houston 26.11.82
Michael Dokes wrsf1 Mike Weaver, Las Vegas 10.12.82
(WBA title)
Larry Holmes wpts12 Lucien Rodriguez, Scranton 27.3.83
Larry Holmes wpts12 Tim Witherspoon, Las Vegas 20.5.83
Michael Dokes drew15 Mike Weaver, Las Vegas 20.5.83
(WBA title)
Larry Holmes wrsf5 Scott Frank, Atlantic City 10.9.83
Gerrie Coetzee wko10 Michael Dokes, Richfield 23.9.83
(WBA title)
Holmes relinquished WBC title and accepted recognition by the newly formed International Boxing Federation
Tim Witherspoon wpts12 Greg Page, Las Vegas 9.3.84
(vacant WBC title)
Pinklon Thomas wpts12 Tim Witherspoon, Las Vegas 31.8.84
(WBC title)
Larry Holmes wrsf12 James Smith, Las Vegas 9.11.84
(IBF title)
Greg Page wko8 Gerrie Coetzee, Sun City 1.12.84
(WBA title)
Larry Holmes wrsf10 David Bey, Las Vegas 15.3.85
(IBF title)

Tony Tubbs wpts15 Greg Page, Buffalo, NY 29.4.85
(WBA title)
Larry Holmes wpts15 Carl Williams, Reno 20.5.85
(IBF title)
Pinklon Thomas wko8 Mike Weaver, Las Vegas 15.6.85
(WBC title)
Michael Spinks wpts15 Larry Holmes, Las Vegas 21.9.85
(IBF title)
Tim Witherspoon wpts15 Tony Tubbs, Atlanta 17.1.86
(WBA title)
Trevor Berbick wpts12 Pinklon Thomas, Las Vegas 22.3.86
(WBC title)
Michael Spinks wpts15 Larry Holmes, Las Vegas 19.4.86
(IBF title)
Tim Witherspoon wrsf11 Frank Bruno, London 19.7.86
(WBA title)
Michael Spinks wrsf4 Steffen Tangstad, Las Vegas 6.9.86
(IBF title)
Spinks relinquished the IBF title after refusing to defend against Tony Tucker
Mike Tyson wrsf2 Trevor Berbick, Las Vegas 22.11.86
(WBC title)
James Smith wrsf1 Tim Witherspoon, New York 12.12.86
(WBA title)
Mike Tyson wpts12 James Smith, Las Vegas 7.3.87
(WBA/WBC titles)
Mike Tyson wrsf6 Pinklon Thomas, Las Vegas 30.5.87
(WBA/WBC titles)
Tony Tucker wrsf10 James Douglas, Las Vegas 30.5.87
(Vacant IBF title)
Mike Tyson wpts12 Tony Tucker, Las Vegas 1.8.87
(Undisputed title)
Mike Tyson wrsf7 Tyrell Biggs, Atlantic City 16.10.87
Mike Tyson wrsf4 Larry Holmes, Atlantic City 22.1.88
Mike Tyson wrsf2 Tony Tubbs, Tokyo 21.3.88
Mike Tyson wko1 Michael Spinks, Atlantic City 27.6.88
Mike Tyson wrsf5 Frank Bruno, Las Vegas 25.2.89

Francesco Damiani wko3 Johnny Duplooy, Syracuse 6.5.89
(Vacant WBO title)
Mike Tyson wrsf1 Carl Williams, Atlantic City 31.7.89
Francesco Damiani wret2 Daniel Netto, Cesena 16.12.89
(WBO title)
James Douglas wko10 Mike Tyson, Tokyo 11.2.90
Evander Holyfield wko3 James Douglas, Las Vegas 25.10.90
Ray Mercer wko9 Francesco Damiani, Atlantic City 11.1.91
(WBO title)
Evander Holyfield wpts12 George Foreman, Atlantic City 9.4.91
Ray Mercer wrsf5 Tommy Morrison, Atlantic City 18.10.91
(WBO title)
Mercer was stripped of the WBO title because he signed to fight Larry Holmes; 7.2.92. Holmes won on points
Evander Holyfield wrsf7 Bert Cooper, Atlanta 23.11.91
Michael Moorer wrsf5 Bert Cooper, Atlantic City 15.5.92
(Vacant WBO title)
Evander Holyfield wpts12 Larry Holmes, Las Vegas 19.6.92
Riddick Bowe wpts12 Evander Holyfield, Las Vegas 13.11.92
Bowe relinquished WBC title after refusing to defend against Lennox Lewis who was named WBC champion on the basis of his second-round stoppage of Donovan 'Razor' Ruddock in London, 31.10.92
Riddick Bowe wrsf1 Michael Dokes, New York 6.2.93
(WBA/IBF titles)
Lennox Lewis wpts12 Tony Tucker, Las Vegas 8.5.93
(WBC title)
Riddick Bowe wrsf2 Jesse Ferguson, Washington 22.5.93
(WBA/IBF titles)
Moorer relinquished WBO title to pursue other belts
Tommy Morrison wpts12 George Foreman, Las Vegas 7.6.93
(Vacant WBO title)
Tommy Morrison wrsf4 Tim Tomashek, Kansas City 30.8.93
(WBO title)
The WBO later rescinded the decision to sanction the fight because of Tomashek's lack of experience

Lennox Lewis wrsf7 Frank Bruno, Cardiff 1.10.93
(WBC title)
Michael Bentt wrsf1 Tommy Morrison, Tulsa 29.10.93
(WBO title)
Evander Holyfield wpts12 Riddick Bowe, Las Vegas 6.11.93
(WBA/IBF titles)
Herbie Hide wko7 Michael Bentt, London 19.3.94
(WBO title)
Michael Moorer wpts12 Evander Holyfield, Las Vegas 22.4.94
(WBA/IBF titles)
Lennox Lewis wrsf8 Phil Jackson, Atlantic City 6.5.94
(WBC title)
Oliver McCall wrsf2 Lennox Lewis, London 24.9.94
(WBC title)
George Foreman wko10 Michael Moorer, Las Vegas 5.11.94
(WBA/IBF titles)

Foreman stripped of the WBA title for agreeing to defend against the unrated German, Axel Schulz. Tony Tucker and Bruce Seldon are nominated to fight for the vacant title

Riddick Bowe wko6 Herbie Hide, Las Vegas 11.3.95
(WBO title)

COMPUTER RATINGS

THE FIRST 50 YEARS

These computer ratings for the first 50 years of gloved world title fights cover the champions from John L. Sullivan to James J. Braddock. Among the factors taken into account when feeding the computer program were skill, power, strength, stamina, title defences, bodyweight, complete ring records and the calibre of opponents. The authors also added personal feelings to go with the facts.

1. **JACK JOHNSON**
2. **GENE TUNNEY**
3. **JACK DEMPSEY**
4. **JAMES J. JEFFRIES**
5. **BOB FITZSIMMONS**
6. **JAMES J. CORBETT**
7. **JOHN L. SULLIVAN**
8. **TOMMY BURNS**
9. **MAX SCHMELING**
10. **MAX BAER**

COMPUTER RATINGS

THE SECOND 50 YEARS

These computer ratings for the second 50 years of gloved world heavyweight title fights cover the champions from Joe Louis to George Foreman.

1. **JOE LOUIS**
2. **MUHAMMAD ALI**
3. **ROCKY MARCIANO**
4. **MIKE TYSON**
5. **GEORGE FOREMAN**
6. **LARRY HOLMES**
7. **SONNY LISTON**
8. **JOE FRAZIER**
9. **JERSEY JOE WALCOTT**
10. **EZZARD CHARLES**

THE AUTHORS

REG GUTTERIDGE OBE travels thousands of miles every year covering the world boxing beat for Independent Television. He has been ITV's 'Voice of Boxing' for more than 30 years and is one of the most respected commentators in the business on both sides of the Atlantic. His partnership at the microphone with Jim Watt is rated the best double act in television sport. Reg has a thoroughbred boxing pedigree. His grandfather, Arthur, was the first professional to box at the original National Sporting Club, and he later became the club's chief second. His father and uncle – the famous Gutteridge Twins – were outstanding coaches and cornermen. Among the champions they trained were Primo Carnera, Ben Foord and Albert Finch. Reg was an outstanding amateur prospect, but his boxing career finished when he lost an argument with a German landmine during the Normandy invasion. A Cockney with a sharp sense of humour, Reg claims that he played 'a bit part' in the film *The Longest Day*. He was chief boxing reporter for the London *Evening News* for more than 40 years and is now a regular contributor to many publications including *Boxing News*. He has seen every world heavyweight champion since Rocky Marciano and counts greats such as Muhammad Ali and Sugar Ray Leonard among his personal friends. He was awarded the OBE in the 1995 New Year Honours List for his services to boxing, broadcasting and journalism.

NORMAN GILLER, a former *Daily Express* sportswriter, is one of Fleet Street's leading freelance journalists and a prolific author with more than 40 sports books to his name. He has written 16 books in partnership with his close friend Jimmy Greaves and has had boxing books published in harness with Henry Cooper, Jim Watt and Frank Bruno. He is a regular scriptwriter for *This Is Your Life,* and devised the Thames Television sports series *Who's The Greatest?* Reg and Norman have had a working relationship and friendship that goes back more than 40 years to when Norman was Reg's copy-boy at the *London Evening News.* He puts Reg's staying power down to what he used to put in his tea. Norman had long experience in newspapers with *Boxing News,* the *London Evening Standard, Daily Herald* and *Daily Express* before becoming a freelance writer in 1973. A PR for the Ali-Dunn and Witherspoon-Bruno world title fights, he is a computer freak as well as a boxing buff and this book drips with computerized data that adds statistical facts to Reg's unequalled authority.

65
135
200